T0368393

Lecture Notes in Computer Science   15466

Founding Editors

Gerhard Goos
Juris Hartmanis

The series Lecture Notes in Computer Science (LNCS), including its subseries Lecture Notes in Artificial Intelligence (LNAI) and Lecture Notes in Bioinformatics (LNBI), has established itself as a medium for the publication of new developments in computer science and information technology research, teaching, and education.

LNCS enjoys close cooperation with the computer science R & D community, the series counts many renowned academics among its volume editors and paper authors, and collaborates with prestigious societies. Its mission is to serve this international community by providing an invaluable service, mainly focused on the publication of conference and workshop proceedings and postproceedings. LNCS commenced publication in 1973.

Belgacem Ben Hedia · Mohamed Ghazel ·
Bruno Monsuez

Editors

Verification and Evaluation of Computer and Communication Systems

17th International Conference, VECoS 2024
Djerba, Tunisia, October 16–18, 2024
Proceedings

 Springer

Editors
Belgacem Ben Hedia ⓘ
CEA LIST Institute
Paris, France

Mohamed Ghazel ⓘ
Gustave Eiffel University
Paris, France

Bruno Monsuez
ENSTA
Paris, France

ISSN 0302-9743   ISSN 1611-3349 (electronic)
Lecture Notes in Computer Science
ISBN 978-3-031-85355-5   ISBN 978-3-031-85356-2 (eBook)
https://doi.org/10.1007/978-3-031-85356-2

Preface

This volume contains the papers presented at the 17th International Conference on Verification and Evaluation of Computer and Communication Systems (VECoS 2024), held during October 16–18, 2024 in Djerba, Tunisia.

The event of this year continues the tradition of previous editions held 2007 in Algiers, 2008 in Leeds, 2009 in Rabat, 2010 in Paris, 2011 in Tunis, 2012 in Paris, 2013 in Florence, 2014 in Bejaïa, 2015 in Bucharest, 2016 in Tunis, 2017 in Montreal, 2018 in Grenoble, 2019 in Porto, 2020 in Xi'an (virtual), 2021 in Beijing (virtual), and 2023 in Marrakech.

As in previous editions, VECoS provided a forum for researchers and practitioners in the areas of verification, control, performance, and dependability evaluation in order to discuss the state of the art and challenges in modern computer and communication systems in which functional and extra-functional properties are strongly interrelated. The main motivation is to encourage the cross-fertilization between various formal verification and evaluation approaches, methods, and techniques, and especially those developed for concurrent and distributed hardware/software systems.

The Program Committee of VECoS 2024 was composed of 77 researchers from 21 countries. We received 42 full submissions from 7 countries. After a thorough and lively discussion phase, the committee decided to accept 16 regular papers. The topics presented covered a range of subjects, including approaches to improving the scalability and efficiency of formal verification and its applications to blockchain, smart contracts, and neural networks. The conference also included two invited talks, one on fault diagnosis of discrete-event systems using Petri nets and the other on descriptive and prescriptive system models formalised in Event-B.

We are grateful to the Program and Organizing Committee members, to the reviewers for their cooperation, and to Springer for their professional support during the production phase of the proceedings. We are also thankful to all authors of submitted papers, to the invited speakers, and to all participants of the conference. Their interest in this conference and contributions are greatly appreciated.

October 2024

Belgacem Ben Hedia
Mohamed Ghazel
Bruno Monsuez

Organization

Executive Committee

Program Co-chairs

Mohamed Ghazel   Gustave Eiffel University, France
Bruno Monsuez   ENSTA Paris, France

Publicity Co-chair

Belgacem Ben Hedia   CEA-LIST, Saclay, France

Local Organizers

Belgacem Ben Hedia   CEA-LIST, Saclay, France
Mohsen Erouel   ISIM Medenine, Tunisia
Olfa Hamrouni   ISET Djerba, Tunisia
Dhaou Brini   ISET Djerba, Tunisia
Ali Oukhay   Djerba Civil Society, Tunisia

Steering Committee

Djamil Aissani   Université de Bejaia, Algeria
Mohamed Faouzi Atig   Uppsala University, Sweden
Kamel Barkaoui (Chair)   CEDRIC CNAM Paris, France
Hanifa Boucheneb   Polytechnique Montréal, Canada
Gabriel Ciobanu   Romanian Academy, Romania
Karim Djouani   Tshwane University of Technology, South Africa
Francesco Flammini   Ansaldo STS, Italy
Belgacem Ben Hedia   CEA-LIST Saclay, France
Antonín Kučera   Masaryk University, Czech Republic
Zhiwu Li   Xidian University, China
Yassine Maleh   Sultan Moulay Slimane University, Morocco
Ali Mili   New Jersey Institute of Technology, USA

Bruno Monsuez   ENSTA UIIS, Palaiseau, France
Geguang Pu   East China Normal University, China
Riadh Robbana   INSAT, Tunisia

Program Committee

D. Aissani	A. Jemai
Y. Ait Ameur	M. Jmaiel
R. Ammour	C. Jerad
M. Asavoae	J. Julvez
M. Faouzi Atig	K. Klai
K. Barkaoui	M. Krichen
F. Belala	L. Kristensen
M. Belguidoum	A. Kucera
I. Ben Dhaou	M. Lahami
I. Ben Hafaiedh	A. Legay
B. Ben Hedia	O. Lengal
I. Ben Dhaou	A. Lisitsa
S. Bensalem	G. Liu
A. Benzina	L. Ma
B. Binder	Y. Maleh
P. Bonhomme	A. Methni
A. Bouajjani	R. Meyer
H. Boucheneb	A. Mili
A. Boudguiga	B. Monsuez
Z. Chen	M. Mosbah
G. Ciobanu	A. Nouri
J. Couvreur	S. Ouchani
S. Dal Zilio	C. Palamidessi
I. Demongodin	A. Rabéa
M. Escheikh	R. Robbana
A. Fantechi	R. J. Rodríguez
A. Geniet	O. H. Roux
M. Ghazel	Z. Sbaï
S. Haddad	L. Sliman
A. Harbaoui	T. Touili
R. Iosif	X. Yin

Additional Reviewers

N. Ali
C. Ameur
Y. Benchaib
A. Benkaci
F. Boudardara
F. Boukour
H. Boussi
A. Boussif
M. Chaabane
B. Charroux
P. Chevalier
P. Courtieu
A. Elaoud
S. Faci
F. Fakhfakh
T. Haas
V. Havlena
T. Joven
M. Kalaagi
E. Keskin

J. Lazaro
H. Mahmood
O. Marsi
I. Mastour
A. Oarga
W. Ouarda
B. Pascariu
H. Sakli
D. Seetheramdoo
F. Sekak
H. Shaiek
D. Sodoyer
M. Taha
S. Tollec
K. Trabelsi
S. van
M. Wahl
B. Xu
L. Yin

Sponsoring Institutions

Keynote Speakers

Descriptive and Prescriptive System Models Formalised in Event-B

Yamine Ait Ameur

ENSEEIHT Toulouse INP, ANR,, France
`yamine@enseeiht.fr`

Abstract. The Event-B method has shown its effectiveness in the rigorous development of complex systems, whether these systems are software, hardware or hybrid. A system model is formalized as a machine that encodes a state-transition system. This machine relies on a set of definitions and theorems defined in a context. A set of proof obligations is automatically generated. When discharged, these proof obligations guarantee the consistency of a model as well as its correctness. Recently, the Event-B method has been extended with the possibility to define new types, being either constructive or axiomatic, described using algebraic theories. These theories are particularly useful for defining generic data types and associated operators, as well as for proving theorems reflecting their properties. This extension paves the way for the formalization of models of complex systems and makes it possible to reduce the proof effort thanks to the exploitation of the new proof obligations induced by the definition of these types. Indeed, axioms and theorems borrowed from these theories are useful to discharge designed models' proof obligations and contribute to reduce the proof effort as the theorems of the theories are proved once and for all. In this presentation, we show how Event-B machines and algebraic theories are set up to formalize prescriptive models for defining particular systems as well as descriptive models, to describe domain knowledge or system environments.

Fault Diagnosis of Discrete-Event Systems Using Petri Nets

Zhiwu Li

Macau University of Science and Technology, China
`ali.mili@njit.edua`

Abstract. Fault diagnosis and diagnosability analysis in cyber-physical systems have received much attention from researchers and practitioners. This talk touches upon this problem from the lens of discrete-event systems that are a technical abstract or model of cyber-physical systems, where a plant is modeled with a labeled Petri net. We present two lines of fault diagnosis in this particular formalism: structural analysis and reachability analysis. The former addresses the problem by integer linear programming, while the latter employs a compact reachable space presentation approach called a basis reachability graph. Diagnosability enforcement is recapitulated using the basis reachability graph. Finally, future exploration in the community is regularly platitudinized.

Contents

Formal Verification of Coupled Transmission Lines using Theorem Proving

Elif Deniz$^{(\boxtimes)}$, Adnan Rashid, and Sofiène Tahar

Department of Electrical and Computer Engineering, Concordia University,
Montreal, QC, Canada
{e_deniz,rashid,tahar}@ece.concordia.ca

Abstract. Coupled transmission lines are essential components of modern electronic systems, which facilitate a reliable and an efficient transmission of high-frequency signals from source to destination and are widely used in various industries, including telecommunications, aerospace, and automotive. Moreover, their dynamics are generally represented by a set of differential equations involving voltages and currents, known as the telegrapher's equations. This paper proposes to use Higher-Order Logic (HOL) theorem proving for formal modeling and verification of coupled transmission lines. In particular, we formalize the equations capturing the line voltages and currents, and their relationship in a system of coupled transmission lines. We then formally verify the equivalence between these equations and their matrix representations. Finally, we conduct a formal proof of the correctness of the general solutions of these generalized telegrapher's equations using the HOL Light theorem prover.

Keywords: Coupled Transmission Lines · Telegrapher's Equations · Higher-Order Logic · Theorem Proving · HOL Light

1 Introduction

The transmission of electrical signals and power is a pivotal achievement of engineering technology, significantly advancing modern civilization. These electrical systems transmit a wide range of communication signals, including data and control over distances reaching thousands of miles. Furthermore, electrical transmission engineering encompasses not only long transmission systems but also a vast array of shorter transmission line segments that perform numerous functions within the terminal units of the system [1]. Beyond their role in carrying information and energy, they can be also used as circuit elements for passive circuits such as impedance transformers [2], resonators [3] and baluns [4]. Coupled transmission lines (CTLs), in particular, play an important role in building the functionality of modern high speed communication systems.

B. Ben Hedia et al. (Eds.): VECoS 2024, LNCS 15466, pp. 1–15, 2025.
https://doi.org/10.1007/978-3-031-85356-2_1

Electromagnetic coupling occurs when two or more unshielded transmission lines are in close proximity due to the interaction of their electric and magnetic fields. This effect is particularly noticeable when the line axes are parallel, defining them as CTLs [5]. CTLs typically consist of two transmission lines but may include more than two. Furthermore, coupled line structures are applicable to all forms and types of transmission lines. For instance, microstriplines [6] and coplanar waveguides [7] are among the most popular planar forms [8]. When the coupled lines are identical (also known as symmetrical coupled lines), they can be analyzed in terms of *even* and *odd* modes to understand their behavior and characteristics. By applying even- and odd-mode excitations separately and then combining their solutions, engineers conveniently analyze the behavior of symmetric coupled transmission lines. This simplifies the problem by breaking it down into two more manageable parts, making it easier to understand and design transmission lines for specific applications.

Traditionally, the analysis of coupled transmission lines involves paper-and-pencil and simulation techniques. In the former approach, the lines are modeled using the telegrapher's equations [9], and the resulting system of coupled transmission line equations is expressed in matrix form. Although this analytical method provides closed-form mathematical solutions, conducting such analyses manually is prone to human error, especially when dealing with complex transmission line configurations. The latter method, which includes commonly used numerical techniques such as the finite-difference time-domain (FDTD) modeling of electromagnetic equations [10] and the transmission line modeling (TLM) method [11], has been shown to be quite time-consuming in many electromagnetic and transmission line problems, such as waveguide structures and high-frequency circuit designs. In addition to requiring a significant amount of memory and computational time, these techniques cannot provide perfectly accurate results because of the discretization of continuous parameters and the use of unverified numerical algorithms.

To address the inaccuracy problems mentioned earlier, formal methods-based techniques are capable of overcoming these issues. In the most pertinent related study on formally analyzing transmission systems using theorem proving [12], the authors formalized the telegrapher's equations for single Transmission Line (TL) and verified the analytical solutions of the equations. Moreover, they formally analyzed the terminated transmission line and its special cases, i.e., short- and open-circuited lines in the HOL Light theorem prover[1]. However, it should be noted that single TL may not offer the same level of versatility as CTLs, which allow for signal interaction and are therefore better suited for more complex applications such as power transmission from Power Grids to users [13].

The primary objective of this paper is to enhance the formal reasoning support within the domain of transmission lines. In this paper, we propose to use Higher-Order Logic (HOL) theorem proving to formally model and analyze CTLs. In particular, HOL Light was selected due to the availability of a library for single TL and its potential to connect this library with CTLs. More-

---

[1] https://www.cl.cam.ac.uk/~jrh13/hol-light/

over, the HOL Light theorem prover offers users the flexibility to develop and apply customized automation methods.

The rest of the paper is organized as follows: In Sect. 2, we present some of the fundamental formal definitions of the multivariate calculus theories of HOL Light that are necessary for understanding the rest of the paper. Section 3 describes the mathematical modeling of CTLs. In Sect. 4, we provide the formal modeling of CTLs. In Sect. 5, we present the formal verification of the analytical solutions of the generalized telegrapher's equations, which are used to model CTLs. Finally, Sect. 6 concludes the paper.

2 Preliminaries

In this section, we present some HOL Light definitions that are used in our proposed formalization and are important to understand the rest of the paper.

2.1 Complex Vectors and Matrices

Here, we explain some of the commonly used HOL Light fuctions in the proposed formalization as follows:

Definition 1. *Vector*
⊢ ∀l. vector l = (lambda i. EL (i - 1) l)

The function `vector` takes an arbitrary list `l`: α `list` and returns a vector having each component of data-type α. It uses the function `EL i l`, which accepts an index `i` and a list `l`, and returns the ith element of a list `l`. In HOL Light, the lambda operator is utilized to construct a vector from its individual components. A complex vector is defined as a vector having every elements as a complex number.

In HOL Light, matrices are fundamentally formalized as vectors of vectors, where a $M \times N$ matrix is formally represented as of type $(\texttt{complex}^N)^M$. For example, a 2×2 complex matrix can be formalized as follows:

Definition 2. 2×2 *Complex Matrix*
⊢ ∀a b c d. cmat2x2 a b c d = vector [vector [a; b]; vector [c; d]]

where `cmat2x2` accepts the complex numbers a:$\mathbb{C}$, b:$\mathbb{C}$, c:$\mathbb{C}$ and d:$\mathbb{C}$, and returns the corresponding 2×2 matrix.

2.2 Complex Analysis Library

This library includes fundamental concepts in complex analysis, including complex derivatives and transcendental functions.

Definition 3. Cx *and* ii
⊢ ∀a. Cx a = complex (a, &0)
⊢ ii = complex (&0, &1)

Cx is a type casting function with a data-type $\mathbb{R} \to \mathbb{C}$. It accepts a real number and returns its corresponding complex number with the imaginary part as zero. The & operator has data-type $\mathbb{N} \to \mathbb{R}$ and is used to map a natural number to a real number. Similarly, the function ii (iota) represents a complex number with a real part equal to 0 and the magnitude of the imaginary part equal to 1.

Definition 4. *Exponential Functions*
⊢ ∀x. exp x = Re (cexp (Cx x))

The HOL Light functions exp and cexp with data-types $\mathbb{R} \to \mathbb{R}$ and $\mathbb{C} \to \mathbb{C}$ represent the real-valued and complex-valued exponential functions, respectively.

Definition 5. *Complex Derivative*
⊢ ∀f x. complex_derivative f x =
                (@f'.(f has_complex_derivative f') (at x))

The function complex_derivative describes the complex derivative in functional form. It accepts a function f: $\mathbb{C} \to \mathbb{C}$ and a complex number x, which is the point at which f has to be differentiated, and returns a variable of data-type $\mathbb{C}$, providing the derivative of f at x. Here, the term at indicates a specific point at which the differentiation is being evaluated, namely, at the value of x.

Definition 6. *Complex Derivative for Vectors*
⊢ ∀f x. complex_derivative_vector Fn x =
                (lambda i.complex_derivative (λx. (Fn$_i$) x) x)

The function complex_vector_derivative takes a vector Fn, whose elements are complex functions of data type $\mathbb{C} \to \mathbb{C}$ and a complex number x, which is the point at which every element of Fn has to be differentiated, and returns a vector data-type Fn: $(\mathbb{C} \to \mathbb{C})^N$, where each element corresponds to the derivatives of the complex functions. It is important to note that throughout the paper, we use a combination of HOL Light code and mathematical notation to enhance readability.

3 Mathematical Modeling of Coupled Transmission Lines

In various transmission line applications, the proximity of neighboring lines often results in a level of coupling. This close proximity leads to modifications in the electromagnetic fields, consequently influencing the propagating voltage and current waves and in turn, altering the characteristic impedance of the transmission line. While this coupling may pose a drawback where it leads to undesired signals, commonly referred to as "cross-talk," it can also serve as a mean of intentionally transferring a set amount of signal to another circuit for various purposes such as monitoring, measurement, or signal processing [9]. There exist two forms of coupling, namely electric and magnetic. The electric coupling results from charges on one line inducing charges on another, often explained by mutual capacitance.

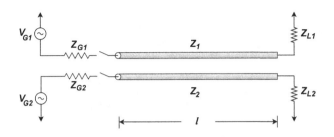

Fig. 1. Coupled Transmission Lines [14]

The magnetic coupling, on the other hand, arises from the interaction of magnetic flux between the lines and is typically described by mutual inductance. Figure 1 shows a generic circuit model for the CTLs. Under the assumption of lossless conditions, we consider two isolated transmission lines characterized by distributed inductances and capacitances per unit length, represented as L_i and C_i for $i = 1, 2$. The respective propagation velocities and characteristic impedances are defined as $v_i = 1/\sqrt{L_i C_i}$ and $Z_i = \sqrt{L_i/C_i}$, respectively. To model an interaction between these lines, mutual inductance and capacitance per unit length, denoted as L_m and C_m, are introduced.

The dynamics of the CTLs can then be mathematically described as follows [9]:

$$\frac{\partial V_1}{\partial z} = -L_1 \frac{\partial I_1}{\partial t} - L_m \frac{\partial I_2}{\partial t} \tag{1}$$

$$\frac{\partial V_2}{\partial z} = -L_2 \frac{\partial I_2}{\partial t} - L_m \frac{\partial I_1}{\partial t} \tag{2}$$

$$\frac{\partial I_1}{\partial z} = -C_1 \frac{\partial V_1}{\partial t} + C_m \frac{\partial V_2}{\partial t} \tag{3}$$

$$\frac{\partial I_2}{\partial z} = -C_2 \frac{\partial V_2}{\partial t} + C_m \frac{\partial V_1}{\partial t} \tag{4}$$

These equations are generalizations of the telegrapher's equations incorporating the mutual inductance and capacitance, which were originally developed for a single transmission line.

To overcome the considerable challenges of solving time-domain PDEs [15], we utilize the *phasor* concept to transform them into a set of coupled Ordinary Differential Equations (ODEs) for the voltages and currents. For sinusoidal steady-state (*phasor*) excitation of the lines, we obtain by replacing $\partial/\partial t \Rightarrow j\omega$ [16]:

$$\frac{dV_1}{dz} = -j\omega L_1 I_1(z) - j\omega L_m I_2(z) \tag{5}$$

$$\frac{dV_2}{dz} = -j\omega L_m I_1(z) - j\omega L_2 I_2(z) \tag{6}$$

$$\frac{dI_1}{dz} = -j\omega C_1 V_1(z) + j\omega C_m V_2(z) \tag{7}$$

$$\frac{dI_2}{dz} = j\omega C_m V_1(z) - j\omega C_2 V_2(z) \tag{8}$$

Any system of linear equations can be represented in a compact form by a matrix-vector multiplication equation. For our case, we present Eqs. (5)–(8), in matrix form describing the relationship between the currents and voltages on the coupled transmission line as [9]:

$$\frac{d\mathbf{V}}{dz} = -j\omega \underbrace{\begin{bmatrix} L_1 & L_m \\ L_m & L_2 \end{bmatrix}}_{\mathbf{L}} \mathbf{I} \tag{9}$$

$$\frac{d\mathbf{I}}{dz} = -j\omega \underbrace{\begin{bmatrix} C_1 & -C_m \\ -C_m & C_2 \end{bmatrix}}_{\mathbf{C}} \mathbf{V} \tag{10}$$

where $\mathbf{V}$ and $\mathbf{I}$ are the column vectors. Moreover, the specific line inductance L and capacitance C in single transmission line have been replaced with 2×2 matrices denoted as $\mathbf{L}$ and $\mathbf{C}$. This modification provides a more detailed representation of the interaction between two coupled transmission lines, and hence a more comprehensive understanding of their dynamics.

4   Formal Modeling of Coupled Transmission Lines

In order to formalize the telegrapher's equations (Eqs. (5)–(8)) and their matrix-based representations (Eqs. (9) and (10)), we first model voltages and currents in HOL Light. Furthermore, we model the distributed and mutual inductance as well as the distributed and mutual capacitance using the feature of type abbreviation as follows:

```
new_type_abbrev (''vol'',':(V1 × V2)')
new_type_abbrev (''cur'',':(I1 × I2)')
new_type_abbrev (''vol_cur'',':(V1 × V2) × (I1 × I2)')
new_type_abbrev (''ind_ctls'',':(L1 × L2) × Lm')
new_type_abbrev (''cap_ctls'',':(C1 × C2) × Cm')
```

Here, V_1, V_2 are of types voltage functions and I_1 and I_2 are of types current functions and they are modeled in HOL Light as:

```
new_type_abbrev (''vol_fun'',':(ℂ → ℂ)')
new_type_abbrev (''cur_fun'',':(ℂ → ℂ)'))
```

Here, the vol_fun type is employed to represent a voltage function $V_1(z)$, where z is a variable of complex type $\mathbb{C}$.

Now, we formalize Eqs. (5) and (6) capturing the voltages on CTLs in HOL Light as follows:

Definition 7. *First Equation for Voltage*
```
⊢ ∀V1 V2 I1 I2 L1 L2 Lm w z.
   coupled_vol_ode_fst ((V1,V2),(I1,I2))((L1,L2),Lm) w z ⇔
     complex_derivative (λz. V1(z)) z =
         --ii * Cx w * (Cx L1 * I1(z) + Cx Lm * I2(z))
```

Definition 8. *Second Equation for Voltage*
```
⊢ ∀V1 V2 I1 I2 L1 L2 Lm w z.
   coupled_vol_ode_snd ((V1,V2),(I1,I2))((L1,L2),Lm) w z ⇔
     complex_derivative (λz. V2(z)) z =
         --ii * Cx w * (Cx Lm * I1(z) + Cx L2 * I2(z))
```

where `coupled_vol_ode_fst` and `coupled_vol_ode_snd` use the complex-derivative function in HOL Light to model the telegrapher's equations. The variables $L1:\mathbb{R}$ and $Lm:\mathbb{R}$ represent the distributed and mutual inductance per unit length, respectively. Here, the variables $z:\mathbb{C}$ refers to the spatial coordinate, while $w:\mathbb{R}$ denotes the angular frequency.

Similarly, we can formalize Eqs. (7) and (8) capturing the currents on CTLs as:

Definition 9. *First Equation for Current*
```
⊢ ∀V1 V2 I1 I2 C1 C2 Cm w z.
   coupled_cur_ode_fst ((V1,V2),(I1,I2))((C1,C2),Cm) w z ⇔
     complex_derivative (λz. I1(z)) z =
         --ii * Cx w * (Cx (C1) * V1(z) - Cx (Cm) * V2(z))
```

Definition 10. *Second Equation for Current*
```
⊢ ∀V1 V2 I1 I2 C1 C2 Cm w z.
   coupled_cur_ode_snd ((V1,V2),(I1,I2))((C1,C2),Cm) w z ⇔
     complex_derivative (λz. I2(z)) z =
         --ii * Cx w * (--Cx (Cm) * V1(z) + Cx (C2) * V2(z))
```

Next, we formalize the matrix representations of the linear system of equations for voltage and current (Eqs. (9) and (10)) as follows:

Definition 11. *Matrix Characterization of ODE System for Voltage*
```
⊢ ∀V1 V2 I1 I2 L1 L2 Lm w z.
   vol_ode_mat_rep ((V1,V2),(I1,I2))((L1,L2),Lm) w z ⇔
   (let ind = ((L1,L2),Lm):ind_ctls in
       complex_derivative_vector (vector [V1;V2]) z =
         (--ii * Cx w) %% inductance_mat_const ind ** cur_vec (I1,I2) z)
```

where `%%` and `**` model the scalar-matrix and matrix-vector multiplications, respectively.

Definition 12. *Matrix Characterization of ODE System for Current*
```
⊢ ∀V1 V2 I1 I2 C1 C2 Cm w z.
   cur_ode_mat_rep ((V1,V2),(I1,I2))((C1,C2),Cm) w z ⇔
```

```
(let cap = ((C1,C2),Cm):cap_ctls) in
    complex_derivative_vector (vector [I1;I2]) z =
        (--ii * Cx w) %% capacitance_mat_const cap ** vol_vec (V1,V2) z)
```

Now, we formally verify the equivalence between the system of linear differential equations for the voltages (Eqs. (5) and (6)) and their matrix characterizations (Eq. (9)) as the following HOL Light theorem:

Theorem 1. *Equivalence between ODE Systems and their Matrix Characterizations for Voltages*
⊢ ∀V1 V2 I1 I2 L1 L2 Lm w z.
    let vlcr = ((V1,V2),(I1,I2):vol_cur) and
        ind = ((L1,L2),Lm):ind_tls) in
        [A1] coupled_vol_ode_fst vlcr ind w z ∧
        [A2] coupled_vol_ode_snd vlcr ind w z ⇔
                vol_ode_mat_rep vlcr ind w z

Assumptions **A1** and **A2** present the telegrapher's equations for the voltages, in phasor domain, i.e., Eqs. (5) and (6). The proof of Theorem 1 is based on properties of complex derivative, complex vectors and complex matrices alongside some complex arithmetic reasoning.

Next, we formally verify the equivalence of the telegrapher's equations for the current (Eqs. (7) and (8)) and their matrix representation (Eq. (10)).

Theorem 2. *Equivalence between ODE Systems and their Matrix Characterizations for Currents*
⊢ ∀V1 V2 I1 I2 C1 C2 Cm w z.
    let vlcr = ((V1,V2),(I1,I2):vol_cur) and
        cap = ((C1,C2),Cm):cap_tls) in
        [A1] coupled_cur_ode_fst V1 vlcr cap z w ∧
        [A2] coupled_cur_ode_snd V2 vlcr cap z w ⇔
                cur_ode_mat_rep vlcr cap w z

The verification of the above theorem is very similar to that of Theorem 1.

5 Formal Verification of Coupled Transmission Lines

To simplify the analysis of the telegrapher's equations, we consider the scenario of the identical transmission lines. In this case, we have $L_1 = L_2 \equiv L_0$ and $C_1 = C_2 \equiv C_0$, so that $\beta_1 = \beta_2 = \omega\sqrt{L_0 C_0} \equiv \beta$ and $Z_1 = Z_2 = \sqrt{L_0/C_0} \equiv Z_0$. Additionally, the wave propagation speed is defined as $v_0 = 1/\sqrt{L_0 C_0}$. If two lossless coupled lines have the same self-inductance parameters $L_1 = L_2 \equiv L_0$ and self-capacitance parameters $C_1 = C_2 \equiv C_0$, the coupled-line structure is considered symmetric. The final solution for symmetric coupled lines can be efficiently derived by combining two single-line scenarios. This is achieved by applying two specific types of excitations: *even* and *odd* mode excitations. In the *even* mode, currents in the conductors exhibit equal magnitudes and flow in parallel directions, while in the *odd* mode, currents in the conductors possess equal magnitudes but flow in opposite directions. It is important to emphasize that this paper primarily focuses on verifying the final solution of the telegrapher's equation rather than the derivation process of the solution.

We now mathematically express the final solutions of the telegrapher's equations for the CTLs in terms of even and odd modes for the voltages and currents as follows:

$$V_1(z) = \underbrace{\frac{e^{-j\beta_+ z} + \Gamma_{L+}e^{-2j\beta_+ l}e^{j\beta_+ z}}{1 - \Gamma_{G+}\Gamma_{L+}e^{-2j\beta_+ l}}V_+}_{\text{even}} + \underbrace{\frac{e^{-j\beta_- z} + \Gamma_{L-}e^{-2j\beta_- l}e^{j\beta_- z}}{1 - \Gamma_{G-}\Gamma_{L-}e^{-2j\beta_- l}}V_-}_{\text{odd}} \quad (11)$$

$$V_2(z) = \underbrace{\frac{e^{-j\beta_+ z} + \Gamma_{L+}e^{-2j\beta_+ l}e^{j\beta_+ z}}{1 - \Gamma_{G+}\Gamma_{L+}e^{-2j\beta_+ l}}V_+}_{\text{even}} - \underbrace{\frac{e^{-j\beta_- z} + \Gamma_{L-}e^{-2j\beta_- l}e^{j\beta_- z}}{1 - \Gamma_{G-}\Gamma_{L-}e^{-2j\beta_- l}}V_-}_{\text{odd}} \quad (12)$$

Similarly, the general solutions for the currents can be mathematically express as:

$$I_1(z) = \frac{1}{Z_+}\left[\underbrace{\frac{e^{-j\beta_+ z} - \Gamma_{L+}e^{-2j\beta_+ l}e^{j\beta_+ z}}{1 - \Gamma_{G+}\Gamma_{L+}e^{-2j\beta_+ l}}V_+}_{\text{even}} + \underbrace{\frac{e^{-j\beta_- z} - \Gamma_{L-}e^{-2j\beta_- l}e^{j\beta_- z}}{1 - \Gamma_{G-}\Gamma_{L-}e^{-2j\beta_- l}}V_-}_{\text{odd}}\right] \quad (13)$$

$$I_2(z) = \frac{1}{Z_-}\left[\underbrace{\frac{e^{-j\beta_+ z} - \Gamma_{L+}e^{-2j\beta_+ l}e^{j\beta_+ z}}{1 - \Gamma_{G+}\Gamma_{L+}e^{-2j\beta_+ l}}V_+}_{\text{even}} - \underbrace{\frac{e^{-j\beta_- z} - \Gamma_{L-}e^{-2j\beta_- l}e^{j\beta_- z}}{1 - \Gamma_{G-}\Gamma_{L-}e^{-2j\beta_- l}}V_-}_{\text{odd}}\right] \quad (14)$$

In this context, the parameters $\beta_\pm$ and $Z_\pm$ indicate the wave numbers and the impedances, respectively and they can be mathematically express as follows:

$$\beta_+ = \omega\sqrt{(L_0 + L_m)(C_0) - C_m} \quad (15) \qquad \beta_- = \omega\sqrt{(L_0 - L_m)(C_0) + C_m} \quad (16)$$

and

$$Z_+ = \sqrt{\frac{L_0 + L_m}{C_0 - C_m}} \qquad (17) \qquad\qquad Z_- = \sqrt{\frac{L_0 - L_m}{C_0 + C_m}} \qquad (18)$$

Table 1. Data Types of Coefficients

Parameter Description	Standard Symbol	HOL Light Symbol: Type
Reflection coefficient at the load in even mode	Γ_{L+}	g1: $\mathbb{C}$
Reflection coefficient at the generator in even mode	Γ_{G+}	g2: $\mathbb{C}$
Reflection coefficient at the load in odd mode	Γ_{L-}	g3: $\mathbb{C}$
Reflection coefficient at the generator in odd mode	Γ_{G-}	g4: $\mathbb{C}$
Complex constant	V_+	Vm: $\mathbb{C}$
Complex constant	V_-	Vp: $\mathbb{C}$

In order to formalize the general solutions of telegrapher's equations for the voltages and currents, we first define the types of the reflection coefficients, i.e., g1, g2, g3, g4 denoted by Γ_{L+}, Γ_{G+}, Γ_{L-} and Γ_{G-} and the transmission line constants for identical lines as 4-tuples, and the complex constants associated with V_+ and V_- in HOL Light. Also, the types of the coefficients are given in Table 1.

```
new_type_abbrev (''ref_cons'',':(g1 × g2 × g3 × g4)')
new_type_abbrev (''ind_cap'',':(L1 × L2 × C1 × C2)')
new_type_abbrev (''vol_const'',':(Vp × Vm)'))
```

We now present the formalization of the general solutions of the telegrapher's equations (Eqs. (9) and (10)) for voltage and current. For brevity, we only provide the solutions for the first voltage and current, i.e., Eqs. (11) and (13). These solutions are formalized in HOL Light as follows:

Definition 13. *First Voltage Solution*
⊢ ∀Vm Vp L0 Lm C0 Cm g1 g2 g3 g4 z l w.
vol_sol_fst (Vm,Vp)((L0,Lm),(C0,Cm))(g1,g2,g3,g4) z l w =
(let tlc = ((L0,Lm),(C0,Cm)) in

$$Vm * \frac{e^{-jCx(wn\_fst\ tlc\ w)z} + g1 * e^{-Cx(\&2)jCx(wn\_fst\ tlc\ w)Cx(1)} * e^{jCx(wn\_fst\ tlc\ w)z}}{Cx(\&1) - g2 * g1 * e^{-Cx(\&2)jCx(wn\_fst\ tlc\ w)Cx(1)}} +$$

$$Vp * \frac{e^{-jCx(wn\_fst\ tlc\ w)z} + g3 * e^{-Cx(\&2)jCx(wn\_fst\ tlc\ w)Cx(1)} * e^{jCx(wn\_fst\ tlc\ w)z}}{Cx(\&1) - g4 * g3 * e^{-Cx(\&2)jCx(wn\_fst\ tlc\ w)Cx(1)}}$$

Definition 14. *First Current Solution*
⊢ ∀Vm Vp L0 Lm C0 Cm g1 g2 g3 g4 z l w.
cur_sol_fst (Vm,Vp)((L0,Lm),(C0,Cm))(g1,g2,g3,g4) z l w =
(let tlc = ((L0,Lm),(C0,Cm)) in $Cx(\frac{\&1}{char\_imp\_fst\ tlc})$ *

$$Vm * \frac{e^{-jCx(wn\_fst\ tlc\ w)z} - g1 * e^{-Cx(\&2)jCx(wn\_fst\ tlc\ w)Cx(1)} * e^{jCx(wn\_fst\ tlc\ w)z}}{Cx(\&1) - g2 * g1 * e^{-Cx(\&2)jCx(wn\_fst\ tlc\ w)Cx(1)}} -$$

$$Vp * \frac{e^{-jCx(wn\_fst\ tlc\ w)z} - g3 * e^{-Cx(\&2)jCx(wn\_fst\ tlc\ w)Cx(1)} * e^{jCx(wn\_fst\ tlc\ w)z}}{Cx(\&1) - g4 * g3 * e^{-Cx(\&2)jCx(wn\_fst\ tlc\ w)Cx(1)}}$$

where `vol_sol_fst` and `cur_sol_fst` accept the inductances $L1:\mathbb{R}$, $L2:\mathbb{R}$, the capacitances $C1:\mathbb{R}$, $C2:\mathbb{R}$, the complex constants `Vm` and `Vp`, the reflection coefficients `g1`, `g2`, `g3`, `g4`, the spatial coordinate `z`, the angular frequency $\omega:\mathbb{R}$ and the boundary condition $1:\mathbb{R}$ and return the corresponding definitions. Moreover, `wn_fst` and `wn_snd` refer to the wave numbers in Eq. (15) and (16), respectively. In addition, `char_imp_fst` and `char_imp_snd` correspond to the characteristic impedances in Eq. (17) and (18), respectively. The second voltage and current solutions, i.e., Eqs. (12) and (14) are formalized in a similar manner. The details about these definitions can be found in the HOL Light proof script [17].

Next, utilizing Definitions 13 and 14, we formalize the general solutions for voltages and currents in vector form for more compact representation:

Definition 15. *Vector Forms of the General Solutions for the Voltages*
⊢ ∀Vm Vp V1 V2 L0 Lm C0 Cm I1 I2 g1 g2 g3 g4 z l w.
  vol_sol_vec ((V1,V2),(I1,I2))(Vm,Vp)((L0,Lm),(C0,Cm))(g1,g2,g3,g4) z l w
⇔
  (let vlcr = ((V1,V2),(I1,I2)) and
       tlc = ((L0,Lm),(C0,Cm)) and
     rc = (g1,g2,g3,g4) and
     vc = (Vm,Vp) in
     vector[V1 z; V2 z] = vector[vol_sol_fst vc tlc rc z l w;
                               vol_sol_snd vc tlc rc z l w])

Here, `vol_sol_fst` and `vol_sol_snd` represent the general solutions for the voltages.

Definition 16. *Vector Forms of the General Solutions for the Currents*
⊢ ∀Vm Vp V1 V2 L0 Lm C0 Cm I1 I2 g1 g2 g3 g4 z l w.
  vol_sol_vec ((V1,V2),(I1,I2))(Vm,Vp)((L0,Lm),(C0,Cm))(g1,g2,g3,g4) z l w
⇔
  (let vlcr = ((V1,V2),(I1,I2)) and
       tlc = ((L0,Lm),(C0,Cm)) and
     rc = (g1,g2,g3,g4) and
     vc = (Vm,Vp) in
     vector[I1 z; I2 z] = vector[cur_sol_fst vc tlc rc z l w;
                               cur_sol_snd vc tlc rc z l w])

Similarly, `cur_sol_fst` and `cur_sol_snd` denote the general solutions for the currents. The final step is to formally verify the correctness of the solutions of the generalized telegrapher's equations as the following HOL Light theorem:

Theorem 3. *Verification of the General Solutions of the Telegrapher's Equation*
⊢ ∀V1 V2 I1 I2 C1 C2 L1 L2 Vm Vp L0 Lm C0 Cm g1 g2 g3 g4 l w.
  let tlc = ((L0,Lm),(C0,Cm)) and ind = ((L1,L2),Lm)
    and cap = ((C1,C2),Cm) and vlcr = ((V1,V2),(I1,I2))
    and rc = (g1,g2,g3,g4) and vc = (Vm,Vp) in

```
[A1] &0 < L1 ∧ [A2] &0 < L2 ∧ [A3] &0 < C1 ∧ [A4] &0 < C2
[A5] Cm < CO ∧ [A6] Lm < LO ∧ [A7] &0 < Cm ∧ [A8] &0 < Lm
[A9] L1 = LO ∧ [A10] L2 = LO ∧ [A11] C1 = CO ∧ [A12] C2 = CO
[A13] (∀z. vol_sol_vec vlcr tlc rc z l w) ∧
[A14] (∀z. cur_sol_vec vlcr tlc rc z l w)
   ⇒ vol_ode_mat_rep vlcr ind w z ∧ cur_ode_mat_rep vlcr cap w z
```

Assumptions A1-A4 ensure that the inductances and capacitances are positive quantities. Assumptions A5-A6 indicate that the distributed capacitance and inductance are greater than the mutual inductance and capacitance, respectively. Assumptions A7-A8 guarantee that the mutual capacitance and inductance are greater than zero. Assumptions A9-A12 model the conditions pertaining identical transmission lines. Assumptions A13 and A14 provide the general solutions of the telegrapher's equations for the voltages and the currents in vector form. Finally, the conclusion of the theorem presents the generalized telegrapher's equations, i.e., Eqs. (9) and (10). The verification of Theorem 3 is mainly based on the following four important formally verified lemmas about the complex derivatives of the general solutions.

Lemma 1. *Verification of the First Voltage Solution*
```
⊢ ∀I1 I2 V1 Vm Vp g1 g2 g3 g4 LO L1 Lm CO Cm z l w.
   let vlcr = ((V1,V2),(I1,I2)) and tlc = ((LO,Lm),(CO,Cm))
      and ind = ((L1,L2),Lm) and rc = (g1,g2,g3,g4) and vc = (Vm,Vp) in
   [A1] L1 = LO ∧ [A2] Cm < CO ∧ [A3] Lm < LO ∧ [A4] &0 < Cm ∧
   [A5] &0 < Lm ∧ [A6] (∀z. V1 z = vol_sol_fst vc tlc rc z l w) ∧
   [A7] (∀z. I1 z = cur_sol_fst vc tlc rc z l w) ∧
   [A8] (∀z. I2 z = cur_sol_snd vc tlc rc z l w)
      ⇒ coupled_vol_ode_fst vlcr ind z w
```

Assumption A1 is the condition for the identical lines. Assumptions A2–A5 are same as those of Assumptions A5–A8 of Theorem 3. Assumption A6 provides the first voltage solution (Eq. (11)) of the telegrapher's equation. Assumptions A7 and A8 provide the general solutions of the telegrapher's equations for the currents (Eqs. (13) and (14)). The conclusion of the lemma provides the telegrapher's equation for the first voltage (Eq. (5)). The proof of Lemma 1 is mainly based on the properties of transcendental functions [18], complex derivatives [19] along with some complex arithmetic reasoning.

Lemma 2. *Verification of the Second Voltage Solution*
```
⊢ ∀I1 I2 V1 Vm Vp g1 g2 g3 g4 LO L2 Lm CO Cm z l w.
   let vlcr = ((V1,V2),(I1,I2)) and tlc = ((LO,Lm),(CO,Cm))
      and ind = ((L1,L2),Lm) and rc = (g1,g2,g3,g4) and vc = (Vm,Vp) in
   [A1] L2 = LO ∧ [A2] Cm < CO ∧ [A3] Lm < LO ∧ [A4] &0 < Cm ∧
   [A5] &0 < Lm ∧ [A6] (∀z. V2 z = vol_sol_snd vc tlc rc z l w) ∧
   [A7] (∀z. I1 z = cur_sol_fst vc tlc rc z l w) ∧
   [A8] (∀z. I2 z = cur_sol_snd vc tlc rc z l w)
      ⇒ coupled_vol_ode_snd vlcr ind z w
```

Assumption A1 is the condition for the identical lines. A2-A5 are the same as those of Lemma 1. Assumption A6 provides the second voltage solution (Eq. (12)) of the telegrapher's equation. Assumptions A7-A8 are also the same as those of Lemma 1. The lemma concludes by providing the telegrapher's equation for the second voltage, as shown in Eq. (6). The proof of the above lemma is similar to that of Lemma 1.

In the next two HOL Light lemmas, we formally verify the derivatives of the general solutions for currents.

Lemma 3. *Verification of the First Current Solution*
```
⊢ ∀I1 I2 V1 V2 Vm Vp g1 g2 g3 g4 L0 C0 C1 Lm Cm z l w.
    let vlcr = ((V1,V2),(I1,I2)) and tlc = ((L0,Lm),(C0,Cm))
      and cap = ((C1,C2),Cm) and rc = (g1,g2,g3,g4) and vc = (Vm,Vp) in
    [A1] C1 = C0 ∧ [A2] Cm < C0 ∧ [A3] Lm < L0 ∧ [A4] &0 < Cm ∧
    [A5] &0 < Lm ∧ [A6] (∀z.I1 z = cur_sol_fst vc tlc rc z l w) ∧
    [A7] (∀z.V1 z = vol_sol_fst vc tlc rc z l w) ∧
    [A8] (∀z.V2 z = vol_sol_snd vc tlc rc z l w)
        ⇒ coupled_cur_ode_fst vlcr cap z w
```

Assumption A1 is the condition for the identical lines. Assumptions A2-A5 are the same as those of the above lemmas. Assumption A6 provides the first current solution (Eq. (13)) of the telegrapher's equation. Assumptions A7-A8 provide the general solutions for the voltages (Eqs. (11) and (12)). The conclusion of Lemma 3 provides the telegrapher's equation for the first current (Eq. (7)). The verification of the above lemma is very similar to those of Lemmas 1 and 2.

Lemma 4. *Verification of the Second Current Solution*
```
⊢ ∀I1 I2 L1 V1 V2 Vm Vp g1 g2 g3 g4 L0 Lm C0 C2 Cm z l w.
    let vlcr = ((V1,V2),(I1,I2)) and tlc = ((L0,Lm),(C0,Cm))
      and cap = ((C1,C2),Cm) and rc = (g1,g2,g3,g4) and vc = (Vm,Vp) in
    [A1] C2 = C0 ∧ [A2] Cm < C0 ∧ [A3] Lm < L0 ∧ [A4] &0 < Cm ∧
    [A5] &0 < Lm ∧ [A6] (∀z.I2 z = cur_sol_snd vc tlc rc z l w) ∧
    [A7] (∀z.V1 z = vol_sol_fst vc tlc rc z l w) ∧
    [A8] (∀z.V2 z = vol_sol_snd vc tlc rc z l w)
        ⇒ coupled_cur_ode_snd vlcr cap z w
```

Assumption A1 is the condition for the identical lines. Assumptions A2-A5 are the same as those of the above lemmas. Assumption A6 provide the second current solution (Eq. (14)) of the telegrapher's equation. Assumptions A7-A8 provide the general solutions for the voltages (Eqs. (11) and (12)). The conclusion of the lemma provides the telegrapher's equation for the second current (8)). The verification of the above lemma and the other lemmas and theorems can be found in our proof script [17].

Discussion

In this paper, we proposed to use the HOL Light proof assistant for the formal verification of coupled transmission lines. An important aspect of our work is the utilization of theorem proving into a domain that has been traditionally dominated by numerical techniques. The analysis of coupled transmission lines requires to understand various fundamental aspects, ranging from electromagnetic theory to microwave engineering. In particular, for those of us who are not experts in electromagnetics, it has been challenging to comprehend the formal definitions used to model transmission systems and phenomena. Another challenge encountered during this formalization was the mathematical proof itself. We relied on snippets of proofs gathered from the literature including textbooks, articles and courses. However, we frequently found these traditional pen-and-paper proofs to be somewhat incomplete or lack rigorous details. Due to the nature of the analysis, we had to develop our own proof with all necessary details for the verification process. The primary benefit of this work includes the accuracy of verified results and the revelation of hidden assumptions, which are often omitted in textbooks and engineering literature. Furthermore, every verified theorem and lemma is made general, allowing for further extensions. We believe our work to be useful in the design and analysis of systems involving transmission lines from various engineering and physical science disciplines such as communication systems, electromagnetics, RF and microwave engineering.

6   Conclusion

Coupled transmission lines are traditionally described by a system of differential equations. In this paper, we first formalized the dynamics of the CTLs using the telegrapher's equations in phasor domain. Since the behavior of the line can be fully characterized using circuit theory parameters, such as matrices representing inductances, capacitances, resistances, and conductances per unit length, we modeled these equations in matrix forms for a more compact representation and ease of the formal analysis. We then formally verified the analytical solutions of the telegrapher's equations for the CTLs. It is important to note that our analysis is conducted under the assumption of lossless lines, where resistances and conductances are assumed to be zero. Our research revealed numerous promising directions for future work. Our first goal is to extend the phasor domain solutions into the time domain and verify their correctness for the time domain partial differential equations. Second, we intend to explore the possibility of formally analyzing the results to determine crosstalk in communication circuits. Finally, we aim to formally analyze cable coupling, which is significant in industrial automation systems where precise control and monitoring of machinery and processes are crucial.

References

1. Chipman, R.A.: Theory and Problems of Transmission Lines. McGraw-Hill (1968)
2. Jensen, T., Zhurbenko, V., Krozer, V., Meincke, P.: Coupled transmission lines as impedance transformer. IEEE Trans. Microw. Theory Tech. **55**(12), 2957–2965 (2007)

3. Cohn, S.B.: Parallel-coupled transmission-line-resonator filters. IRE Trans. Microw. Theory Tech. **6**(2), 223–231 (1958)
4. Yeung, L.K., Wu, K.L.: A dual-band coupled-line balun filter. IEEE Trans. Microw. Theory Tech. **55**(11), 2406–2411 (2007)
5. Pozar, D.M.: Microwave Engineering. Wiley, Hoboken (2011)
6. Garg, R., Bahl, I.: Characteristics of coupled microstriplines. IEEE Trans. Microw. Theory Tech. **27**(7), 700–705 (1979)
7. Martel, J., Fernández-Prieto, A., del Río, J.L.M., Martín, F., Medina, F.: Design of a differential coupled-line directional coupler using a double-side coplanar waveguide structure with common-signal suppression. IEEE Trans. Microw. Theory Tech. **69**(2), 1273–1281 (2020)
8. Mongia, R., Bahl, I.J., Bhartia, P.: RF and Microwave Coupled-Line Circuits. Artech House, Norwood (1999)
9. Collier, R.: Transmission Lines: Equivalent Circuits, Electromagnetic Theory, and Photons. Cambridge University Press, Cambridge (2013)
10. Bondeson, A., Rylander, T., Ingelström, P.: Computational Electromagnetics. Springer, Cham (2012)
11. Christopoulos, C.: The Transmission-line Modeling Method: TLM. Springer, Cham (2012)
12. Deniz, E., Rashid, A., Hasan, O., Tahar, S.: Formalization of the telegrapher's equations using higher-order-logic theorem proving. J. Appl. Logics-IfCoLog J. Log. Appl. **11**(2) (2024)
13. da Silva Costa, L.G., de Queiroz, A.C.M., Adebisi, B., da Costa, V.L.R., Ribeiro, M.V.: Coupling for power line communications: a survey. J. Commun. Inf. Syst. **32**(1) (2017)
14. Orfanidis, S.J.: Electromagnetic Waves and Antennas. Rutgers University (2002)
15. Strauss, W.A.: Partial Differential Equations: An Introduction. Wiley, Hoboken (2007)
16. Magnusson, P.C., Weisshaar, A., Tripathi, V.K., Alexander, G.C.: Transmission Lines and Wave Propagation. CRC Press, Boca Raton (2017)
17. Deniz, E.: Formal verification of coupled transmission lines, HOL Light script (2024). https://hvg.ece.concordia.ca/code/hol-light/pde/te/ctl.ml
18. HOL Light Multivariate Calculus (2024). https://github.com/jrh13/hol-light/blob/master/Multivariate/transcendentals.ml
19. HOL Light Multivariate Calculus (2024). https://github.com/jrh13/hol-light/blob/master/Multivariate/canal.ml

Optimizing Label Coverage Using Regular Expression-Based Linear Programming

Kais Klai[1], Mohamed Taha Bennani[2], Jaime Arias[1]([⊠]), Hanen Ochi[1],
and Hadhami Elouni[1]

[1] Université Sorbonne Parid Nord, LIPN UMR CNRS 7030, Villetaneuse, France
{kais.klai,jaime.arias,ochi,hadhami.ouni}@lipn.univ-paris13.fr
[2] Faculty of Sciences of Tunis, University of Tunis El Manar, Tunis, Tunisia
taha.bennani@fst.utm.tn

Abstract. In this paper, we propose a new linear-time complexity algorithm that generates the regular expression of a labelled transition system (LTS), *i.e.*, its language. The LTS represents the behaviour of a system such that each path witnesses a possible execution, and such that the language consists of all the possible executions. This contribution is then used to ensure the well-known label coverage criterion in model-based testing. Given an LTS under test, the objective is to find as few and as short paths as possible that cover all the labels/actions of the system to generate significant test inputs. To reach this goal, our second contribution in this paper is to formulate this problem as an Integer Linear Program (ILP) involving the set of finite paths of the system that will be extracted from the regular expression of the LTS. Our approach is validated through a prototype and evaluated on some toy examples, as well as randomly generated LTS, to highlight its feasibility and limits.

Keywords: label coverage · LTS · test path generation

1 Introduction

Testing is an essential phase in the system development life cycle. Its main objective is to reveal the presence of faults to eliminate them [2]. The test phase does not only involve generating test inputs; it also includes activities such as test selection, test prioritization, test minimization, among others [15]. Although they are part of the same phase and share the same objective, these activities have specific needs. The selection activity aims to identify the tests required to validate the system alterations. Prioritization seeks to specify a test execution order to increase the probability of fault revelation, while minimization aims to eliminate redundant tests. The optimization techniques are essential to reduce the effort, in terms of time and resources, required by the test activities. The optimization problems associated with these activities can be formulated single- or multi-objective based. Furthermore, they can use various methods such as linear or dynamic programming, greedy, evolutionary or stochastic algorithms, and hybrid approaches [5].

B. Ben Hedia et al. (Eds.): VECoS 2024, LNCS 15466, pp. 16–31, 2025.
https://doi.org/10.1007/978-3-031-85356-2_2

According to [18], model-based testing (MBT) has three dimensions: *model specification*, *test generation* and *test execution*. For the third dimension, only two types of test execution are possible: *online* and *offline*. While the online approach generates tests based on the system under test (SUT) response, the offline approach is independent. *The model specification* can describe the inputs and outputs of the system, their evolution, and the means that manage this evolution. For instance, the evolution may depend on time or previous processes, and its values may be continuous or discrete. The evolution definition could be functional, stochastic or transition-based, such as a labelled transition system (LTS). *The generation of test inputs* relies on a selection criterion and a generation technology. The former depends on the structural coverage of the model, the data coverage, and the fault identification. The technology deployed leans on random generation, search algorithms, and model checking. MBT relies on models of a SUT and/or its environment to derive test cases for the system. The test paths characterize abstract test cases, whereas specific input test data must be provided to make them concrete.

Figure 1 shows an LTS that will be used throughout the paper to demonstrate the results delivered by each proposed algorithm. The main features of this LTS are its nested and interleaved loop structure.

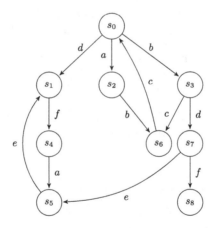

Fig. 1. Running Example

In this paper, we focus on the model specification paradigm that governs the system input and output values evolution by describing the system as an LTS. If the test generation selection relies on transition coverage, the identification of the test paths relies on a combination of search algorithms, and their minimization uses constraint solving. The main contributions of this paper are:

1. A novel method to generate test paths using regular expressions;
2. A revised version of the objective function related to the linear program aiming to find an exact solution that minimizes the cost of the test paths;

3. A supporting tool that can generate optimal test paths from an LTS.

The paper is organized as follows. Section 2 gives background about regular expressions and labelled transition systems. Section 3 introduces the main contributions of this paper. It begins by presenting our approach to generate regular expressions from LTS. It then shows the identification of representative paths, ending with linear programming to optimize the number and size of paths while ensuring coverage of all labels in the original LTS. Section 4 presents the experiments conducted on a selection of toy examples of LTS and randomly generated ones. Before concluding and showing the future work, we present related works on path selection optimization and the extended regular expressions used to model test paths.

2   Preliminaries

In this section, we recall the definition of regular expressions and labelled transition systems. We also introduce some notations used throughout the paper.

2.1   Regular Expressions

Let Σ be a given (non-empty) alphabet, and let $\{0, 1, +, \cdot,^*\}$ be five function symbols. The operations $+$ and $\cdot$ are binary, * is unary, and 0 and 1 are constants.

Definition 1 (Regular Expression [17]). *A regular expression over Σ is a formula obtained inductively from 0, 1, the letters of Σ, and the functions $\{+, \cdot,^*\}$ in the following manner:*

- *0, 1, and a, for $a \in \Sigma$, are regular expressions;*
- *if E and F are regular expressions, then $(E + F)$, $(E \cdot F)$, and (E^*) are regular expressions.*

$Reg(\Sigma^*)$ denotes the set of regular expressions over Σ. To each regular expression $E \in Reg(\Sigma^*)$, we assign a corresponding language of Σ^*, denoted by $|E|$.

2.2   Labelled Transition Systems

A labelled transition system (LTS) consists of a set of states and a set of transitions between those states. These transitions are labelled by actions, and one state is designated as the initial state. More formally:

Definition 2 (Labelled Transition System). *A labelled transition system (LTS) is a 4-tuple $\langle S, Act, \rightarrow, s_0 \rangle$, where:*

- *S is a (finite) set of states;*
- *Act is a (finite) set of actions (also known as labels);*
- *$\rightarrow \in S \times Act \times S$ is a transition relation; and*
- *s_0 is the initial state.*

Given $(s, a, s') \in \rightarrow$, $\ell(s, s')$ gives the label a associated with the transition.

Figure 1 shows an example of LTS. An action a is enabled by a state s (denoted by $s \xrightarrow{a}$) iff $\exists s'$ such that $(s, a, s') \in \rightarrow$. By extension, given a finite sequence of actions $\sigma = a_1 \ldots a_n \in Act^*$, the sequence $s \xrightarrow{\sigma}$, iff $\exists s_1, s_2, \ldots, s_n$ where $s \xrightarrow{a_1} s_1 \xrightarrow{a_2} s_2 \ldots \xrightarrow{a_n} s_n$. A sequence σ is said to be a run, iff $s_0 \xrightarrow{\sigma}$. The language of an LTS T is defined as follows: $L(T) = \{\sigma \in Act^* \mid s_0 \xrightarrow{\sigma}\}$. In this paper, we consider that the language contains maximal sequences only, *i.e.*, any prefix of an element of $L(T)$ is in $L(T)$ as well. Such languages are called prefix-closed.

Before we proceed to the next section, it is necessary to introduce some notations that will be used throughout the paper. Given a state s, an alphabet Σ, a sequence $\sigma \in \Sigma^*$, and the symbol $\perp$ denoting an undefined value:

- $Lg(s) = \{\langle seq, s' \rangle \in Reg(\Sigma^*) \times (S \cup \{\perp\}) \mid s \xrightarrow{seq}\}$
- $\sigma \cdot Lg(s) = \{\langle \sigma \cdot seq, s' \rangle \mid \langle seq, s' \rangle \in Lg(s)\}$
- $Cy(s) = \{\langle seq, s' \rangle \in Lg(s) \mid s' = s\}$
- $\overline{Cy(s)} = Lg(s) \setminus Cy(s)$

Given $e \in Lg(s)$, we shall use e_{seq} and e_{state} to denote the sequence (*i.e.*, *seq*) and the state (*i.e.*, s') elements for e, respectively.

3 Optimal Transition Coverage

This section introduces the three steps required to generate test paths covering all LTS transitions. The first step generates from an LTS a regular expression that models all paths starting from the initial state. Then, we present a grammar with a set of semantic actions, with which the parsing process of the regular expression computes the representative paths. The last part describes the problem of an Integer Linear Program (ILP) that selects optimal representative paths that cover all the labels in the LTS.

3.1 On-the-Fly Language Generation

In the following, we present a new algorithm that generates the regular expression representing the language of the system.

Algorithm 1 is based on a depth-first and recursive traversal of the LTS associated to the SUT. It takes as input a stack (we assume that it is firstly called with a stack containing the initial state only). Each traversed state of the graph is either completely treated, in that case it is saved in a map, or partially treated (or to be treated), in that case it belongs to the stack.

To help to better understand the algorithm, we consider the LTS presented in Fig. 1 where the above three situations are present. Figure 2 illustrates the application of the algorithm on this LTS. We assume that we traverse the graph by considering the paths on the left-hand side first, *i.e.*, first the path s_0, s_1, s_4, s_5 is explored and stopped at s_5 because its successor is s_1 that belongs already to

---

Algorithm 1: RegularExpressionGeneration function

Input: st ;   /* a stack containing the initial state s_0 */
Output: $Lg(s_0)$

1 **if** $st \neq \emptyset$ **then**
2     $cur = st.top()$
3   **if** $succ(cur) = \emptyset$ **then**
4        $Lg(cur) = \{\langle 0, \bot \rangle\}$
5   **else**
6        $Lg(cur) = \emptyset$
7   **foreach** $next \in succ(cur)$ **do**
8   **if** $next \in st$ **then**
9              $Lg(cur) = Lg(cur) \cup \{\langle \ell(cur, next), next \rangle\}$
10   **else**
11   **if** $next$ *is visited* **then**
12   UpdateLg(next)
13   **else**
14   st.push(next)
15   RegularExpressionGeneration(st)
16             $Lg(cur) = Lg(cur) \cup \{\ell(cur, next) \cdot Lg(next)\}$
17   **if** $Cy(cur) \neq \emptyset$ **then**
18   **if** $\overline{Cy(cur)} \neq \emptyset$ **then**
19             $Lg(cur) = \bigcup_{e \in \overline{Cy(cur)}} \{\langle (\Pi_{e' \in Cy(cur)} e_{seq}'^{*})^{*} \cdot e_{seq}, e_{state} \rangle\}$
20   **else**
21             $Lg(cur) = \{\langle (\Pi_{e \in Cy(cur)} e_{seq}^{*})^{*}, \bot \rangle\}$

22 $cur = st.pop()$
23 add cur to the map
24 **return** $Lg(cur)$

Algorithm 2: UpdateLg function

Input: state s
Output: update $Lg(s)$;   /* as well as Lg(s') s.t. Lg(s) depends on Lg(s') */

1 **if** s *is in the map* **then**
2   **foreach** $e \in Lg(s)$ **do**
3   **if** $e_{state} \neq \bot$ *and* $e_{state} \neq s_0$ **then**
4   UpdateLg(e_{state})
5           $Lg(s) \cdot$ replace($e, e_{seq} \cdot Lg(e_{state})$)

---

the current path. Similarly, the second path s_0, s_2, s_6 is stopped at s_6 since the unique successor of s_6 is s_0 which belongs to the current path. In Fig. 2, solid arrows represent the different calls, while dashed ones are the returned values.

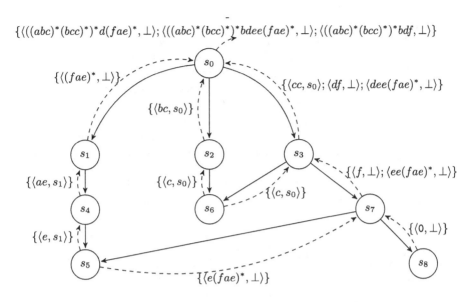

Fig. 2. Execution of the Algorithm 1 on the LTS of Fig. 1

Back to the explanation of Algorithm 1 that starts by checking if the stack is not empty (line 1). If it is the case, the top of the stack is copied in $curr$ (without removing it from the stack) (line 2). In case the current state is terminal (no successor), its language is set to $\{\langle 0, \bot \rangle\}$ (line 4). This is for instance the case of state s_8. Otherwise, its language is initialized to empty, and the list of successors of the current state is treated by considering the following three cases (line 7):

1. If the successor is in the stack (*i.e.*, belongs to the current path), then we update the language of the current state by adding the pair $\langle a, next \rangle$ (line 9) where a is the label of the transition $(curr, next)$. Intuitively, it means that (1) there is a cycle involving $next$ and cur, and (2) that from cur, label a can be concatenated to the language starting from $next$ (that is not completed yet). For instance, in Fig. 2, this is the case at state s_5 whose successor s_1 is still in the stack (current path), then the language of s_5 (*i.e.*, $Lg(s_5)$) is saved as $\{\langle e, s_1 \rangle\}$. The same case stands when traversing the second path. Indeed, at s_6 discovering that the successor s_0 belongs to the stack, the language of s_6 is saved as equal to $\{\langle c, s_0 \rangle\}$.
2. If the successor is not in the current language but has been visited, then function UpdateLg is called (line 12) in order to update/compute the language of this successor before updating the language of the current state (line 16). This is an interesting case that we explain through Figs. 1 and 2. We encounter this case at two occasions:
   (a) At state s_3, label c leads to state s_6 that has been completely treated and thus left the stack. Its language has been computed as equal to $\{\langle c, s_0 \rangle\}$. Since s_0 is still present in the stack, it is not possible to completely compute the language of s_6. The call to UpdateLg for s_6 will have no effect,

and the language of s_6 remains equal to $\{\langle c, s_0 \rangle\}$ (condition at line 3 of Algorithm 2 is false for the unique element of $Lg(s_6)$). The language of s_7 will also depend on the language of s_0 (line 16) which be solved later (by backtracking) when we come back to s_0.

(b) At state s_7, label e leads to state s_5 that left the stack and is completely treated. Note that "*completely treated*" does not mean that the corresponding language is definitely computed. Indeed, in this case, the language of s_5 is saved as $\{\langle e, s_1 \rangle\}$. Thus, it has to be updated as soon as s_5 is reached by another path (*e.g.*, from s_7). Calling UpdateLg for s_5 implies a recursive call to UpdateLg for s_1. It turns out that the language of s_1 is completely computed as $\{\langle (fae)^*, \bot \rangle\}$ (this will be explained later) which makes the language of s_5 updated as $\{\langle e(fae)^*, \bot \rangle\}$ thanks to replace($\langle e, s_1 \rangle$) that will replace $\langle e, s_1 \rangle$ by $\langle (fae)^*, \bot \rangle$ in $Lg(s_5)$ (line 5 of Algorithm 2). Coming back to line 16 of Algorithm 1, adds the pair $\langle ee(fae)^*, \bot \rangle$ to the language of $Lg(s_7)$.

3. If the successor is not in the stack nor visited before, it is pushed into the stack and treated by a recursive call (lines 14 and 15) before updating the language of the current state (line 16). For instance, the call with s_1 on the top of the stack will imply a recursive call with s_4 on the top of the stack, then a call with s_5 on the top of the stack. As explained above, the call with s_5 will return the language $\{\langle e, s_1 \rangle\}$, then the language of s_4 is updated as $\{\langle ae, s_1 \rangle\}$ and the language of s_1 update as $\{\langle fae, s_1 \rangle\}$ (both by line 16).

Now, it is time to explain statements inside the conditional at line 17. Once the language $Lg(cur)$ of all the successors of the current state cur is computed as a set of pairs $\langle seq, state \rangle$, we consider two disjoint subsets $Cy(cur)$ and $\overline{Cy(cur)}$. When it is not empty (line 17), $Cy(cur)$ contains (as defined in Sect. 2) couples of type $\langle seq, cur \rangle$ which intuitively witnesses the loops involving the state cur. This means that, from cur the loop $(seq)^*$ is possible. This is the case, for instance, of s_1 whose language will be set to $\{\langle fae, s_1 \rangle\}$ after the recursive call with s_4 on the top of the stack is achieved. Here, $\overline{Cy(s_1)} = \emptyset$ which leads to $Lg(s_1) = \{\langle (fae)^*, \bot \rangle\}$ (line 21). In case $\overline{Cy(cur)} \neq \emptyset$, $Lg(cur)$ is computed by line 19. This is the case of state s_0. When all the recursive calls are finished, $Lg(s_0)$ is computed first (before line 17) as $\{\langle d(fae)^*, \bot \rangle; \langle abc, s_0 \rangle; \langle bcc, s_0 \rangle; \langle bdee(fae)^*, \bot \rangle; \langle bdf, \bot \rangle\}$. Thus, $Cy(s_0) = \{\langle abc, s_0 \rangle; \langle bcc, s_0 \rangle\}$ and $\overline{Cy(s_0)} = \{\langle d(fae)^*, \bot \rangle; \langle bdee(fae)^*, \bot \rangle; \langle bdf, \bot \rangle\}$. So one can repeat, in any order and infinitely often, the loops $(abc)^*$ and $(bcc)^*$ before joining the one of the three finite paths $d(fae)^*$, $bdee(fae)^*$, and bdf. The role of line 19 is then to compute the $Lg(s_0)$ as $\{\langle ((abc)^*(bcc)^*)^* d(fae)^*, \bot \rangle; \langle ((abc)^*(bcc)^*)^* bdee(fae)^*, \bot \rangle; \langle ((abc)^*(bcc)^*)^* bdf, \bot \rangle\}$. Finally, it is easy to deduce that the whole language of the system is the sum of the first parts of the pairs composing $Lg(s_0)$, *i.e.*, $Lg(s_0) = ((abc)^*(bcc)^*)^* d(fae)^* + ((abc)^*(bcc)^*)^* bdf + ((abc)^*(bcc)^*)^* bdee(fae)^*$.

Table 1 gives $Lg(s_i)$ for each state s_i ($i = 0 \ldots 8$) of the LTS of Fig. 1. It is worth noting that some states are left with incomplete languages such as s_2, s_3, s_4 and s_6, whose languages still depend on the languages of other states.

Table 1. Result of the Algorithm 1 for the LTS of Fig. 1

State	Language
s_0	$\{\langle((abc)^*(bcc)^*)^*d(fae)^*,\bot\rangle; \langle((abc)^*(bcc)^*)^*bdf,\bot\rangle;$ $\langle((abc)^*(bcc)^*)^*bdee(fae)^*,\bot\rangle\}$
s_1	$\{\langle(fae)^*,\bot\rangle\}$
s_2	$\{\langle bc,s_0\rangle\}$
s_3	$\{\langle cc,s_0\rangle; \langle df,\bot\rangle; \langle dee(fae)^*,\bot\rangle\}$
s_4	$\{\langle ae,s_1\rangle\}$
s_5	$\{\langle e(fae)^*,\bot\rangle\}$
s_6	$\{\langle c,s_0\rangle\}$
s_7	$\{\langle f,\bot\rangle; \langle ee(fae)^*,\bot\rangle\}$
s_8	$\{\langle 0,\bot\rangle\}$

Remember that our objective is to compute the language of the initial state s_0. Thus, the language of any state is either completed or expressed as a function of the language of s_0. The latter is only necessary when it is visited by a second path. For instance, the language of state s_5 was first expressed as $\{\langle e,s_1\rangle\}$, and then updated to $\{\langle e(fae)^*,\bot\rangle\}$ when it was visited again from state s_7.

Finally, our algorithm can easily be extended to handle final states. Given a state s, the corresponding language $Lg(s)$ can be analysed to ignore elements (pairs) that do not lead to final states. One can add a boolean component to each pair of $Lg(s)$ whose value determines whether the corresponding branch leads to terminal states or not. If not, that branch will not be considered in the computation of the language of state s.

Complexity of the Regular Expression Generation. In Algorithm 1, the language of each state is computed (although incompletely) once from line 17 to line 21. This leads to n computations if n is the number of states in the LTS. However, function UpdateLg is invoked for a state s each time s is visited starting from the second time (the first time s is considered as a new state, so lines 14 and 15 are executed). Also, the first time the function UpdateLg is called for a state s, the language of s is definitely calculated (although depending on some states that are still present in the stack). Thus, visiting a state x times will not cost more than visiting it once. Thus, in the worst scenario the number of computations will be $2 * n$ (n by RegularExpressionGeneration + n by UpdateLg) which leads to a complexity of $\mathcal{O}(n)$, where n is the number of states in the graph. It is worth noting that we consider here the number of times the computation of the language Lg of each state is performed, and not the number of times each state is visited by our algorithm (that is quadratic).

3.2   Representative Paths' Generation

Once the regular expressions have been generated, the next step is to enumerate all their representative paths. By representative paths, we mean a set of transition sequences where each one contains, at most, a single iteration of a given loop. The advantage is the optimization of the test cost, as the addition of another sequence of the same loop does not improve the coverage rate of transitions. A more formal description is provided in the following definition.

Definition 3 (Representative Paths). Representative paths *constitute the language of a* representative expression (RE), *which is a regular expression where the unary operator* $*$ *is replaced by the binary operator* $+$. *The first operand of the latter operator is the operand of the unary operator* $*$, *and the second operand is the constant 0.*

For instance, the regular expression $r_1 = a^*b(ba^*b)$ has a representative expression $RE(r_1) = (a + 0)(b(a + 0)b)$. The representative paths of r_1 constitute the language of $RE(r_1)$, which is $|RE(r_1)| = \{bb, bab, abb, abab\}$.

To generate the set of representative paths, we use a syntactic analysis. In the abstract syntax tree (AST), the concatenation operation node has two children. The semantic action related to reducing the concatenation operation concatenates the elements of the sets related to each of the children. When reducing the closure operation, the semantic action associated with the AST's star node adds the empty word to the set of words related to the operand associated with the closure, *i.e.,* the one found in the closure operation's child node. The grammar G used to generate the AST of the representative path calculus is shown below.

$$\langle A \rangle ::= (\langle A \rangle)* \mid \langle S \rangle$$
$$\langle S \rangle ::= \langle A \rangle \langle A \rangle \mid \langle S \rangle \; tr \mid tr$$

This grammar has two layers. The first, associated with the non-terminal A, ensures the reduction of the closure operation of an operand or the call to the second layer. The layer related to the non-terminal S secures recognition of the concatenation operation and a single transition tr (*i.e.,* an element of the alphabet Σ). This analysis can concatenate two expressions with closure or an expression with a transition tr.

Moreover, the proposed grammar has three shift/reduce conflicts. The first relates to the kernel item set of the $LR(0)$ automaton made up of $\{A \rightarrow S\bullet, S \rightarrow S\bullet tr\}$. Indeed, when reading a transition, the parser can shift to another item set or reduce the closure operation. In our implementation, we have fixed this problem by assigning the priority to the shift operation, since reducing the closure is associated with reading the closing parenthesis. The last two shift/reduce conflicts are associated with the kernel item set $\{A \rightarrow A \bullet A, \; S \rightarrow AA\bullet\}$ of $LR(0)$'s automaton. When reading the opening parenthesis token, we have given priority to reducing the non-terminal S, as we are detecting the beginning of a closure expression. Additionally, when the next token is a transition, we perform the shift operation. The time complexity of the representative paths generation process is equal to the complexity of the $LALR(1)$ analyser, which is $O(n)$, where n is the length of the regular expression generated by the previous process.

Figure 3 shows the process of generating the representative paths of a regular expression. As the construction is bottom-up and left-to-right, we start by reducing the first transition a, which is not represented in this abstract syntax tree for the sake of clarity. The first concatenation operation identification, which has two children, a and b, is linked to concatenating an expression with a transition. This identification generates a set with a single word $\{ab\}$. This operation is repeated at the next level up, using the concatenation of an expression and a transition to generate the set $\{abc\}$. When reducing the closing expression, we add the empty word ϵ to the previous set, giving the set $\{\epsilon, abc\}$the multiplication operation on the sets generates the product set $\{\epsilon, abc, bcc, abcbcc\}$, which groups together all the concatenation combinations of the elements of the two previous sets. As the empty word is in the generated set, the reduction of the closing operation, which adds the empty word to the set of words of the previous stage, has no effect at this stage of analysis. Before reaching the root node of this AST, the product of two sets of words is generated, $\{\epsilon, fae\}$ and $\{d, abcd, bccd, abcbccd\}$. The latter set was constructed by concatenating the set $\{\epsilon, abc, bcc, abcbcc\}$ and the node containing the singleton $\{d\}$.

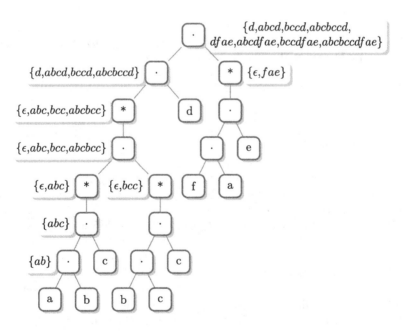

Fig. 3. Representative paths generation from $((abc)^*(bcc)^*)^*d(fae)^*$

3.3 Problem Formulation Using Integer Linear Programming

Integer Linear Programming (ILP) is a linear programming type where the variables can only take on the integer values. The solvers for this problem, where the number of constraints is fixed, are pseudopolynomial-time [16]. In our case, each variable x_j symbolizes a path in a given LTS. The coefficient a_{ij} indicates the number of occurrences of the label t_i in the path x_j. If the coefficient a_{ij} is greater than 1, the path x_j contains at least one occurrence of the label t_i. Otherwise, the label does not belong to the path. Every constraint of the linear program denotes a LTS-covered label. Therefore, the constraints' number is equal to the number of labels. All constraints' expressions must be greater or equal to 1, as each label must belong to at least one path. Every objective coefficient c_i represents the length of a path. This coefficient is also equal to the sum of the constraint coefficients of the path: $\Sigma_{i=1}^{m} a_{ij}$. The objective function reduces the coverage cost, as the sum of the length of the selected paths covering the LTS labels is minimal.

$$
\begin{array}{ll}
\textbf{Minimize} & c_1 x_1 + \ldots + c_n x_n \\
\textbf{Subject to} & a_{11} x_1 + \ldots + a_{1n} x_n \geq 1 \\
& \qquad \vdots \qquad\qquad\qquad\qquad\qquad x_j \in \{0,1\}, j = 1, \ldots, n \\
& a_{m1} x_1 + \ldots + a_{mn} x_n \geq 1
\end{array}
$$

For our running example, we have six labels and the path generation process provides 20 paths, which leads to an ILP program with six rows and 20 columns. For the second generated path "a_b_c_b_d_f", the column $(A_i^2)^T$ is equal to $[1, 2, 1, 1, 0, 1]$. The objective function to be minimized is:

$$
x_1 + 6x_2 + 6x_3 + 6x_4 + x_5 + \ldots + 6x_{20}
$$

4 Experiments

Our approach has been implemented in the open-source tool OptLP [1], that is written in C++. In this section, we shall present some experimental results to evaluate its performance. We conducted all the experiments on a Dell Precision 7560 laptop equipped with an Intel(R) Core(TM) i7-11850H 8-core processor running at 2.5 GHz, 32 GiB of memory, and Ubuntu 20.04. The reader can find the files needed to reproduce our experiments at https://depot.lipn.univ-paris13.fr/PMC-SOG/experiments/regex-lp.

First, we use a set of toy examples, presented in the tool's repository [1]. Table 2 presents preliminary results focusing on pathfinding metrics where the first column contains the identifier of each LTS of the twelve toy examples. Column 2 indicates the size of ILP algorithm, represented by the couple (r, c), where r is the number of rows and c is the number of columns. The former indicates the number of labels to be covered, while the latter denotes the number of generated paths. The time in milliseconds needed to generate the regular expression, extract the paths, and solve the ILP problem is represented by column 3, 4, and 5, respectively. The obtained optimal sequences are presented in the last column. Notice that the optimal sequences are not unique. For instance, for G_4, another optimal sequence is $t_7\_t_{10}\_t_8\_t_{11}$.

The ILP resolution process has the most significant impact on the processing time for generating optimal paths as it has a polynomial complexity. For small LTS, for instance G_1, ILP resolution takes 60% of the whole process against 96% for large LTS like G_{11}.

Table 2. Preliminary results for toy examples

LTS	ILP Size(r,c)	RegExp(ms)	Paths(ms)	ILP(ms)	Optimal Paths
G_1	(3,1)	0.020	3.515	5.32	a_b_c_
G_2	(5,161)	0.04	4.27	10.22	a_c_d_b_f_b_
G_3	(3,3)	0.027	3.883	5.963	a_b_c_
G_4	(4,24)	0.042	4.024	6.365	t8_t10_t7_t11_
G_5	(8,4)	0.031	3.614	7.64	t5_t14_t24_t22_t17_t2_t12_t10_
G_6	(6,20)	0.068	3.814	6.999	a_b_c_d_f_a_e_
G_7	(5,18)	0.044	3.698	6.825	t1_t3_t2_t5_t1_t3_t2_t3_t4_t1_ t3_t2_t3_t2_
G_8	(9,16)	0.058	3.674	6.219	t3_t5_t9_t11_t7_t12_t6_t4_t10_ t12_
G_9	(6,12)	0.06	3.755	8.724	t1_t13_t15_t1_t23_t1_t5_t21_t7_
G_{10}	(5,74529)	0.074	101.511	927.126	a_c_d_b_f_d_a_a_b_
G_{11}	(9,115248)	0.086	92.731	2259.67	d_h_a_i_g_b_f_a_e_c_f_a_b_
G_{12}	(6,14)	0.065	3.81	6.253	b_c_b_f_h_b_a_b_g_

To check the correctness of our algorithm by executing the approach on small test cases, we have manually analysed these toy examples. The identified optimal paths of all graphs are equal to those generated by the implementation of our approach, except for G_7, G_8, G_{10}, and G_{11}. We noticed that manually crafted optimal path (*e.g.*, a_c_d_b_f_d in G_{10}) is a prefix of the automatically generated one (*i.e.*, a_c_d_b_f_d_a_a_b). This weakness is related to the path generation process from regular expression.

We conducted a second analysis presented in Table 3, using randomly generated deterministic LTS. For each experiment, we varied the number of states (column 1) from 1000 to 4000, and adjusted the number of transitions (column 2) accordingly. We also performed random selections from a fixed set of 1000 labels. Additionally, we show the following information: total execution time in column 3, ILP size in column 4, average size of generated paths in column 5, number of optimal paths in column 6, and average size of optimal paths in the last column.

These results highlight the variability in computational complexity and path structures across different random LTS as the number of states and transitions grows. Our proof of concept shows a memory overflow (*i.e.,* MO) indicating that the memory limit was exceeded during the execution process, leading to an abrupt termination of the process. This interruption occurs after path generation, which highlights the limit of using ILP for very large LTS.

Table 3. Preliminary results for random LTS

# States	# Trans.	Time(s)	ILP Size (r, c)	Avg. Size	# Opt. Paths	Opt. Avg. Size
1000	1000	0.04005	(315, 490)	7	119	21
	1200	0.088201	(481, 1903)	12	166	21
	1250	0.086095	(328, 2172)	11	108	19
2000	2000	0.537548	(355, 1004)	7	104	22
	2400	14.9252	(349, 3651)	13	82	23
	2600	MO	(386, 566285)	78	–	–
3000	3000	0.087241	(572, 1482)	7	188	21
	3400	7.61547	(586, 6660)	18	174	24
	3700	154.404	(598, 24875)	24	148	27
4000	4000	3.18056	(586, 2054)	8	192	22
	4400	4.60993	(597, 3662)	13	166	27
	4600	1110.66	(584, 638452)	25	150	25

5   Related Work

Several approaches have proposed solutions to generate regular expressions from a LTS. The algorithm known as state-elimination method [3] takes as input an automaton. It removes the states one after the other while transforming the labels of the transitions so that the language accepted by the resulting automaton is unchanged. This method involves systematic removal of states while adjusting transitions, which can lead to very large intermediate expressions. Other approaches, namely McNaughton Yamada [13] and Conway methods [4], share a common foundation in the algebraic approach to solving a system of regular expression equations. The McNaughton-Yamada Algorithm iteratively eliminates states in a manner similar to state-elimination, maintaining the same complexity characteristics. The second one uses a more structured approach by solving a system of linear equations, potentially managing expression size better despite similar complexity. All these previous cited methods have a worst-case time complexity $\mathcal{O}(n^3)$ [7] and can experience significant space complexity due to the potential exponential growth of intermediate regular expressions. A common feature of these approaches is the specification of final states in the automaton accepting the language related to the regular expression. Our approach releases this constraint, as we generate a regular expression for an automaton by specifying only its initial node.

Miao et al. [14] have used a graph of relationships to describe a web application. This graph, which models the interactions between web pages, is extended by introducing a virtual page and then labelling the nodes. The authors have defined two conversion rules and two other deduction rules to generate test paths from elementary relationships between two web pages. According to this study, a test path has three characteristics: initial page, path length, and path content. A test path starts from the default page and stops at a page that points to the virtual page. Also, it should contain at least two transitions. Finally, it must not have a test path as a prefix or postfix, and must not contain redundant pages. These constraints, which may be coherent for web applications, drastically reduce the specification of test paths for more general-purpose applications.

Extended Regular Expressions (ERE) [10] use the classical algebraic operations of regular expressions to which they add the "range" operator to model the number of cycles. The authors have defined six modelling rules to transform a program into an ERE model. Then, from the ERE model, they have generated executable paths (*i.e.,* test paths) whose objective is to satisfy a coverage criterion. These test paths are then transformed into test inputs. The MTTool [12] implements this method by covering states, transitions and pairs of transitions. Generating test paths from the ERE model requires the following three steps: expression decomposition, algebraic processing and sub-expression combinations [9]. In addition to the initial six modelling rules, the authors have added four rules to handle complex loops [11]. In contrast to this process, our approach relies on dynamic programming, which we believe is more efficient, as it does not search for the loop pattern before applying the transformation rule.

6   Conclusion

The main contribution of this paper is a linear-time complexity generation of a regular expression from an LTS using dynamic programming. Also, we have proposed a syntactic approach with linear complexity for representative paths generation whose objective is to enumerate the set of abstract test paths related to a given LTS. Finally, we formulated an ILP problem to select test paths, minimizing the length and the number (*i.e.,* the global label number) while covering all the LTS labels. We demonstrated the effectiveness of this approach on elementary examples, and then verified its ability to solve the scaling problem through a random generation of LTS whose size includes up to 4000 states, 1000 labels and 4600 transitions.

Two perspectives will be considered in the near future. First, we intend to combine this approach with the one proposed in [8] to handle Petri net transition coverage using symbolic observation graphs [6]. Second, to face the state space explosion problem, and to be able to manage huge or even infinite state space graphs, we are going to count on deep learning approaches to help us explore and analyse such systems.

References

1. Arias, J., Bennani, M.T., Elouni, H., Klai, K., Ochi, H.: OptLp: optimizing label coverage using regular expression-based linear programming (2024). https://depot.lipn.univ-paris13.fr/PMC-SOG/optlp
2. Avizienis, A., Laprie, J., Randell, B., Landwehr, C.E.: Basic concepts and taxonomy of dependable and secure computing. IEEE Trans. Dependable Secur. Comput. **1**(1), 11–33 (2004). https://doi.org/10.1109/TDSC.2004.2
3. Brzozowski, J.A., McCluskey, E.J.: Signal flow graph techniques for sequential circuit state diagrams. IEEE Trans. Electron. Comput. **12**(2), 67–76 (1963). https://doi.org/10.1109/PGEC.1963.263416
4. Conway, J.H.: Regular Algebra and Finite Machines. Dover Publications (2012)
5. Gupta, N., Sharma, A., Pachariya, M.K.: An insight into test case optimization: ideas and trends with future perspectives. IEEE Access **7**, 22310–22327 (2019). https://doi.org/10.1109/ACCESS.2019.2899471
6. Haddad, S., Ilié, J.-M., Klai, K.: Design and evaluation of a symbolic and abstraction-based model checker. In: Wang, F. (ed.) ATVA 2004. LNCS, vol. 3299, pp. 196–210. Springer, Heidelberg (2004). https://doi.org/10.1007/978-3-540-30476-0_19
7. Hopcroft, J.E., Motwani, R., Ullman, J.D.: Introduction to Automata Theory, Languages, and Computation, 3rd edn., Pearson international edition. Addison-Wesley (2007)
8. Klai, K., Bennani, M.T., Arias, J., Desel, J., Ochi, H.: Symbolic observation graph-based generation of test paths. In: Prevosto, V., Seceleanu, C. (eds.) TAP 2023. LNCS, vol. 14066, pp. 127–146. Springer, Cham (2023). https://doi.org/10.1007/978-3-031-38828-6_8
9. Li, Y., Feng, Y., Guo, C., Chen, Z., Xu, B.: Crowdsourced test case generation for android applications via static program analysis. Autom. Softw. Eng. **30**(2), 26 (2023). https://doi.org/10.1007/S10515-023-00394-W
10. Liu, P., Ai, J., Xu, Z.J.: A study for extended regular expression-based testing. In: Zhu, G., Yao, S., Cui, X., Xu, S. (eds.) 16th IEEE/ACIS International Conference on Computer and Information Science, ICIS 2017, pp. 821–826. IEEE Computer Society (2017). https://doi.org/10.1109/ICIS.2017.7960106
11. Liu, P., Li, Y., Ai, S., Zhang, W.: Four rules for converting complex loops to regular expressions. In: 9th International Conference on Dependable Systems and Their Applications, DSA 2022, pp. 1055–1056. IEEE (2022). https://doi.org/10.1109/DSA56465.2022.00160
12. Liu, P., Xu, Z.: MTTool: a tool for software modeling and test generation. IEEE Access **6**, 56222–56237 (2018). https://doi.org/10.1109/ACCESS.2018.2872774
13. McNaughton, R., Yamada, H.: Regular expressions and state graphs for automata. IRE Trans. Electron. Comput. **9**(1), 39–47 (1960). https://doi.org/10.1109/TEC.1960.5221603
14. Miao, H., Qian, Z., Song, B.: Towards automatically generating test paths for web application testing. In: Second IEEE/IFIP International Symposium on Theoretical Aspects of Software Engineering, TASE 2008, pp. 211–218. IEEE Computer Society (2008). https://doi.org/10.1109/TASE.2008.26
15. Pan, R., Bagherzadeh, M., Ghaleb, T.A., Briand, L.C.: Test case selection and prioritization using machine learning: a systematic literature review. Empir. Softw. Eng. **27**(2), 29 (2022). https://doi.org/10.1007/S10664-021-10066-6

16. Papadimitriou, C.H.: On the complexity of integer programming. J. ACM **28**(4), 765–768 (1981). https://doi.org/10.1145/322276.322287
17. Sakarovitch, J.: Elements of Automata Theory. Cambridge University Press (2009)
18. Utting, M., Pretschner, A., Legeard, B.: A taxonomy of model-based testing approaches. Softw. Test. Verif. Reliab. **22**(5), 297–312 (2012). https://doi.org/10.1002/STVR.456

Formal Verification of Declarative Specifications of BPs: DCR2CPN-Based Approach

Ikram Garfatta[1]([⊠]), Kaïs Klai[2], and Walid Gaaloul[1]

[1] Institut Mines-Télécom, Télécom SudParis, SAMOVAR UMR 5157, Évry, France
ikram_garfatta@telecom-sudparis.eu
[2] University Sorbonne Paris North, LIPN UMR CNRS 7030, Villetaneuse, France

Abstract. Declarative business process models, notably Dynamic Condition Response (DCR) graphs, have gained traction as an alternative to traditional imperative approaches. However, adequate verification tools for such models remain scarce. This paper proposes a model-checking approach for DCR graphs verification using Coloured Petri Nets (CPN) as a pivot language. The transformation from DCR to CPN is proven to preserve semantics, ensuring the resulting model aligns with the original. Once transformed, the CPN model can be checked by any model checker to verify specific properties. We have automated this process via a C++ prototype that generates CPNs in the specification language of *Helena*, the model checker that we choose to leverage in our work.

Keywords: DCR · Business Process Management · Model Checking · Coloured Petri Nets · Temporal properties

1 Introduction

The most commonly used Business Process Model representations have long relied on imperative workflow descriptions, such as BPMN [20], YAWL [2], and Petri Nets [1]. Such representations are a convenient choice when operations are set and organized in a well-structured manner, allowing designers to define the control flow by specifying *how* tasks are executed. However, when processes must operate under unforeseeable circumstances, determining the order of operations becomes complicated. This is due to imperative models' limitations in providing enough flexibility for ad hoc processes and suitable tools to manage uncertainty and dynamics. To address this, researchers have proposed declarative approaches for business process representation, which are more suitable in such cases [24]. In recent years, these approaches have gained traction among BP designers, especially in sectors requiring high workflow flexibility, such as healthcare and case management [22]. Declarative representations succeed by implicitly describing processes through rules and constraints that govern tasks without specifying a fixed sequential order. They focus on *what* should be enacted rather than *how*.

B. Ben Hedia et al. (Eds.): VECoS 2024, LNCS 15466, pp. 32–46, 2025.
https://doi.org/10.1007/978-3-031-85356-2_3

ConDec [22] and DecSerFlow [3] were among the first declarative languages proposed for process modeling, both supported by DECLARE [23], a prototype workflow management system. In this work, we are interested in Dynamic Condition Response (DCR) graphs [12] as a means for business process representation as this language was proposed to improve on the execution efficiency problems encountered in the former languages [4].

The verification phase is crucial in the business process (BP) life cycle to ensure it meets specified requirements and avoids execution errors. This topic has been extensively studied for imperative representations, as highlighted in the survey conducted in [17]. BPMN, one of the most widely used modeling languages for BPs, has inspired numerous studies focusing on the formal verification of various aspects of BPMN models [6,8,10,21,26,30]. These studies frequently employ Petri nets as a formalism to enhance BPMN semantics. For example, in [8], the authors propose a mapping of BPMN's core elements into labeled Petri net patterns, which was implemented in a tool that automates Petri net generation and assists semantic analysis. Another approach in [21] analyzes BPMN processes using Colored Petri nets [15] as the target formal representation, using a modified BPEL4WS representation as a pivot language. YAWL, also based on Petri nets, extends the formalism to model complex workflows. An automation of transforming BPMN models into YAWL was proposed in [30] for verification using tools like Woflan [29].

These foundational studies marked the beginning of BP verification research, with subsequent studies using extensions of Petri nets to accommodate more complex models [16] and focusing on specific aspects, as in [5,14]. Other formal methods for BP verification include π-calculus [26], event calculus [10], and theorem proving [6].

Similar to the imperative languages of BP modelling, the emergence of the declarative modelling mode needs to be backed up by suitable tools that would allow the verification of its models. In fact, the implicit nature of the representation of the workflow makes it less obvious to be interpreted by the designers and therefore makes it easier for simple modelling errors to pass unnoticed. Moreover, the dynamic and complex nature of the domains that require flexible models puts more at stake and adds to the importance of having a verification tool that would insure the correctness of the process model. However, compared to the rich state of research on imperative business process model verification, there is a notable scarcity of studies on declarative model verification. To address this gap, we propose a model checking approach for DCR graphs using Coloured Petri Nets as a pivot language. We focus on DCR graphs because they offer simplicity and accessibility, with a graphical notation that enhances interpretability compared to models like EM-BrA^{2}CE [11], and fewer rule types than similar representations such as DECLARE [23], while maintaining expressiveness [28].

This expressive power presents challenges for formal verification, as it must manage the complexity of declarative models, which may have conflicting goals or requirements, leading to potential inconsistencies. Our approach involves defining a CPN model (CPN4DCR) that represents a DCR graph with equivalent semantics, allowing for state-based and event-based temporal property verification. We also propose an extension to model DCR choreographies, ensuring correctness through temporal property verification using the *Helena* [9] model checker. The semantic equivalence between DCR graphs and our CPN model has been proven, with the translation implemented via our *DCR2CPN* tool[1].

It is worth noting that the closest approach that could be compared to ours was proposed in [7], where the authors transform DCR graphs into safe Petri nets with inhibitor arcs and read arcs to facilitate formal verification. However, the use of inhibitor arcs can be simplified by using complementary places, especially given that safe Petri nets are inherently bounded. Additionally, while the inclusion of read arcs aims to support concurrency, this feature is not practically implemented in their transformation since the model checker TAPAAL that they use does not support it. Their transformation often results in complex Petri net models, necessitating pruning to manage the size of the reachability graphs. This pruning complicates the verification process, as their bisimilarity proof, which ensures semantic equivalence between DCR and Petri nets, is conducted before pruning, leaving no guarantee of bisimilarity post-pruning. In contrast, our approach offers greater expressiveness since it not only supports the transformation of DCR choreographies but is also more extensible, allowing for future incorporation of additional DCR features such as time constraints, sub-processes, and data elements.

The paper is structured as follows: Sect. 2 defines key concepts (DCR, CPN, LTL). Section 3 introduces a running example. Section 4 presents our main contribution for formal modeling and verification of DCR graphs. Section 5 details the implementation of *DCR2CPN*. Finally, Sect. 6 concludes and discusses future directions.

2   Background

2.1   DCR Graphs and Choreographies

We start by defining DCR graphs before giving the definition of DCR choreographies.

Definition 1. *A DCR graph is a tuple $Gr = (E, M, Act, \rightarrow\bullet, \bullet\rightarrow, \rightarrow+, \rightarrow\%, \rightarrow\diamond, l)$ where $\mathcal{M}(Gr) = (2^E \times 2^E \times 2^E)$ is the set of all markings:*

1. *E is the set of events, ranged over by e.*
2. *$M \in \mathcal{M}(Gr)$ is the marking of the graph (explained below).*
3. *Act is the set of actions.*
4. *$\rightarrow\bullet, \bullet\rightarrow \subseteq E \times E$ are the condition and response relations, respectively. In general, e is a condition for e' ($e \rightarrow\bullet e'$) means that e must have been executed at least once before executing e'. Having e' as a response for e ($e\bullet\rightarrow e'$) means that e' should be executed at least once after having executed e.*

---

[1] https://github.com/Sol2CPN/DCR2CPN.

5. $\rightarrow+, \rightarrow\% \subseteq E \times E$ *are the dynamic include and exclude relations, respectively,*
   satisfying that $\forall e \in E . e \rightarrow+ \cap e \rightarrow\% = \emptyset$.
6. $\rightarrow\diamond \subset E \times E$ *is the milestone relation.*
7. $l : E \rightarrow Act$ *is a labelling function mapping every event to an action.*

DCR Graph: Semantics. A marking $M = (Ex, Re, \text{In}) \in \mathcal{M}(Gr)$ is a triplet
of event sets where Ex represents the set of events that have previously been
executed, Re the set of events that are pending responses required to be executed
or excluded, and In the set of events that are currently included. The idea
conveyed by the dynamic inclusion/exclusion relations is that only the currently
included events are considered in evaluating the constraints. In other words, if e
is a condition for e' ($e \rightarrow\bullet e'$), but is excluded from the graph then it no longer
restricts the execution of e'. Moreover, if e' is the response for e ($e\bullet\rightarrow e'$) but is
excluded from the graph, then it is no longer required to happen for the flow to
be acceptable. The inclusion relation $e \rightarrow+ e'$ (resp. exclusion relation $e \rightarrow\% e'$)
means that, whenever e is executed, e' becomes included in (resp. excluded from)
the graph. The milestone relation is similar to the condition relation in that it
is a blocking one. The difference is that it is based on the events in the pending
response set. In other words, if e' is a milestone of e ($e' \rightarrow\diamond e$), then e cannot be
executed as long as e' is in Re.

DCR Choreography: Syntax. A DCR choreography is a DCR graph that
can be executed in a distributed way. An event in a DCR choreography has an
initiator and can potentially have one or more *receivers*. In the following, we
adapt the definition given in [13] on account of simplicity and better adequacy
with our work.

Definition 2. *A DCR choreography is a couple* (Gr, R) *where R is a set of roles
and Gr a DCR graph whose labelling function l is defined as follows:* $l : E \rightarrow$
$(Act \times R \times \mathcal{P}(R))$.

DCR Choreography: Semantics. A DCR choreography has the same semantics as a DCR graph with the added condition that only the *initiator* of an event
can execute it. For more details on DCR Graphs we refer the readers to [18].
   An example of a distributed DCR graph is given in Fig. 1. Visually, such a
model can be represented as a directed graph with events (boxes) as nodes and
five types of arrows for the five types of relations that can link them. We use the
upper part of a box to indicate the *initiator* of the event and the bottom part
to indicate the *receiver(s)*.

2.2   Coloured Petri Nets

A Petri net [19] is a formal model with mathematics-based execution semantics. It is a directed bipartite graph with two types of nodes: places (drawn

as circles) and transitions (drawn as rectangles). Despite its efficiency in modelling and analysing systems, a basic Petri net falls short when the system is too complex, especially when representation of data is required. To overcome such limitations, *Coloured Petri nets* [15] were proposed as an extension equipping the tokens with colours or types allowing them to hold values.

The formal definition of CPN's syntax is given in Definition 3.

Definition 3 (Coloured Petri net). *A* Coloured Petri Net *is a nine-tuple* $CPN = (P, T, A, \Sigma, V, C, G, E, I)$, *where:*

1. P *is a finite set of* places.
2. T *is a finite set of* transitions *such that* $P \cap T = \emptyset$.
3. $A \subseteq (P \times T) \cup (T \times P)$ *is a set of directed* arcs.
4. Σ *is a finite set of non-empty* colour sets.
5. V *is a finite set of* typed variables *such that* $Type[v] \in \Sigma$, $\forall v \in V$.
6. $C : P \to \Sigma$ *is a* colour set function *that assigns a colour set to each place.*
7. $G : T \to EXPR_V$, *where* $EXPR_V$ *is the set of expressions with variables in* V, *is a* guard function *that assigns a guard to each transition t.*
8. $E : A \to EXPR_V$ *is an* arc expression function *that assigns an arc expression to each arc a such that* $Type[E(a)] = C(p)_{MS}$ *(i.e., the type of an expression corresponds to the multiset of the colour of the arc's place).*
9. $I : P \to EXPR_\emptyset$ *is an* initialisation function *that assigns an initialisation expression to each place p such that* $Type[I(p)] = C(p)_{MS}$.

CPN: Semantics. For CPN $(P, T, A, \Sigma, V, C, G, E, I)$, we note:

- A *marking* is a function M that maps each place into a multiset of tokens.
- The *initial marking* M_0 is defined by $M_0(p) = \langle I(p) \rangle$ for all $p \in P$.
- The *variables of a transition* t are denoted by $Var(t) \subseteq V$.
- A *binding* of a transition t is a function b that maps each variable $v \in Var(t)$ into a value $b(v) \in Type[v]$. It is written as $\langle var_1 = val_1, ..., var_n = val_n \rangle$. The set of all bindings for a transition t is denoted $B(t)$.
- A *binding element* is a pair (t, b) such that $t \in T$ and $b \in B(t)$. The set of all binding elements $BE(t)$ for a transition t is defined by $BE(t) = \{(t, b) | b \in B(t)\}$. The set of all binding elements in a CPN model is denoted BE.

For more details on CPN we refer readers to [15].

2.3 Linear Temporal Logic

The approach presented in this paper is primarily based on model checking of CPN models w.r.t formulae expressed in Linear Temporal Logic (LTL). This logic was first introduced in [25] as a means to reason about concurrent programs.

In LTL, a classical timeline that starts "now" is considered, where every moment has a unique possible future. In other words, a model of LTL is an infinite sequence of indexed states ($i = 0, 1, 2, ...$) where each point in time has a unique successor. An LTL formula is evaluated over such a sequence of states starting from an i'th state. It contains a finite set *Prop* of atomic propositions, the usual Boolean operators $\neg$, $\wedge$, $\vee$, and $\to$, in addition to temporal operators:

- Until ($\mathcal{U}$): $\varphi\ \mathcal{U}\ \psi$ is true if ψ is true *now* or φ is true *now* and remains so until ψ holds.
- Next ($\mathcal{X}$ or $\circ$): $\mathcal{X}\ \varphi$ is true if φ is true in the next step.
- Globally ($\mathcal{G}$ or $\square$): $\mathcal{G}\varphi$ is true if φ is true in every step.
- Future ($\mathcal{F}$ or $\Diamond$): $\mathcal{F}\ \varphi$ is true if φ is true now or in some future time step.

3 Running Example

In this section, we present a running example inspired from the BPMN choreography in [27], through which we will be explaining our proposed approach and the different notions therein used. We will also use this example to discuss the nature of the properties that we are interested in verifying. Our example is depicted by the DCR choreography shown in Fig. 1, and represents a simplified process for care provision in an Integrated Home Care (*IHC*). Three participants take part in this choreography, namely a *General Practitioner* (*GP*) who is typically a physician in charge of the patient, a *Specialist Physician* (*SP*) who is a doctor certified in a specific area of medical practice and a *Nurse* (*Nu*) who is a licensed general health-care provider. For lack of space, we refer the readers to [27] for a more details on this example.

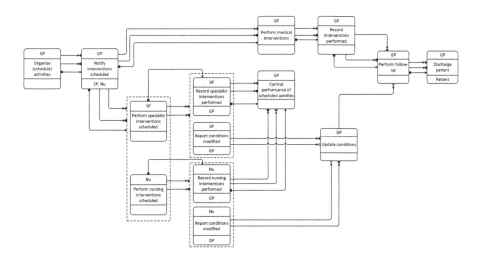

Fig. 1. IHC DCR choreography

4 A CPN Model for DCR Choreographies

As was mentioned in Sect. 1, the approach that we propose for the verification of DCR graphs is based on their transformation into CPN models that hold the same semantics. To this end, we start by presenting, in Sect. 4.1 a CPN model that allows the verification of state-based LTL properties. This models is then extended in Sect. 4.2 to allow the verification of both state- and event-based LTL properties. Finally, we present in Sect. 4.3 a second extension to our model that consists in a transformation of a DCR choreography by taking into account the concept of *roles*.

4.1 CPN4DCR Initial Model

Definition 4 (CPN4DCR). *Given a DCR graph* $Gr = (E, M, Act, \rightarrow\bullet, \bullet\rightarrow,$ $\rightarrow+, \rightarrow\%, \rightarrow\diamond, l)$, *a corresponding CPN model* $CPN4DCR = (P, T, A, \Sigma, V, C,$ $G, E, I)$ *(depicted in Fig. 2a) is defined s.t.:*

- $P = \{S\}$, *where S is the single place of the model representing its state*
- $T = \{t_i, \forall i \in [1, n]\}$, *with* $n = |E|$ *the number of events in* Gr
- $A = \{(t_i, S), \forall t_i \in T\} \cup \{(S, t_i), \forall t_i \in T\}$
- $\Sigma = \{C_E, (C_E \times C_E \times C_E)\}$, *s.t.,* C_E *is defined as a set of integers type s.t., an event* $e_i \in E$ *is represented in* C_E *by its index i.*
- $V = \{Ex, Re, In, Ex', Re', In'\}$, *with* $Type[v] = C_E, \forall v \in V$
- $C = \{S \rightarrow (C_E \times C_E \times C_E)\}$
- $G = \{t_i \rightarrow guard_i, \forall i \in [1, n]\}$, *with* $n = |E|$
- $E = \{(S, t_i) \rightarrow \langle Ex, Re, In\rangle, \forall(S, t_i) \in A \cap (P \times T)\} \cup \{(t_i, S) \rightarrow$ $\langle Ex', Re', In'\rangle, \forall(t_i, S) \in A \cap (T \times P)\}$ *with*
  - $\star$ $Ex' = Ex \cup \{i\}$,
  - $\star$ $Re' = (Re\backslash\{i\}) \cup \{j, \forall e_j \in e_i\bullet\rightarrow\}$ *and*
  - $\star$ $In' = (In \cup \{j, \forall e_j \in e_i \rightarrow+\})\backslash\{j, \forall e_j \in e_i \rightarrow\%\}$
- $I = \{S \rightarrow \langle S_1, S_2, S_3\rangle\}$ *with* $\langle S_1, S_2, S_3\rangle$ *the initial marking M of* Gr

For all $t_i \in T$ *representing an event* e_i *in the DCR graph, we further precise:*

- $guard_i$ *is the conjunction of the conditions defining the enabling of the corresponding event* e_i:
  1. $i \in In$,
  2. $(\{j, \forall e_j \in \rightarrow\bullet e_i\} \cap In) \subseteq Ex$ *and*
  3. $\{j, \forall e_j \in \rightarrow\diamond e_i \cap In\} \subseteq (E\backslash Re)$
- *the expression* $\langle Ex', Re', In'\rangle$ *on its output arc is defined such that:*
  1. $Ex' = Ex \cup \{i\}$,
  2. $Re' = (Re\backslash\{i\}) \cup \{j, \forall e_j \in e_i\bullet\rightarrow\}$ *and*
  3. $In' = (In \cup \{j, \forall e_j \in e_i \rightarrow+\})\backslash\{j, \forall e_j \in e_i \rightarrow\%\}$

Applying this definition on the DCR graph that would be obtained if we were to omit the concept of *roles* from our choreography in Fig. 1 is shown in Fig. 2b.

Definition 5 (Marking Equivalence). *A marking* $M^{Gr} = \langle Ex, Re, In\rangle$ *of a DCR graph Gr is said to be equivalent to a marking* $M^C = \langle S \rightarrow \langle S_1, S_2, S_3\rangle\rangle$ *of a CPN model C iff*

- $\forall e_i \in Ex$ (respectively Re and In), $\exists i \in S_1$ (respectively S_2 and S_3), and
- $\forall i \in S_1$ (respectively S_2 and S_3), $\exists e_i \in Ex$ (respectively Re and In)

We note $M^{Gr} \equiv M^C$.

Definition 6 (Execution Sequence Equivalence). *An execution sequence of length k, $\sigma_k^{Gr} = \langle e_i, ..., e_j \rangle$ of a DCR graph Gr is said to be equivalent to an execution sequence of length k, $\sigma_k^C = \langle t_i, ..., t_j \rangle$ of a CPN model C iff*

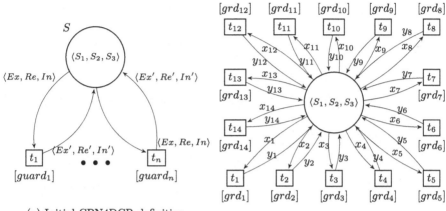

(a) Initial CPN4DCR definition

(b) Initial CPN4DCR of the IHC example

Fig. 2. Initial CPN4DCR

- $(M_1^{Gr} \equiv M_1^C \wedge M_1^{Gr} \xrightarrow{\sigma_k^{Gr}} M_2^{Gr} \wedge M_1^C \xrightarrow{\sigma_k^C} M_2^C) \implies M_2^{Gr} \equiv M_2^C$

We note $\sigma_k^{Gr} \equiv \sigma_k^C$.

Theorem 1. *Let Gr be a DCR graph and C the corresponding CPN model generated by following Definition 4, then Gr and C are semantically equivalent.*

Proof. Let Gr be a DCR graph and C the corresponding CPN model generated by following Definition 4. In order to prove that Gr and C are semantically equivalent we need to prove that

1. $\forall \sigma_k^{Gr} = \langle e_1, ..., e_k \rangle, \exists \sigma_k^C = \langle t_1, ..., t_k \rangle$, and
2. $\forall \sigma_k^C = \langle t_1, ..., t_k \rangle, \exists \sigma_k^{Gr} = \langle e_1, ..., e_k \rangle$

such that $\sigma_k^{Gr} \equiv \sigma_k^C$, $\forall k \in [1, m]$ with m the length of the longest execution sequence. We start by proving *(1)*:

- Let $P(n)$ be the statement: $\forall \sigma_n^{Gr} = \langle e_1, ..., e_n \rangle, \exists \sigma_n^C = \langle t_1, ..., t_n \rangle$ such that $\sigma_n^{Gr} \equiv \sigma_n^C$.
- $P(1) : \forall \sigma_1^{Gr} = \langle e_1 \rangle, \exists \sigma_1^C = \langle t_1 \rangle$ such that $\sigma_1^{Gr} \equiv \sigma_1^C$. This can be derived from Definition 4. In fact, the initial marking of C (M_0^C) being defined as

equivalent to that of Gr (M_0^{Gr}), and the guard of each transition $t_i \in T$ being defined as to correspond to the enabling conditions of the relative event $e_i \in E$, we can deduce that the set of fireable transitions $(M_0^C \rightarrow)$ corresponds to the set of enabled events $(M_0^{Gr} \rightarrow)$. Additionally, the marking M_i^C obtained by firing t_i is equivalent to that obtained by executing e_i $(M_i^C \equiv M_i^{Gr})$ since the elements of M_i^C are defined as to correspond to the effect of the execution of e_i in Gr.

- Assume that $P(k) : \forall \sigma_k^{Gr} = \langle e_1, ..., e_k \rangle, \exists \sigma_k^C = \langle t_1, ..., t_k \rangle$ such that $\sigma_k^{Gr} \equiv \sigma_k^C$ is true for some $k \in [2, m-1]$. We will prove that $P(k+1) : \forall \sigma_{k+1}^{Gr} = \langle e_1, ..., e_{k+1} \rangle, \exists \sigma_{k+1}^C = \langle t_1, ..., t_{k+1} \rangle$ such that $\sigma_{k+1}^{Gr} \equiv \sigma_{k+1}^C$ is true.

$$\sigma_{k+1}^{Gr} \equiv \sigma_{k+1}^C \implies \exists e_{k+1} \in E, t_{k+1} \in T \text{ such that } \sigma_k^{Gr} \cdot e_{k+1} \equiv \sigma_k^C \cdot t_{k+1} \quad (1)$$

$$\sigma_k^{Gr} \equiv \sigma_k^C \iff (M_0^{Gr} \xrightarrow{\sigma_k^{Gr}} M_k^{Gr} \wedge M_0^C \xrightarrow{\sigma_k^C} M_k^C \wedge M_k^{Gr} \equiv M_k^C) \quad (2)$$

Analogously to the reasoning in the previous point, we can deduce that:

$$\forall e_{k+1} \in E \text{ such that } M_k^{Gr} \xrightarrow{e_{k+1}} M_{k+1}^{Gr},$$
$$\exists t_{k+1} \in T \text{ such that } (M_k^C \xrightarrow{t_{k+1}} M_{k+1}^C \wedge M_{k+1}^{Gr} \equiv M_{k+1}^C) \quad (3)$$

And therefore:

$$\forall \sigma_{k+1}^{Gr} = \langle e_1, ..., e_{k+1} \rangle, \exists \sigma_{k+1}^C = \langle t_1, ..., t_{k+1} \rangle \text{ such that } \sigma_{k+1}^{Gr} \equiv \sigma_{k+1}^C \quad (4)$$

The second part (2) is provable following a similar reasoning.

Discussion. It is evident to see that a DCR graph is a model based on *events* or *tasks*, which in our corresponding CPN model we represent by transitions. It is therefore sensible to assume that the users would want to formulate the properties to be verified based on those tasks. Such properties can refer to (i) the execution of an event, which would translate into a property about the firing of its corresponding transition in the CPN model, or to (ii) the possibility of executing an event, which would translate into a property about the fireability of its corresponding transition. The nuance between the two cases might seem subtle, but the difference is rather plain when it comes to their expression in LTL. To explain this, we will refer to the simple example in Fig. 3. In fact, it would be easy to express a property on the firing of a transition (e.g., if transition t_1 is fired, transition t_2 *will* be fired in the future) using event-based LTL. Such a property would be, in that case, simply expressed as follows: $\mathcal{G}(t_1 \implies \mathcal{F}t_2)$. Expressing the same property using state-based LTL cannot be

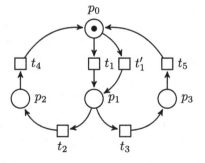

Fig. 3. LTL property example

accomplished in such a straightforward and intuitive way. In general, to express the firing of a transition in state-based LTL we would have to resort to *markings*. Thus, "a transition t is fired" is expressed by the fact that we reach a marking m' that is the immediate successor of a marking m and where the difference between the two markings corresponds to the effects of firing t. More rigorously, t is fired if $\exists m'$ s.t $m \rightarrow m'$ with $m \wedge \mathcal{X} m - pre(t) + post(t)$. On the other hand, it can be intuitive to express properties on the fireability of a transition (e.g., transition t_2 *may* be fired in the future) using state-based LTL as follows: $\mathcal{G}(\mathcal{F} p_1)$. Trying to express the same property in event-based LTL can be very hard to do in complex models as it is counter-intuitive. To be able to express both kinds of properties, we would ideally have a model checker that supports both event-based and state-based LTL formulae. In reality, model checkers only support one kind of LTL properties. To get around this technical limitation, we propose a second CPN model for DCR graphs that allows to easily and efficiently express event-based properties as state-based ones.

4.2 CPN4DCR Generalization for Event-Based Properties

If we go back to the example in Fig. 3, we note that, if we remove the transition t_1', we can find a much simpler state-based LTL property to express the event-based one that we had given as example ($\mathcal{G}(t_1 \implies \mathcal{F} t_2)$). In fact, we would not have to resort to expressing a property on the markings of the model, and the following expression: $\mathcal{G}(p_1 \implies \mathcal{F} p_2)$ would be enough to express an equivalent state-based property to the former one. This is mainly due to the fact that by removing the transition t_1', the place p_1 can only be marked by the firing of t_1, and therefore having a token in p_1 forcibly implies that t_1 has been fired. The idea behind our second model is inspired by this particular case and consists mainly in introducing a set of additional places P^T to the first model, such that we would have one and only one place $p^T \in P^T$ marked when a transition (corresponding to an event in the DCR graph) is fired. We also add a set of *fake* transitions T^F whose role is solely to connect the added places to the main place S of our first model. The definition of our second model can then be given as follows:

Definition 7 (CPN4DCR2).   *Given a DCR graph* $Gr = (E, M, Act,$ $\rightarrow \bullet, \bullet \rightarrow, \rightarrow+, \rightarrow\%, \rightarrow\diamond, l)$ *and its corresponding initial CPN4DCR model* $CPN4DCR = (P, T, A, \Sigma, V, C, G, E, I)$ *as defined in Definition 4, an event-oriented generalization CPN4DCR model* $G\_CPN4DCR = (P', T', A', \Sigma',$ $V', C', G', E', I')$ *(depicted in Fig. 4a) is defined s.t.:*

- $P' = P \cup P^T$ *where* $P^T = \{p_i^T, \forall i \in [1, n]\}$, *with* $n = |E|$ *the number of events in* Gr
- $T' = T \cup T^F$ *where* $T^F = \{t_i^F, \forall i \in [1, n]\}$, *with* $n = |E|$ *the number of events in* Gr
- $A' = \{(S, t_i), \forall t_i \in T\} \cup \{(t_i, p_i^T), \forall t_i \in T \text{ and } p_i^T \in P^T\} \cup \{(p_i^T, t_i^F), \forall p_i^T \in P^T \text{ and } t_i^F \in T^F\} \cup \{(t_i^F, S), \forall t_i^F \in T^F\}$

- $\Sigma' = \Sigma$
- $V' = V \cup \{X\}$, with $Type[X] = (C_E \times C_E \times C_E)$
- $C' = C \cup \{p_{T_i} \rightarrow (C_E \times C_E \times C_E), \forall p_i^T \in P^T\}$
- $G' = G$
- $E' = \{a \rightarrow \langle Ex, Re, In \rangle, \forall a \in A \cap (\{S\} \times T)\} \cup \{(t_i, p_i^T) \rightarrow \langle Ex', Re', In' \rangle, \forall (t_i, p_i^T) \in A \cap (T \times P^T)\} \cup \{a \rightarrow X, \forall a \in A \cap (P^T \times T^F) \cup (T^F, \{S\})\}$ with (1) $Ex' = Ex \cup \{i\}$, (2) $Re' = (Re \backslash \{i\}) \cup \{j, \forall e_j \in e_i \bullet \rightarrow\}$ and (3) $In' = (In \cup \{j, \forall e_j \in e_i \rightarrow +\}) \backslash \{j, \forall e_j \in e_i \rightarrow \%\}$
- $I' = I$

Optimization of the Model. Adding *fake* transitions and places to our CPN model would indeed increase the size of its state space since we are basically creating intermediate states between the original states from the initial model. This would degrade the performance of the model checker that is supposed to take in charge the verification of the model. In order to minimize the number of extra states to be created, we only create *fake* transitions for the events involved in the property to be verified. For instance, let us consider the following property on the *IHC* example in Fig. 1: $prop_{DCR} : \mathcal{G}((ReportConditionsModifiedSP \vee ReportConditionsModifiedNu) \implies \mathcal{F} \ UpdateConditionsGP)$ which basically expresses the fact that if any change in the conditions of the patient is reported by either the *SP* or the *Nu*, the *GP* has to update the conditions of the patient in their report. The application of this definition on the DCR graph that would be obtained if we were to omit the concept of *roles* from this choreography, with the aim of verifying the property $prop_{DCR}$ is shown in Fig. 4b.

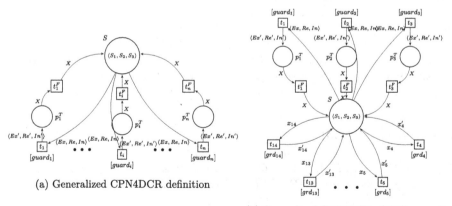

(a) Generalized CPN4DCR definition

(b) Generalized CPN4DCR of IHC example

Fig. 4. Generalized CPN4DCR

4.3   CPN4DCR Extension for DCR Choreographies

In order to be able to verify properties on DCR choreographies, we need to take into account the concept of *roles* in our CPN4DCR model. To do so, we mainly add a place R, initially containing the set of $\langle initiator, receivers \rangle$ in the DCR choreography model, linked to all transitions representing events.

Definition 8 (CPN4DCR3). *Given a DCR choreography (Gr, R) where $Gr = (E, M, Act, \to\bullet, \bullet\to, \to+, \to\%, \to\diamond, l)$, the corresponding initial CPN4DCR model for Gr: $CPN4DCR = (P, T, A, \Sigma, V, C, G, E, I)$ as in Definition 4, and its generalization $G\_CPN4DCR = (P', T', A', \Sigma', V', C', G', E', I')$, the extended CPN4DCR model for choreographies $E\_CPN4DCR = (P'', T'', A'', \Sigma'', V'', C'', G'', E'', I'')$ (depicted in Fig. 5) is defined s.t.:*

- $P'' = P' \cup \{R\}$
- $T'' = T'$
- $A'' = A' \cup \{(R, t_i), \forall t_i \in T\} \cup \{(t_i, R), \forall t_i \in T\}$
- $\Sigma'' = \Sigma \cup \{C_R, (C_R \times \mathcal{P}(C_R))\}$, *where C_R is a colour defined as a string type ($C_R = STRING$) to represent* roles *in DCR*
- $V'' = V' \cup \{V_R, V_{SR}\}$, *with $Type[V_R] = C_R$ and $Type[V_{SR}] = \mathcal{P}(C_R)$*
- $C'' = C' \cup \{R \to (C_R \times \mathcal{P}(C_R))\}$
- $G'' = G'$
- $E'' = E' \cup \{a \to \langle V_R, V_{SR} \rangle, \forall a \in A'' \cap (\{R\} \times T) \cup (T \times \{R\})\}$
- $I'' = I' \cup \{R \to \{r_i, \forall i \in [1..k]\}$, *where each r_i being a token representing the initiator ans potential receivers of an event $e \in E$ with $k = |\bigcup_{j=1}^{|E|} l(e_j)|$.*

For all $t_i \in T$ representing an event e_i in the DCR graph, we further precise that the expression $\langle V_R, V_{SR} \rangle$ on the arcs connecting t_i to R is defined such that $\langle V_R, V_{SR} \rangle = l(e_i)$. For lack of space, the figure of the CPN model obtained by the application of this definition on the DCR choreography in Fig. 1 is included in our online repository[2].

5   Proof of Concept

To demonstrate the feasibility of our approach we implemented a proof of concept in C++ that applies the formal definitions proposed in this paper. Our *DCR2CPN* prototype, available online in our repository (see footnote 2), can be used to generate Coloured Petri Nets written in the specification language of *Helena* [9] from DCR graphs introduced as *XML* files[3]. The implementation consists of a parser for DCR graphs, a translator for converting DCR graphs to CPN models, and a CPN specification files generator. The output of our tool can then be fed, along with an LTL property to be verified, into *Helena* which will either confirm that the property holds or provide a counter-example if it does not. Our tool has been tested on the running example as well as a few

---

[2] See footnote 1.

[3] https://documentation.dcr.design/documentation/dcr-xml/.

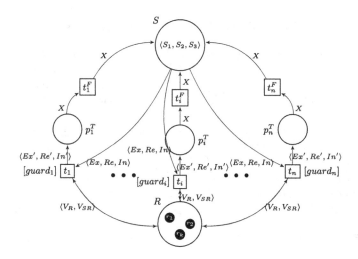

Fig. 5. Extended CPN4DCR for choreographies

other DCR models (see the repository for the artifacts). Leveraging *Helena* we were able to verify a variety of properties such as: *absence of dead activities:* there are no activities that can never be executed, *absence of incomplete process executions:* a process instance can always complete its execution, *reachability of an activity:* all executions of a process must pass by a certain activity (e.g., in our *IHC* example, we can check that all executions must pass by the "Discharge patient" activity), *acceptance of the flow:* the process execution always terminates in an accepting state (i.e., all pending responses are eventually executed or excluded), *other case-specific properties:* for example, in our use case, we can check that if any change in the conditions of the patient is reported by either the *SP* or the *Nu*, the *GP* has to update the conditions of the patient in their report. An exhaustive evaluation using a benchmark of DCR graphs is indeed to be carried out, but these preliminary results bode well as to the validity and efficiency of our approach.

6   Conclusion

Our work proposes a formal verification approach for DCR graphs based on CPN as a pivot formalism. We propose CPN4DCR, a CPN model that we have proven to be semantically equivalent to a DCR graph. This initial model shows some limitations when it comes to the verification of event-based LTL properties, which we solve by proposing a generalization of this model that allows us to verify both state- and event-based properties. Then we propose an extension that allows to additionally represent DCR choreographies in CPN. The endgame is to develop a verification tool that would leverage our CPN4DCR model as well as the *Helena* model checker to verify properties expressed on DCR models. This tool would hide the intricacies of CPN and model checking from the user in order to be accessible to non formal modelling experts. At the time being, we have automated the transformation of a DCR graph into the initial CPN4DCR model. Our next step is to complete the automation of the generalized and extended CPN4DCR models. We will also work on a transformation module for the property to be verified. This module would automatically generate an LTL property expressed on the CPN4DCR elements, given a property that the user would express on the input DCR model. The *Helena* model checker needs to be integrated in the tool to be invoked on the CPN4DCR model along with the generated LTL property. The final step is to present the result returned by *Helena* (i.e., the counter example given in case of violation of the verified property, which is expressed on the elements of CPN4DCR) into a result comprehensible by the user (i.e., expressed on the elements of the DCR).

References

1. van der Aalst, W.M.P.: The application of petri nets to workflow management. J. Circ. Syst. Comput. **8**(1), 21–66 (1998)
2. van der Aalst, W.M.P., ter Hofstede, A.H.M.: YAWL: yet another workflow language. Inf. Syst. **30**(4), 245–275 (2005)
3. van der Aalst, W.M.P., Pesic, M.: Decserflow: towards a truly declarative service flow language. In: Web Services and Formal Methods, Third International Workshop, WS-FM 2006 Vienna, Austria, 8–9 September 2006. LNCS, vol. 4184, pp. 1–23. Springer (2006)
4. van der Aalst, W.M.P., Pesic, M., Schonenberg, H.: Declarative workflows: balancing between flexibility and support. Comput. Sci. Res. Dev. **23**(2), 99–113 (2009)
5. Boubaker, S., Klai, K., Kortas, H., Gaaloul, W.: A formal model for business process configuration verification supporting OR-join semantics. In: On the Move to Meaningful Internet Systems, OTM. LNCS, vol. 11229, pp. 623–642 (2018)
6. Bryans, J.W., Wei, W.: Formal analysis of BPMN models using event-B. In: Formal Methods for Industrial Critical Systems - 15th International Workshop, FMICS. LNCS, vol. 6371, pp. 33–49. Springer (2010)
7. Cosma, V.P., Hildebrandt, T.T., Slaats, T.: Transforming dynamic condition response graphs to safe petri nets. In: Application and Theory of Petri Nets and Concurrency - 44th International Conference, PETRI NETS 2023, Lisbon, Portugal, 25–30 June 2023. LNCS, vol. 13929, pp. 417–439. Springer (2023)
8. Dijkman, R.M., Dumas, M., Ouyang, C.: Semantics and analysis of business process models in BPMN. Inf. Softw. Technol. **50**(12), 1281–1294 (2008)
9. Evangelista, S.: High level petri nets analysis with Helena. In: Applications and Theory of Petri Nets 2005, pp. 455–464. Berlin, Heidelberg (2005)
10. Gaaloul, W., Bhiri, S., Rouached, M.: Event-based design and runtime verification of composite service transactional behavior. IEEE Trans. Serv. Comput. **3**(1), 32–45 (2010)
11. Goedertier, S., Vanthienen, J.: Declarative process modeling with business vocabulary and business rules. In: On the Move to Meaningful Internet Systems 2007: OTM 2007 Workshops, Part I, vol. 4805, pp. 603–612. Springer (2007)
12. Hildebrandt, T.T., Mukkamala, R.R.: Declarative event-based workflow as distributed dynamic condition response graphs. In: Proceedings Third Workshop on Programming Language Approaches to Concurrency and communication-cEntric Software. EPTCS, vol. 69, pp. 59–73 (2010)

13. Hildebrandt, T.T., Slaats, T., López, H.A., Debois, S., Carbone, M.: Declarative choreographies and liveness. In: Formal Techniques for Distributed Objects, Components, and Systems FORTE 2019. LNCS, vol. 11535, pp. 129–147. Springer (2019)
14. Houhou, S., Baarir, S., Poizat, P., Quéinnec, P., Kahloul, L.: A first-order logic verification framework for communication-parametric and time-aware BPMN collaborations. Inf. Syst. **104**, 101765 (2022)
15. Jensen, K., Kristensen, L.M.: Coloured Petri Nets: Modelling and Validation of Concurrent Systems, 1st edn. Springer (2009)
16. Kheldoun, A., Barkaoui, K., Ioualalen, M.: Formal verification of complex business processes based on high-level petri nets. Inf. Sci. **385**, 39–54 (2017)
17. Morimoto, S.: A survey of formal verification for business process modeling. In: Computational Science - ICCS 2008, 8th International Conference. LNCS, vol. 5102, pp. 514–522. Springer (2008)
18. Mukkamala, R.R.: A formal model for declarative workflows dynamic condition response graphs. Ph.D. thesis (2012)
19. Murata, T.: Petri nets: properties, analysis and applications. Proc. IEEE **77**(4), 541–580 (1989)
20. OMG: Business process model and notation (BPMN) 2.0 (2014). https://www.omg.org/spec/BPMN/
21. Ou-Yang, C., Lin, Y.D.: BPMN-based business process model feasibility analysis: a petri net approach. Int. J. Prod. Res. **46**, 3763–3781 (2008)
22. Pesic, M., van der Aalst, W.M.P.: A declarative approach for flexible business processes management. In: BPM 2006 International Workshops, BPD, BPI, ENEI, GPWW, DPM, semantics4ws. LNCS, vol. 4103, pp. 169–180. Springer (2006)
23. Pesic, M., Schonenberg, H., van der Aalst, W.M.P.: DECLARE: full support for loosely-structured processes. In: 11th IEEE International Enterprise Distributed Object Computing Conference, pp. 287–300. IEEE Computer Society (2007)
24. Pichler, P., Weber, B., Zugal, S., Pinggera, J., Mendling, J., Reijers, H.A.: Imperative versus declarative process modeling languages: an empirical investigation. In: Business Process Management Workshops - BPM 2011 International Workshops, Clermont-Ferrand, France, 29 August 2011, vol. 99, pp. 383–394 (2011)
25. Pnueli, A.: The temporal logic of programs. In: Annual Symposium on Foundations of Computer Science, Providence, pp. 46–57. IEEE Computer Society (1977)
26. Puhlmann, F., Weske, M.: Using the *pi*-calculus for formalizing workflow patterns. In: Business Process Management, 3rd International Conference, BPM 2005, Nancy, France, 5–8 September 2005, vol. 3649, pp. 153–168 (2005)
27. Russo, V., Ciampi, M., Esposito, M.: A business process model for integrated home care. In: The 6th International Conference on Emerging Ubiquitous Systems and Pervasive Networks. Procedia Computer Science, vol. 63, pp. 300–307 (2015)
28. Schönig, S., Jablonski, S.: Comparing declarative process modelling languages from the organisational perspective. In: Business Process Management Workshops - BPM 2015, 13th International Workshops, Innsbruck, Austria, 31 August–3 September 2015, Revised Papers. LNBIP, vol. 256, pp. 17–29. Springer (2015)
29. Verbeek, E., van der Aalst, W.M.P.: Woflan 2.0: a petri-net-based workflow diagnosis tool. In: Application and Theory of Petri Nets 2000, ICATPN 2000. LNCS, vol. 1825, pp. 475–484. Springer (2000)
30. Ye, J., Sun, S., Song, W., Wen, L.: Formal semantics of BPMN process models using yawl. In: 2008 Second International Symposium on Intelligent Information Technology Application, vol. 2, pp. 70–74 (2008)

Toward Green Data Lake Management and Analysis Through a CTMC Model

Marzieh Derakhshannia[1]([⊠]), Julien Grange[2], and Nihal Pekergin[2]

[1] IRIT Laboratory, Paul Sabatier University, 31062 Toulouse, France
`marzieh.derakhshannia@irit.fr`
[2] LACL Laboratory, Paris Est Créteil University, 94010 Créteil, France
{`julien.grange,nihal.pekergin`}`@u-pec.fr`

Abstract. In the realm of big data era, large-scale data processing systems are considered critical energy-consumption sources that exert significant impacts on the ecosystem. With the emergence of big data environments, which leads to the production of multi-structured data, numerous solutions and technologies have arisen to efficiently process vast amounts of data, to capitalize on real-time data generation. Recently, a centralized data repository platform called *Data Lake* has been proposed to manage the heterogeneous data originating from diverse sources, and sustainability issues in data platform management have gained traction. In this article, we intend to design and analyze an energy-aware strategy for a green data lake framework. This strategy prioritizes ecological concerns, particularly energy consumption, ensuring the maintenance of sufficient quality of service in terms of data availability. We present a model based on continuous-time Markov chain (CTMC) to analyze the trade-off between energy efficiency and performance of a green data lake platform.

Keywords: Green Data Lake · Energy Efficiency · CTMC

1 Introduction

Big data has become an omnipresent phenomenon that is characterized by the generation of a considerable volume of data in a glance of time. While the huge amount of varied data maintains potential value for generating useful insights and easing the decision-making, processing heterogeneous data is considered a problematic issue, especially in related to environmental considerations. Big data infrastructures which cover the technologies for data storage and processing, must deal with the challenges of high energy consumption [26].

In view of the critical consequences of big data technologies and infrastructures in terms of environmental awareness, it is crucial to develop sustainable strategies for these platforms to efficiently manage the consumption of energy while maintaining quality services for users [20]. The typology of such green strategies for big data infrastructures is classified based on the data lifecycle within these systems. This classification includes all data lifecycle phases

© The Author(s), under exclusive license to Springer Nature Switzerland AG 2025
B. Ben Hedia et al. (Eds.): VECoS 2024, LNCS 15466, pp. 47–61, 2025.
https://doi.org/10.1007/978-3-031-85356-2_4

like green acquisition, green storage, green computation and green communication [26].

Data lakes serve as modern, heterogeneous data management platforms designed to address the shortcomings of traditional data management systems, like data warehouses, in extracting knowledge from raw data [19]. The integrated data lake infrastructure, typically deployed on the Hadoop environment, allows data to be stored in various formats and structures for future use [6]. The data lake pipeline includes interdependent layers supporting each phase of the data lifecycle: data ingestion, storage, process and access. Consequently, data lakes are recognized as one of the most power-intensive platforms. It is worth mentioning that minimizing power consumption in data management systems often leads to throughput degradation and low quality of service. For this reason, it is imperative to come up with proper green mechanisms and strategies to gain a balance between energy efficiency and quality of service [11].

In this study, we intend to propose a green strategy for a sustainable data lake infrastructure. We first focus on identifying significant events and factors that contribute to high energy consumption, particularly in the storage and processing layers. Our approach involves applying a discrete-event-based system in the form of a continuous-time Markov chain model (CTMC). This model allows to evaluate the various states of power consumption and performance of the data lake layers.

We consider mixed strategies based on two pure strategies, referred to as the *left* and *right* strategies, which manage the job allocation and the configuration of nodes based on three distinct regimes. These regimes represent varying levels of energy consumption and computational power of a node. Our goal is to find an optimal mixed strategy with respect to some objective function, i.e. to specify how nodes should be activated depending on the rate of query arrival in order to achieve a trade-off between energy consumption and data availability in a green data lake. This approach builds on the idea of dynamical scaling of processing capacities, in the line of DVFS [9].

2   Related Work

Due to the significance of environmental concerns in massive data management systems, many recent studies have focused on enhancing energy efficiency in big data infrastructures and platforms. These studies mainly investigate two categories of energy-saving solutions: green hardware design and green software configuration [8]. Considering the broad use of the Hadoop environment and related technologies such as Hadoop Distributed File System (HDFS) and MapReduce, many studies have focused on green strategies for this platform and its components.

In the field of hardware design, several investigations have studied configuration strategies and modern hardware equipment to significantly reduce energy consumption in such systems. The development of modern processors, resource virtualization, task scheduling, node management, and some configuration techniques like Dynamic Voltage Frequency Scaling (DVFS) are among the most common considerations for green hardware design. For example, [9] tackles energy consumption optimization in Hadoop clusters by considering CPU frequency scaling depending on the workload (DVFS). In the same context, [25] implements the DVFS policies to improve energy efficiency in the MapReduce framework. In terms of the configuration methods, [15] proposes an energy-saving model based on storage reconfiguration in a distributed storage system. [12] proposes a green HDFS platform relying on the definition of *cold zones* and *hot zones*, which correspond to sets of idle and active servers, to reduce power consumption in Hadoop clusters.

In terms of the sustainable software solutions, most studies focus on query plan optimization and jobs allocation mechanisms. For instance, [13] proposes a query optimization plan that takes into consideration the various energy states of hardware components to improve energy efficiency in modern databases. In the same context, [16] focuses on improving the database query optimiser to generate power-efficient query plans.

3   Green Data Lake Architecture

Data lake architecture as a modern data management system can be considered as a logistical structure where the flow of raw materials (raw data) is converted into useful products (information) through a pipeline of interconnected members (layers) [17]. In such an interconnected system, the performance of each layer directly impacts the others. To achieve high global performance, a comprehensive paradigm is needed to manage all layers toward a unified objective. In the data lake platform, query execution time and data availability have been considered the most critical factors influencing service quality. In light of environmental issues, sustainability considerations are becoming another important factor that should be properly evaluated and taken into account when defining the service level objectives of big data platforms [1].

Following the data lifecycle in a data lake, it is possible to identify energy-consuming operations during data ingesting, storing, processing and querying. We provide an overview of the logistical architecture of the data lake to pinpoint the function of each layer and how it impacts the power consumption of the system:

Ingestion Layer: Ingestion of massive amounts of data from many different sources and in varied structures is handled during this phase. This layer could be considered highly energy-consuming due to need for normalizing the data structures, which require use of CPU, RAM, and storage devices [22]. However, data ingestion into a data lake is more cost-effective than in traditional systems because it skips the data schema normalization phase required in (ETL) processes.

Storage Layer: In the storage layer, data is stored in its native format for future use. One of the most reliable, scalable and fault-tolerant systems for storing large-scale data in the Hadoop environment is a distributed file system called

HDFS (Hadoop Distributed File System) [12]. HDFS is defined by its ability to store and replicate data across multiple clusters of nodes, providing high data availability and throughput [5]. The cluster architecture of HDFS contains two important types of nodes: a NameNode and multiple DataNodes [18]. Node activity and workload management is one of the main strategies for achieving energy efficiency and power consumption control in the data lake storage layer. Dynamic node management policies, such as adjusting the number of idle or active nodes and servers, CPU frequency control, resource allocation, and DataNodes scheduling, should be considered when analyzing the energy efficiency of the Hadoop environment [3].

Processing Layer: The large amount of heterogeneous data processed in the processing layer makes this layer the most prominent in terms of power consumption. MapReduce is recognized as a big data processing technology that handles large-scale data using parallel computing. A user request is submitted to the framework in the form of *jobs*. Two important MapReduce components, Job-Tracker and TaskTracker, manage the jobs allocation and server configuration to execute the Map and Reduce phases [7]. Hence, various factors like heterogeneous clusters, workload management strategies, calculation algorithms, CPU utilization, task scheduling, and job management can significantly influence the efficiency of this layer in terms of performance and power consumption [15]. In particular, the number of active jobs in the process layer is the parameter which makes a remarkable difference in the CPU rate, execution time, data availability and overall system efficiency [10].

Access Layer: For a specific query, there can be multiple equivalent query plans that produce identical results but differ in power efficiency and response time. In each data management system, the query optimizer aims to choose the best query plan based on a statistical information [8]. Many factors play critical roles in the energy consumption of the query process, such as the number of processed tuples, the number of read and write operations in memory, and the number of I/O communications. Furthermore, each query operation, including *Update, Insert, Delete, Create table, Select, Join*, etc., possesses a distinct energy consumption pattern and cost model depending on the number and order of operations involved. As a result, cost estimation and query optimization for various query plans are among the most relevant topics in the field of green data management systems [27].

Based on the above, the storage, processing and access layers emerge as the most critical ones both in terms of energy consumption and execution time. In this paper, our aim is to present a green node management strategy in storing and processing the data in the data lake pipeline, based on the entry workload. Therefore, we only focus on the storage and processing layers to offer a unified framework.

4 Green Data Lake Management Model

In this section, we construct a discrete-event model in the form of a continuous-time Markov chain model (CTMC) to evaluate the power consumption and performance of a data lake, in order to propose green data lake strategies and provide an acceptable trade-off between energy consumption and data availability. We make several assumptions to simply the data lake structure in order to build our model:

- The data lake is implemented in Hadoop environment [24];
- The storage layer relies on HDFS (Hadoop Distributed File System);
- The DataNode management and scheduling are handled by NameNode, based on HDFS policy;
- The processing layer uses MapReduce technology;
- A MapReduced job is defined as a query operation (corresponding to the one-operation-to-one-job approach) [14];
- The job and node failure are not taken into consideration;
- We consider only one type of computing and storage entities: *nodes*.

Based on the assumptions provided, our primary goal is to establish a policy that manages the energy-efficiency of the node while maintaining an acceptable quality of service and response time. There exist several methods and strategies to monitor the power consumption of the nodes, such as DVFS, which adjusts the voltage frequency [4]. In this study, we propose a related strategy which controls dynamically the frequency (and consequently, the energy consumption) of each node depending on the number of queries the system has to manage. In our model, we consider three distinct node regimes, described below. Reducing the operating mode of a node decreases its storage bandwidth, computing power, and overall power consumption [2]. The three regimes are as follows:

(R_0) **Stand-by regime:** In Stand-by regime, nodes consume a negligible amount of energy, but they are not capable of storing data or do a computation.
(R_1) **Low regime:** In this regime, nodes have limited energy consumption, which leads to a low output rate and make them less efficient for storing and processing data.
(R_2) **High regime:** Nodes in this mode provide a high service rate at the cost of high energy consumption.

As mentioned above, we model strategies both for the storage layer and the processing layer. The storage layer stores data on the nodes, while the processing layer receives client queries as input. Both layers exhibit similar behavior: upon the arrival of input data, they activate a certain number of nodes either for data storage or computation, which allows us to model strategies for these two layers in a unified way. The arrival of such inputs follows a Poisson distribution. Upon arrival, the input is divided into several *jobs*. In the case of a query, each of these jobs represents a MapReduce operation, corresponding to an operation like

Join or *Group by*. This corresponds to the one-operation-to-one-job approach. In the case of incoming data, the number of jobs corresponds to the number of data nodes on which this data is stored. Due to the replication policy, the same data must be stored on several nodes, resulting in that number of jobs.

We represent the internal state of the data lake at time t by a pair of random variables $(J(t), R(t))$:

- $J(t)$ is the number of active jobs in the data lake,
- $R(t) = (R_0(t), R_1(t), R_2(t))$ is the vector representing the number of nodes in each mode at time t.

There are only two events which are relevant to our model: query arrival and job completion. We assume that each kind of event occurs identically and independently with a time-homogeneous exponential rate. Since we assume that the evolution of the state variables due to the occurrence of an event depends only upon their current values, the underlying model is a time-homogeneous continuous-time Markov chain [23].

4.1 Model Parameters

Dimensioning Parameters. The dimension of our data lake is given by the following parameters:

- n: Total number of nodes.
- jn_{Max}: Maximum number of jobs per node.

Hence, the maximal number of jobs that can simultaneously be supported by the data lake is $n * jn_{Max}$. Beyond that number, any arriving query is rejected. Obviously, the number of queries lost will have a negative impact on the quality of service.

Strategies and Decision Variables: Strategies are defined in terms of two decision variables. The first one is the *threshold* thr, which is the maximal number of jobs a node in low regime will be able to service. Thus, we assume that the *capacity* of a configuration (R_0, R_1, R_2), i.e. the maximal number of jobs it can service, is

$$cap(R_0, R_1, R_2) = R_1 * thr + R_2 * jn_{Max}. \tag{1}$$

Beyond that capacity, the configuration must change, meaning that either one node in (R_0) must be upgraded to regime (R_1) or one node must move from (R_1) to (R_2).

Note that this choice is not deterministic. For instance, if the node configuration is $(3, 2, 0)$ (meaning that there are 3 nodes in mode (R_0), 2 in mode (R_1) and none in regime (R_3)) and an arrival query spawns enough jobs to exceed $cap(R_0, R_1, R_2)$, there are two possibilities to increase the processing capacities: either go to configuration $(2, 3, 0)$ or $(3, 1, 1)$. Thus, a strategy needs to decide whether it will prioritize putting stand-by nodes to work (below, the *left strategy*), or increasing the capacity of already active nodes (the *right strategy*). This leads to following two strategies after a query arrival:

Left strategy: When the capacity is exceeded in node configuration (R_0, R_1, R_2) where $R_0 > 0$, the next node configuration is (R_0-1, R_1+1, R_2).
Right strategy: When the capacity is exceeded in node configuration (R_0, R_1, R_2) where $R_1 > 0$, the next node configuration is (R_0, R_1-1, R_2+1).

To allow for more fine-grained strategies, we consider mixed strategies, where each time the capacity is exceeded, the behavior is randomly determined. Such a strategy is defined by the probability r of following a right strategy any time the capacity is exceeded – a left strategy being chosen with probability $1 - r$. This $r \in [0, 1]$ is the second decision variable of our model. Obviously, when the left strategy (resp. right strategy) cannot be applied because $R_0 = 0$ (resp. $R_1 = 0$), we apply the right strategy (resp. left strategy) with probability 1.

Following a job service completion, the load of the system diminishes, thus the regime of a node must be downgraded if possible. In this case, **left strategy** means to downgrade a node in regime (R_2) to (R_1), while **right strategy** means to downgrade a (R_1) node to (R_0). As for mixed strategies, if a job completion brings the load under the capacity of a configuration with lower regimes, a left strategy will be applied if possible with probability $1 - r$, and a right strategy will be applied if possible with probability r. For instance, if a jobs completion occurs in configuration $(3, 1, 1)$ and the new load can be supported by configurations $(4, 0, 1)$ and $(3, 2, 0)$, then the only node in regime (R_2) will be downgraded to (R_1) with probability $1 - r$ (left strategy, leading to configuration $(3, 2, 0)$), while the node in regime (R_1) will go to regime (R_0) with probability r (right strategy, yielding configuration $(4, 0, 1)$).

Event Rates: As mentioned above, we consider two events: *query arrival* and *job completion*. We assume the arrival of queries to the data lake follows a Poisson distribution with rate λ, meaning that the expected time between two queries is $\frac{1}{\lambda}$. As a reminder, a query consists of a set of operations, each generating a job. In our model, each query is divided into several jobs upon arrival, with the probability of an incoming query resulting in i jobs denoted as p_i. To maintain a tractable model, we disregard the relationship between jobs and the queries that spawned them. In other words, once a query arrives, it generates a certain number of jobs, which from then on are indistinguishable from previously running jobs. At any given time, we only track the total number of jobs. Consequently, we do not consider query completion but rather job completion, and we treat each completed job as a step toward the completion of the query that spawned it. We believe that observing job completion provides a reasonable approximation of the desired performance objective, which is to maximize the query completion rate.

We assume that all jobs are identical and that their execution time follows an exponential distribution. The parameter μ_1 represents the service rate for a single job running alone on a node in mode (R_1). Similarly, μ_2 represents the service rate of a node in regime (R_2) running one job. The contention between jobs running on the same node will be taken into account.

With that in mind, we describe how we model the job completion rate, and defer the discussion about rewards for these job completions to a later section. We use the following formula to determine the rate of jobs completion, in the case where j_1 jobs run on the $R_1(t)$ nodes in mode (R_1), and j_2 on the $R_2(t)$ nodes in regime (R_2):

$$R_1(t) * \mu_1 \sqrt{j_1} + R_2(t) * \mu_2 \sqrt{j_2}. \tag{2}$$

Let us now explain the reason behind the choice of formula (2). Recall that the parameter μ_i, for $i \in \{1, 2\}$, represents the completion rate of a single job running alone on a node in state (R_i). The completion rate is composed of two parts: the first one corresponding to regime (R_1), and the second to regime (R_2). Their sum gives the completion rate for the whole system.

The service rate for a job is obviously an increasing function of the number of active nodes, provided there are more jobs than nodes. The job completion rates in nodes of (R_i) regime is multiplied by the number of nodes in (R_i) regime, R_i.

Furthermore, with a constant number of jobs, this rate will increase if nodes are in a higher regime. In formula (2), this amounts to saying $\mu_2 > \mu_1$.

Several jobs may be executed in an interleaving manner on a node, thus an increase in the number of jobs would lead to an increase in the job completion rate. However, there would be an overhead due to the shared resource contention. Therefore the increase of the job completion rate with respect to the increase of the number of jobs can not be linear but rather sublinear. To account for this behavior, we choose as concave function the square root function.

Of course, we do not want to explicitly distribute the jobs on the set of active nodes. Our approach is rather to suppose that MapReduce does this distribution optimally, that is, in a way that maximizes the rate. With this assumption, the rate at time t in the configuration $(J(t), R(t))$ with $R(t) = (R_0(t), R_1(t), R_2(t))$ is estimated as

$$\max_{j_1 + j_2 = J(t)} \left(R_1(t) * \mu_1 \sqrt{j_1} + R_2(t) * \mu_2 \sqrt{j_2} \right). \tag{3}$$

If both $R_1(t)$ and $R_2(t)$ are greater than zero, this maximum is reached for

$$\begin{cases} j_1 = \frac{(\mu_1 R_1(t))^2 \, J(t)}{(\mu_1 R_1(t))^2 + (\mu_2 R_2(t))^2} \\ j_2 = \frac{(\mu_2 R_2(t))^2 \, J(t)}{(\mu_1 R_1(t))^2 + (\mu_2 R_2(t))^2}. \end{cases} \tag{4}$$

Obviously, if one of R_1 and R_2 is zero (say $R_1 > 0$, $R_2 = 0$), then (2) is maximal when $j_1 = J(t)$ and $j_2 = 0$. Injecting these values in (2), we get the optimal service rate of a given configuration $(J(t), R(t))$.

Note that another concave function could have been chosen in (2) instead of square root. Our choice is motivated by the relative ease to estimate an optimal solution for (3).

Discrete-Event Based Evolution of the Model: The event-based evolution of the proposed CTMC model is presented in the following pseudo-code

(Algorithm 1). Recall that the query arrival rates are input parameters while service rate parameters are computed from hardware characteristics of the underlying data lake architecture as explained in the previous section. Let us remark that the proposed model is not restricted to two power consumption regimes and can be extended to a more fine-grained hierarchy of node regimes.

Algorithm 1. Discrete-event evolution of the model

 // J' and R'_i are the updated values after arrival and service events
if event: input query arrival **then**
 the query is split in i jobs with probability p_i
 if $J + i > \mathrm{n} * \mathrm{jn}_{\mathrm{Max}}$ **then**
  $J' = J$ *// reject the query*
 else
  $J' = J + i$ *// update the number of active jobs*
 end if
 // upgrade the regime if possible
 if $J' > \mathrm{cap}(R_0, R_1, R_2)$ **then**
  if $R_0 > 0$ and $R_1 > 0$ **then**
   $R'_0 = R_0 - 1; R'_1 = R_1 + 1$, with probability $1 - r$ *// left strategy*
   $R'_1 = R_1 - 1; R'_2 = R_2 + 1$, with probability r *// right strategy*
  else if $R_0 = 0$ **then**
   $R'_1 = R_1 - 1; R'_2 = R_2 + 1$ *// forced right strategy*
  else
   $R'_0 = R_0 - 1; R'_1 = R_1 + 1$ *// forced left strategy*
  end if
 end if
end if
if event: job completion **then**
 $J' = J - 1$ *// update the number of active jobs*
 // downgrade the regime if possible
 if $R_1 > 0$ and $R_2 > 0$ **then**
  if $J' \leq \mathrm{cap}(R_0 + 1, R_1 - 1, R_2)$ and $J' \leq \mathrm{cap}(R_0, R_1 + 1, R_2 - 1)$ **then**
   $R'_1 = R_1 + 1; R'_2 = R_2 - 1$, with probability $1 - r$ *// left strategy*
   $R'_0 = R_0 + 1; R'_1 = R_1 - 1$, with probability r *// right strategy*
  else if $J' \leq \mathrm{cap}(R_0 + 1, R_1 - 1, R_2)$ and $J' > \mathrm{cap}(R_0, R_1 + 1, R_2 - 1)$ **then**
   $R'_1 = R_1 + 1; R'_2 = R_2 - 1$, with probability $1 - r$ *// left strategy*
  else if $J' > \mathrm{cap}(R_0 + 1, R_1 - 1, R_2)$ and $J' \leq \mathrm{cap}(R_0, R_1 + 1, R_2 - 1)$ **then**
   $R'_0 = R_0 + 1; R'_1 = R_1 - 1$, with probability r *// right strategy*
  end if
 else if $R_2 = 0$ and $J' \leq \mathrm{cap}(R_0 + 1, R_1 - 1, R_2)$ **then**
  $R'_0 = R_0 + 1; R'_1 = R_1 - 1$ *// forced right strategy*
 else if $R_1 = 0$ and $J' \leq \mathrm{cap}(R_0, R_1 + 1, R_2 - 1)$ **then**
  $R'_1 = R_1 + 1; R'_2 = R_2 - 1$ *// forced left strategy*
 end if
end if

4.2 Model Assessment

The underlying CTMC is finite, provided that dimensioning parameters are finite, thus the unique limit (steady-state) distribution exists. We consider the long run power consumption and data availability of the data lake under the proposed strategies. A green data lake management aims to provide low response times and a minimal query loss while maintaining low power consumption.

In our model, the dimension of the data lake is specified by the maximum number of nodes, n and the maximum number of jobs by node, jn_{Max}. We must inject hardware characteristics as input in our model to be able to evaluate the Quality of Service (QoS) and the power consumption. The hardware characteristics are summarized by the service rate for a job, μ_k, if it is executed alone by a node operating in regime (R_k). The power consumption of a node in regime (R_k) is given by c_k. The parameters of the proposed CTMC model are given in Table 1.

Table 1. The model notations

Notation	Definition
n	Number of nodes
jn_{Max}	Maximum number of jobs per node
thr	Maximum number of jobs on a node in (R_1)
r	Probability to choose right strategy
λ	Query arrival rate
p_i	Probability of incoming query that gives rise to i jobs
μ_k	Service rate of a job running on a node at regime $k = \{1, 2\}$
c_k	Power consumption of a node in regime $k = \{0 \cdots 2\}$
$J(t)$	Number of jobs at time t
$R(t)$	Vector representing the number of nodes in each regime at time t

We evaluate two QoS measures: expected response time per job ER and expected query loss, EL in steady-state for a given data lake configuration. The first measure ER is calculated by Little's theorem [23]. We need to compute the expected number of jobs, EJ and the expected throughput, thput. It follows from Little's theorem that $ER = EJ/\text{thput}$. For each state (J, R), we assign a reward J to compute EJ. In order to count job completions, a reward of 1 is allocated to states where a job service occurs. To compute the second QoS measure, expected query loss, we assign a reward of 1 to states in which maximum job capacity (i.e. $jn_{Max} * n$) is exceeded after a query arrival.

We also assign rewards to states depending of the power consumption of the regimes of their nodes. We assume that the energy consumption of a node in (R_0) is negligible. The reward representing the power consumption of a node in mode (R_1) (resp. (R_2)) is defined as c_1 (resp. c_2) where $c_2 > c_1$. Therefore for a state in configuration (R_0, R_1, R_2), the power consumption reward amounts to $c_1 * R_1 + c_2 * R_2$. We denote by EP the expected power consumption of the date lake in steady state.

Through numerical analysis of the underlying CTMC, we compute the steady-state distribution and the corresponding expected rewards. The CTMC model cannot be directly applied for optimisation. However, its analysis provides the expected rewards for fixed decision parameter values (thr and r), indicating the efficiency of the strategy. We can then compute this reward for different values, and retain the parameter values and strategies which minimize the underlying reward.

5   Numerical Experiences

In this section we present some numerical results to illustrate how a trade-off between QoS and power consumption can be obtained through dynamic management of the processing speed (frequency) of the nodes. We use the probabilistic model-checker Prism[1] to construct and analyze the proposed CTMC model. Data lakes are complex systems, and obtaining values for the parameter in different level of abstraction is hard work. We looked into various articles in the literature to obtain relevant estimations of the model parameters.

We analyzed the queries from a dataset containing 103 typical HIVE queries[2]. The probability that a query that will result in i jobs arrives, p_i, is statistically estimated from this dataset. The external query arrival rate, λ, is an input parameter in the following experiments. The expected number of jobs per arrival is approximately 5, with the following probabilities: $p_2 = 0.05$, $p_3 = 0.34$, $p_4 = 0.18$; $p_6 = 0.24$, $p_8 = 0.09$ and $p_{12} = 0.1$.

Let f_1 (resp. f_2) be the frequency for regime (R_1) (resp. (R_2)). The job completion rate when one job executed alone in regime (R_i), μ_i, depends on the frequency of regime (R_i). Obviously, $f_1 < f_2$ entails $\mu_1 < \mu_2$. We assume that this dependency is linear: if $f_2/f_1 = k$ then $\mu_2/\mu_1 = k$. The power consumption of a node increases with its frequency. Let Pow_i be the power consumption of a node in regime (R_i). As $f_1 < f_2$, we have $Pow_1 < Pow_2$. In several articles of the literature, this dependency is stated to be a cubic function (see e.g. [21]). If $f_2/f_1 = k$ then $Pow_2/Pow_1 = k^3$. Following these, we assume such a dependency between the frequency ratio and the power consumption ratio.

We consider two major QoS measures: the expected response time per job, ER, and the expected query loss, EL. In the case when the date lake is not overloaded, EL is negligible and the job completion rate can be considered to be equal to job arrival rate, which is the query arrival rate multiplied by the expected number of jobs per query arrival. Thus ER will be equal to the expected number of jobs, EJ divided by a constant. Smaller EJ values imply then low response times, which indicate better QoS. However, when the date lake is overloaded, EJ cannot accurately represent QoS, and we need to evaluate the expected job loss rate (EL) or a weighted combination of EJ and EL.

In the following numerical experiments, we consider the ratios of Pow_2/Pow_1 and μ_2/μ_1 depending on the ratio of f_2/f_1 rather than precise numerical values.

---

[1] https://www.prismmodelchecker.org.

[2] https://github.com/hortonworks/hive-testbench/tree/hdp3/spark-queries-tpcds.

We take $f_2 = k * f_1, k = \{2,3,4\}$ in each experiment without taking a particular value for f_1. We consider a date lake configuration with n = 5, $jn_{Max} = 30$. By taking $\mu_1 = 1$, we normalize the job completion rate in regime (R_1). The power consumption parameter c_1 is also taken as 1. We take $\lambda = 10$, with strategy parameter r taking values between 0.05 and 0.95 with a step of 0.05. We set thr = 15 in Fig 1 and thr = 13 in Fig 2. In each figure, the x axis corresponds to strategy parameter r; in other words, a high r favors a **right strategy** (which pushed nodes to regime (R_2) as early as possible) while small values of r favor a **left strategy** (thus pushing as many nodes to regime (R_1) before promoting them to (R_2)). The y axis of the various graphics represent expected performances measures in the steady-state; respectively number of jobs, power consumption, query lost probability, and the number of nodes in (R_0), (R_1), (R_2) regimes.

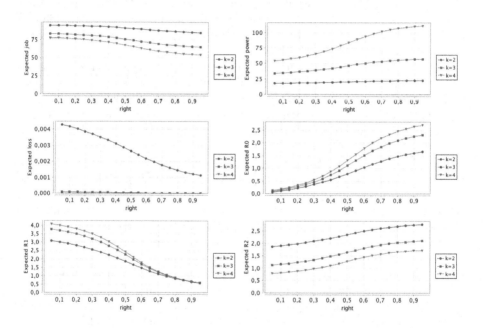

Fig. 1. Performance measures in the steady-state with thr $= 15$

Let us first turn to Fig. 1, namely to the case where thr = 15. It turns out favoring a right strategy (that is, strategies with a high r) has a positive impact on QoS (see the *Expected loss* graphic), at the cost of a higher power consumption (see the *Expected power* graphic). Conversely, the more a strategy veers to the left, the more energy-efficient it becomes, at the cost of QoS.

As to the ration k between the frequency of nodes (R_2) and nodes in (R_1), one can observe that $k = 3$ seems appropriate, since the query loss probability is negligible – as is the case for $k = 4$ – contrary to the case $k = 2$, where some queries cannot be accepted due to the overflow (see the *Expected loss* diagram). The power consumption increase going from $k = 2$ to $k = 3$ is also significantly less than that with $k = 4$. It is thus qualitatively apparent that going from $k = 3$ to $k = 4$ is not justified, as the increase in power consumption is noticeable, and this only yields a negligible improvement on the number of rejected queries, and a small improvement on response time (see the *Expected job* graphic). In the other sub figures, the expected number of nodes in different regimes are given. Remark that the sum of them must be equal to n = 5.

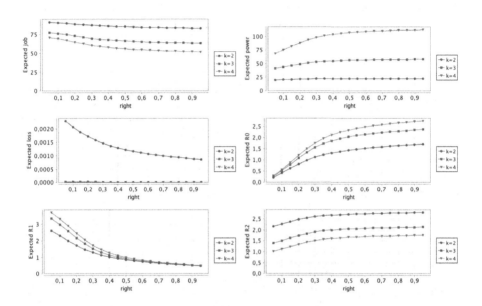

Fig. 2. Performance measures in the steady-state with thr = 13

In Fig. 2, we keep the values of all the parameters, except for thr which is now equal to 13. Intuitively speaking, this means the upgrading mechanism of a node from (R_1) to (R_2) is triggered earlier. The quantitative conclusions obtained by the study of Fig. 1 also apply here. If one decides to go with $k = 3$, there is not much difference between choosing thr = 13 and thr = 15. However, we can observe an significant improvement on the expected query loss when $k = 2$: if one opts for $k = 2$ (for instance because of hardware restrictions, or because one places a high focus energy efficiency in comparison to QoS), then going for a lower value of thr lowers query refusals.

6   Conclusion

In this article, we tackle the essential issue of the environmental impact of data lakes. More precisely, we have taken a first step toward proposing data lake strategies which take into account not only response time but also energy consumption.

Data lakes are complex systems, and having models for such platforms to gain a better insight into their behavior is crucial. We propose a first step model by abstracting and simplifying their various aspects. The numerical examples illustrate that such models are useful to dimension date lake configurations, and evaluate the management mechanisms.

Different extensions are possible, for instance by considering more than 3 node regimes, or by looking into different functions to take into account the contention of several jobs running on a single node. In a second stage, we intend to go from continuous-time Markov chains to Markov decision processes (MDP), which allow to optimize directly on the decision variables.

References

1. Calza, F., Parmentola, A., Tutore, I.: Big data and natural environment. How does different data support different green strategies? Sustain. Futures **2**, 100029 (2020)
2. Chen, J.J., Kuo, C.F.: Energy-efficient scheduling for real-time systems on dynamic voltage scaling (DVS) platforms. In: Proceedings of the 13th IEEE International Conference on Embedded Real-Time Computing Systems and Applications, pp. 28–38. IEEE (2007)
3. Cheng, D., Rao, J., Jiang, C., Zhou, X.: Resource and deadline-aware job scheduling in dynamic hadoop clusters. In: Proceedings of the 2015 IEEE International Parallel and Distributed Processing Symposium, pp. 956–965. IEEE (2015)
4. El Mahjoub, Y.A., Castel-Taleb, H., Le Corre, L.: Stochastic modeling and optimization for power and performance control in DVFS systems (2023)
5. Ghorpade, S.J., Shinde, S.N., Chaudhari, R.S.: A review on big data processing using green hadoop. Int. J. Innov. Comput. Sci. Eng. **4** (2017)
6. Giebler, C., Gröger, C., Hoos, E., Schwarz, H., Mitschang, B.: Leveraging the data lake: current state and challenges. In: Big Data Analytics and Knowledge Discovery, pp. 179–188. Springer (2019)
7. Goiri, Í., Le, K., Nguyen, T.D., Guitart, J., Torres, J., Bianchini, R.: GreenHadoop: leveraging green energy in data-processing frameworks. In: Proceedings of the 7th ACM European Conference on Computer Systems, pp. 57–70 (2012)
8. Guo, B., Yu, J., Liao, B., Yang, D., Lu, L.: A green framework for DBMS based on energy-aware query optimization and energy-efficient query processing. J. Netw. Comput. Appl. **84**, 118–130 (2017)
9. Ibrahim, S., Moise, D., Chihoub, H.E., Carpen-Amarie, A., Bougé, L., Antoniu, G.: Towards efficient power management in MapReduce: investigation of CPU-frequencies scaling on power efficiency in hadoop. In: Adaptive Resource Management and Scheduling for Cloud Computing, pp. 147–164. Springer (2014)
10. Ikken, S., Renault, É., Tahar Kechadi, M., Tari, A.: Toward scheduling I/O requests of MapReduce tasks based on Markov model. In: Proceedings of the International Conference on Mobile Secure Programmable Networking, pp. 78–89. Springer (2015)
11. Kanapram, D., Lamanna, G., Repetto, M.: Exploring the trade-off between performance and energy consumption in cloud infrastructures. In: 2017 Second International Conference on Fog Mobile Edge Computing (FMEC), pp. 121–126. IEEE (2017)

12. Kaushik, R.T., Bhandarkar, M.: GreenHDFS: towards an energy-conserving, storage-efficient, hybrid hadoop compute cluster. In: Proceedings of the USENIX Annual Technical Conference, vol. 109, p. 34 (2010)

13. Lang, W., Kandhan, R., Patel, J.M.: Rethinking query processing for energy efficiency: slowing down to win the race. IEEE Data Eng. Bull. **34**(1), 12–23 (2011)

14. Lee, R., Luo, T., Huai, Y., Wang, F., He, Y., Zhang, X.: YSmart: yet another SQL-to-MapReduce translator. In: Proceedings of the 31st International Conference on Distributed Computing Systems, pp. 25–36. IEEE (2011)

15. Liao, B., Yu, J., Zhang, T., Guo, B., Sun, H., Changtian, Y.: Energy-efficient algorithms for distributed storage systems based on block storage structure reconfiguration. J. Netw. Comput. Appl. **48**, 71–86 (2015)

16. Liu, X., Wang, J., Wang, H., Gao, H.: Generating power-efficient query execution plans. In: Proceedings of the 2nd International Conference on Advances in Computer Science and Engineering (CSE 2013), pp. 286–290. Atlantis Press (2013)

17. Machado, I.A., Costa, C., Santos, M.Y.: Data mesh: concepts and principles of a paradigm shift in data architectures. Procedia Comput. Sci. **196**, 263–271 (2022)

18. Munshi, A.A., Mohamed, Y.A.R.I.: Data lake lambda architecture for smart grids big data analytics. IEEE Access **6**, 40463–40471 (2018)

19. Nargesian, F., Zhu, E., Miller, R.J., Pu, K.Q., Arocena, P.C.: Data lake management: challenges and opportunities. Proc. VLDB Endow. **12**(12), 1986–1989 (2019)

20. Pappas, I.O., Mikalef, P., Giannakos, M.N., Krogstie, J., Lekakos, G.: Big data and business analytics ecosystems (2018)

21. Rizvandi, N.B., Taheri, J., Zomaya, A.Y.: Some observations on optimal frequency selection in DVFS-based energy consumption minimization. J. Parallel Distrib. Comput. **71**(8), 1154–1164 (2011)

22. Roose, P., Valera, H.H.Á., Maurice, A., Ravat, F., Song, J., Vallès-Parlangeau, N.: Energy measurement system for data lake. In: ACIIDS 2024 - 16th Asian Conference on Intelligent Information and Database Systems (2024)

23. Trivedi, K.: Probability and Statistics with Reliability, Queuing and Computer Science Applications (2016). https://doi.org/10.13140/RG.2.1.3432.6009

24. White, T.: Hadoop: The Definitive Guide. O'Reilly Media, Inc. (2012)

25. Wirtz, T., Ge, R.: Improving mapreduce energy efficiency for computation intensive workloads. In: 2011 International Green Computing Conference and Workshops, pp. 1–8. IEEE (2011)

26. Wu, J., Guo, S., Li, J., Zeng, D.: Big data meet green challenges: greening big data. IEEE Syst. J. **10**(3), 873–887 (2016)

27. Xu, Z., Tu, Y.C., Wang, X.: Online energy estimation of relational operations in database systems. IEEE Trans. Comput. **64**(11), 3223–3236 (2015)

A High Parallelization Method
for Automated Formal Verification
of Deep Neural Networks

Imene Ben Hafaiedh[1(✉)], Amira Chouchane[2], Amani Elaoud[3],
Linda Lamouchi[1,2], and Mohamed Ghazel[2]

[1] University of Tunis El Manar (UTM), Institut Supérieur d'Informatique (ISI),
LIPSIC Laboratory, Tunis, Tunisia
`imen.benhafaiedh@isi.utm.tn`
[2] Université Gustave Eiffel, ESTAS, COSYS, Champs-sur-Marne, France
{`amira.chouchane,mohamed.ghazel`}`@univ-eiffel.fr`
[3] LIMTIC Laboratory, École Supérieure de Génie Informatique et de Technologie
(ESGITECH), Tunis, Tunisia
`amani.elaoud@fst.utm.tn`

Abstract. The verification of DNNs has garnered significant attention recently, especially with the growing willingness of their utilization in safety and security-critical applications. Due to the complexity and large size of such networks, ensuring guarantees about their behavior in an automated way remains a challenging task. Despite the challenges, achieving automated formal verification would represent an important step towards their wider adoption. In this paper, we consider the problem of formally verifying DNNs based on an optimized strategy that enables the combination and parallel invocation of a set of existing verification techniques. Our approach involves computing interval over-approximations of the output set for feed-forward neural networks with input uncertainty. We achieve such an over-approximation by leveraging various existing approaches and adapting bound reduction methods for the verification of some desired properties, e.g., robustness. In particular, we propose an automated approach that supports the formal verification of various types of DNN specifications with arbitrary, bounded, multivariate, linear, and non-linear activation functions. We report on the workflow of our approach process, its implementation in a framework, and provide an illustration of the technique using the DNN of the *ACAS Xu* benchmark pertaining to an Airborne Collision Avoidance System.

Keywords: Deep Neural Networks (DNN) · Automated Verification · Formal Verification · Neural Network Robustness

1 Introduction

Deep Neural Networks (DNNs) are one of the most widely used techniques in Machine Learning. Indeed, they are effective learning models that can produce interesting outcomes in a variety of applications such as autonomous

B. Ben Hedia et al. (Eds.): VECoS 2024, LNCS 15466, pp. 62–80, 2025.
https://doi.org/10.1007/978-3-031-85356-2_5

cars [38], games [45], robotics [27] and medecine [16]. Despite their use in a variety of domains, DNNs still have a limited number of applications in situations involving safety and security where assurances regarding networks' performances are required, and concerns about their vulnerability to adversarial perturbations have been accompanying them since their early utilisation [18]. Moreover, because DNNs are black boxes, they are difficult to interpret and correct [34]. This further increases the risk that undesirable behaviors remain undetected. Indeed, in the past years, more and more examples of such weaknesses have been discovered [10]. As a result of this increased awareness about the vulnerability of DNNs and their limited reliability, there is a large and growing body of work in the research community pertaining to DNN verification and, in particular on developing automatic techniques to assist in verifying them [30]. Many of these works include attack and defence techniques for adversarial examples. Such techniques aim to enhance the DNN by identifying or eliminating adversarial attacks [52]. However, they cannot be directly applied to certify DNNs, due to their inability to provide clear assurance evidence with their results. More powerful methods include verification and testing, both of which have been demonstrated as useful in evaluating the reliability of DNNs in the case of real-world software and hardware systems. Testing techniques have been proposed to evaluate the robustness of DNNs against input perturbations [9,39,55]. Such techniques are often effective in finding input samples to demonstrate a lack of robustness, but they cannot prove the absence of such inputs. However, with the expanding use of DNNs in safety-critical applications [24], verification approaches providing formal guarantees about DNN behavior are becoming more and more popular. Such approaches have evolved beyond theoretical consideration [5,6,40], with multiple proposals leveraging various automated reasoning techniques. These include Boolean satisfiability (SAT) solvers [3], Satisfiability Modulo Theories (SMT) solvers [11], and Mixed Integer Programming (MIP) solvers [49]. More specifically, formal verification approaches for DNNs are classified based on their formulation of two types of analysis [32] namely: reachability [5,42], optimization [1].

In the present work, we propose a new formal approach to compute interval over-approximations of the output set of feed-forward deep neural networks [4] with input uncertainty for robustness verification. The developed technique is based on various existing approaches and allows the adaptation of existing bound reduction methods for robustness verification in DNNs. Specifically, during the interval propagation phase, we implement a highly parallelized process that allows the combination of different existing verification methods to refine the obtained results. The implemented algorithm generates the tightest interval over-approximation of the output of each layer obtained while performing the forward propagation. In summary, the key contributions of this paper are three-fold:

- We propose an approach for the formal verification of robustness properties of deep neural networks based on computing interval over-approximations of the output intervals. The approach is based on the idea of combining, in an optimal manner, several existing techniques for robustness verification.

- We develop a framework implementing our method and instantiate it for the parallelization of two well-known existing verifiers, namely ERAN and Planet.
- We conduct experimental evaluations on a popular benchmark and show the effectiveness of our approach in terms of robustness, precision and execution time. We also compare the performance of our framework with the state-of-the-art verification verifiers.

The rest of the paper is structured as follows. In Sect. 2, we introduce some basic notation and definitions to be used throughout the paper. Moreover, we present our approach, detailing the different steps and algorithmic aspects. In Sect. 3, we describe the architecture of the developed framework, while providing some relevant implementation details. Section 4 presents the research questions under investigation, the datasets forming the basis of our experimental analysis, the experimental setup, and discuss the obtained results. Section 5 reviews the related work. We conclude the paper in Sect. 6 with final remarks and suggestions for potential directions in future research.

2   Approach

In this section, we first define the Neural Network Verification (NNV) problem that we aim to solve. Then, we provide a formalization and algorithmic details of our verification approach

2.1   DNN Verification

A DNN $\mathcal{N}$ encodes an approximation of a non-linear and bounded algebraic function $f : \mathcal{R}^n \rightarrow \mathcal{R}^m$ where n is the number of nodes in the input layer, and m represents the number of nodes in the output layer. A DNN $\mathcal{N}$ can be represented as a directed graph $G_\mathcal{N} = < V_\mathcal{N}, E_\mathcal{N} >$ where $V_\mathcal{N}$ is a set of nodes and $E_\mathcal{N}$ is a set of weighted oriented arcs between the nodes. In this paper, we consider the following notations for nodes and arc weights, respectively: $V_\mathcal{N} = \{x_{i,j}; 0 \leq i \leq p-1, 1 \leq j \leq n_i\}$ where p is the number of layers in $\mathcal{N}$ and n_i the number of nodes in the ith layer. In fact, $x_{i,j}$ represents the jth node of the ith layer.

$E_\mathcal{N} = \{w_{k,l}^i; 1 \leq k \leq n_i, 1 \leq l \leq n_{i+1}, 0 \leq i \leq p-1\}$. $w_{k,l}^i$ is the weight of the arc connecting the kth node of the ith layer to the lth node of the $(i+1)^{th}$ layer. It should be noted that, in the context of DNN verification, the weights of all the arcs are known.

DNN verification is the process of ensuring that, for every conceivable input, the neural network output meets some specified criteria. In essence, it involves scrutinizing the relationships between the input and output of the neural network to confirm the persistence of some specific properties of interest. Formally speaking, given a DNN $\mathcal{N}$, a safety property $\phi(\mathcal{N})$ defines a set of corresponding constraints ϕ_I on the DNN inputs (the pre-condition) and a set of constraints

ϕ_O on the DNN outputs (the post-condition). In other words, it seeks for investigating whether the following holds:

$$\forall x \in \mathcal{R}^n : \phi_I(x) \Rightarrow \phi_O(\mathcal{N}(x))$$

where x represents the DNN inputs, $\mathcal{N}(x)$ represents the DNN outputs, $\phi_I(x)$ is the set of constraints on the DNN inputs and $\phi_O(\mathcal{N}(x))$ is the set of constraints on the DNN outputs.

In this paper, we discuss a new approach to compute rigorous bounds on the outputs of a DNN, to formally analyse some properties on the DNN, e.g., robustness.

2.2   Iterative Interval Refinement

The choices of an abstract domain, an upper bound and a lower bound for each DNN node, allows for balancing the precision and scalability of the verification process. For this reason, we have developed an approach that dynamically updates the lower and upper bounds iteratively, layer by layer. During the intervals' propagation phase, we enable a high parallelization process that permits the combination of different existing incomplete verification methods, in order to fine-tune the obtained results. Accordingly, two types of parallelization are considered:

– Intra-layer parallelization: It refers to the concurrent execution of computations among nodes within the same layer of the network. This type of parallelism takes advantage of the fact that the calculations performed by individual nodes within a layer are independent of each other.
– Parallelization of verifiers: It refers to the process of optimizing and accelerating verification tasks by performing the verifiers concurrently or simultaneously. Parallelization of these verifiers aims to exploit the parallel processing capabilities of the computer, enabling multiple computation tasks to be performed at the same time.

We denote by $I_{i,j} = [l_{i,j}, u_{i,j}]$ the interval associated with node $x_{i,j}$, as defined in Subsect. 2.1, where $0 \leq i \leq p-1$ and $1 \leq j \leq n_i$. We denote by $\mathcal{V} = \{V_1, V_2, ..., V_q\}$ the set of q used verifiers for DNN verification, and $I^r_{i+1,j} = [l^r_{i+1,j}, u^r_{i+1,j}]$, with $1 \leq r \leq q$, the bound of node $x_{i+1,j}$ produced by verifier V_r. Our approach involves defining a Verifier, denoted as $V_1 + V_2 + .. + V_q$, which is a combination of the verifiers V_i in $\mathcal{V}$. This verifier takes as an input the output intervals of verifiers V_i, $1 \leq i \leq q$, and produces as an output a lower and upper bounds for node $x_{i+1,j}$ in the $(i+1)^{th}$ layer, defined as follows:

$$[l_{i+1,j}, u_{i+1,j}] = \bigcap_{1 \leq r \leq q} [l^r_{i+1,j}, u^r_{i+1,j}] \tag{1}$$

which means $l_{i+1,j} = \max_{1 \leq r \leq q} l^r_{i+1,j}$, and $u_{i+1,j} = \min_{1 \leq r \leq q} u^r_{i+1,j}$.

The verifier $V_1 + V_2 + .. + V_q$ allows for establishing boundaries for the network nodes outputs, which are more tightly constrained than those obtained by each verifier V_i individually. Consequently, verifier $V_1 + V_2 + .. + V_q$ produces rigorous bounds on the nodes of the output layer. Moreover, the parallelization contributes to the scalability of neural network verification processes, enabling them to handle larger models and datasets more effectively. Specialized hardware, such as GPUs or TPUs, can be utilized to effectively parallelize verifications, capitalizing on their design for superior performance in parallel processing tasks aligned with neural network operations.

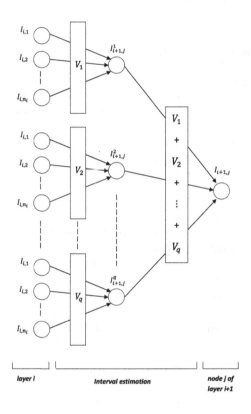

Fig. 1. Principle of the interval estimation

2.3   Verification Algorithm

In this part, we introduce our verification technique as outlined in Algorithm 1. The algorithm presented here takes as input the list of verifiers $\mathcal{V}$, a neural network NN, and the property to be verified P. It outputs the verification verdict, which can be 'Unsat' if property P is deemed satisfactory, 'Sat' if P is considered unsatisfactory, and 'Unknown' if the verifier cannot conclusively determine the satisfaction of property P.

The function $get\_Network\_Infos$ explores the DNN NN and produces the set of known intervals I_0 of the input layer, which are composed of the intervals from $I_{0,1}$ to I_{0,n_0}. It also produces the weight vector W, the number of layers p, the vector N which includes the number of nodes in each layer, and the bias vector b.

Let i be a counter used to traverse the layers of the network from layer 0 to layer $p-2$, layer by layer. For a fixed value of i (layer i). The interval computation is performed in parallel for each node j of layer $i+1$, with $1 \leq j \leq n_{i+1}$ and n_{i+1} is the number of nodes of layer $i+1$. The function $output\_interval$ allows for getting the estimation of the interval $I^r_{i+1,j}$ (as defined in this paper), by the verifier V_r, from the input intervals of layer $i+1$, which is initialized to I_0. This procedure is carried out in parallel for each verifier V_r, with $1 \leq r \leq q$, of the set $\mathcal{V}$. The intervals $I^r_{i+1,j}$ are stored in a vector Q. The estimated interval $I_{i+1,j}$ produced by the verifier $V_1 + V_2 + ... + V_q$ corresponds to the intersection of intervals $Q(r) = I^r_{i+1,j}$ for all $1 \leq r \leq q$. The vector of intervals I includes then the estimated intervals associated with the nodes of layer $i+1$ which, in turn, are the input intervals for layer $i+2$.

For layer $i = p - 2$, the verifier V_r produces an estimation $I^r_{p-1,j}$ for each node j of layer $p-1$ (the DNN output layer). It also produces a verdict for the verification of property P. The estimated intervals $I_{p-1,j}$ for each node j of layer $p-1$ is then not used for the verdict. Therefore, we update the values of $I^r_{p-1,j}$ to determine a new verdict of each verifier using the new estimated interval $I_{p-1,j}$ for each j (replacing the value of $I^r_{p-1,j}$ with the value of $I_{p-1,j}$ for each node j of the last layer). The function $get\_verdict$ provides the verdict of verifier V_r by considering the new estimated values $I^r_{p-1,j}$ for the last layer. The vector R includes then the verdict of different verifiers. The final verdict is based on the different verdicts of the verifiers V_r. If the set of verdicts from different verifiers is either "Sat" or "unknown," then the final verdict is "Sat". Otherwise, if the set of verdicts from different verifiers is either "Unsat" or "unknown," then the final verdict is "Unsat." If all the verdicts are "unknown", then the final verdict is "unknown".

3   Implementation

As a matter of fact, our proof-of-concept implementation of the approach comprises various Python modules, each dedicated to performing one of the aforementioned steps outlined in our proposed method (see Sect. 2). To evaluate our method, we have opted to instantiate it by implementing and integrating two widely recognized DNN verifiers, namely Planet [14] and ERAN [46]. The latter uses abstract interpretation to overapproximate the reachable output region and is considered as the most scalable qualitative verification tool [36]. The former combines techniques from SMT and search-based methods. The choice of these verifiers is driven by the diversity in their underlying approximation techniques.

Algorithm 1. *DNN* Verification

Require: $\mathcal{V} \neq [], NN \neq [], P \neq []$
Ensure: $Vf \in \{Sat, Unsat, Unknown\}$
  $\{I_0, W, N, b, p\} \leftarrow get\_Network\_Infos(NN)$
  $q \leftarrow number\_of\_verifiers(\mathcal{V})$
  $i \leftarrow 0$
  $I \leftarrow I_0$
  while $i \leq p - 2$ **do**
    $n_{i+1} \leftarrow number\_of\_nodes(N, i + 1)$
    $j \leftarrow 1$
    while $j \leq n_{i+1}$ **do**
      $r \leftarrow 1$
      $Q = []$
      while $r \leq q$ **do**
        $I_{i+1,j}^r \leftarrow output\_interval(V_r, I)$ ⎫
        $Q \leftarrow [Q; I_{i+1,j}^r]$ ⎬ in // ⎫
        $r \leftarrow r + 1$ ⎭   ⎪
      end while   ⎪
      $I_{i+1,j} \leftarrow \bigcap\limits_{1 \leq r \leq q} Q(r)$ ⎬ in //
      $I \leftarrow [I; I_{i+1,j}]$ ⎪
      $j \leftarrow j + 1$ ⎪
    end while   ⎭
    $i \leftarrow i + 1$
  end while
  $j \leftarrow 1$
  while $j \leq n_{p-1}$ **do**
    $r \leftarrow 1$
    $R = []$
    while $r \leq q$ **do**   ⎫
      $Verd_r \leftarrow get\_verdict(V_r, I)$ ⎫   ⎪
      $R \leftarrow [R; Verd_r]$ ⎬ in //   ⎬ in //
      $r \leftarrow r + 1$ ⎭   ⎪
    end while   ⎭
    $j \leftarrow j + 1$
  end while
  if (Inclusion(R,Sat,Unknown)=True) **then**
    $Vf \leftarrow Sat$
  else if (Inclusion(R,Unsat,Unknown)=True) **then**
    $Vf \leftarrow Unsat$
  else if (Inclusion(R,Unknown,Unknown)=True) **then**
    $Vf \leftarrow Unknown$
  end if

ERAN, for instance, falls under the class of reachability methods, approximating sets of output values in light of some given input constraints. On the other hand, Planet operates within optimization methods, exploring input space regions to formulate optimization sub-problems. By integrating both verifiers, we leverage the strengths of the two classes of verification techniques. Another motivating factor for instantiating our method with ERAN and Planet lies in their distinct input file requirements. This showcases the extensibility of our framework and its capacity to handle varying input types effectively. Indeed, Planet [15] accepts a unified file as input, encompassing both the network description and the specifications, i.e. the property to be checked. In practice, these properties are encoded as a set of layers appended to the end of the network. The supported properties in this format involve input constraints represented as intervals, and output constraints formulated as linear inequalities over the output neurons. Rather than combining the network and the property to be checked into a single file, ERAN takes in both a network specification and several parameters to specify the property to be checked such as, for instance, the input and output bounds. Our implementation of the proposed approach uses some existing DNN verification tools as a backend. For the evaluation reported here, we used the recently published DNNV framework [43] as the underlying verification engine, which allows us to create and run re-usable verification benchmarks. The overall architecture of our implemented framework is illustrated in Fig. 2. To implement our framework, we have integrated several DNNV modules [44], in such a way as to simplify the execution of our approach. Such modules are mainly used to unify the input files related to the DNN and the properties to be investigated by the implemented verifiers. Indeed, the modules of DNNV that we have integrated in our framework take as an input a network in the common ONNX (Open Neural Network Exchange) [23] input format, a property formulated in an expressive domain-specific language DNNP, and the name of a target verifier. These modules use plugins for the target verifier, and transform the problem by simplifying the network and reducing the property to enable the application of verifiers that otherwise would be unable to run (cf. components *DNN Simplifier* and *Property reducer* highlighted in blue in Fig. 2). Then other modules that we call translators, translate the network and the investigated property to the input format of the desired verifier. In Fig. 2, the modules we have implemented are highlighted in red, and they allow implementing the different steps of our method detailed previously in Sect. 2. Figure 3 shows the matching between the different implemented modules and the typical workflow of our approach. Each module implements some specific steps of Algorithm 1. Technically, the *Input module* splits the input DNN into a unique layer to be merged together with the property to check. Each implemented verifier is then given the corresponding input in the appropriate format. Then, the verifiers (here ERAN and Planet) are run in parallel over this particular layer. The output intervals that are given by each of the verifier are treated through the *Output Optimization* module with respect to the refinement step of our method. The obtained computed interval is given as an input to the computed next layer of the DNN, with the corresponding unification implemented in the *Input Module*. The invocation of our implemented modules is reiterated iteratively until reaching the final layer of the DNN. At this stage, the DNNV module, referred to as the *Output Translator*, is triggered to consolidate and produce the verification result.

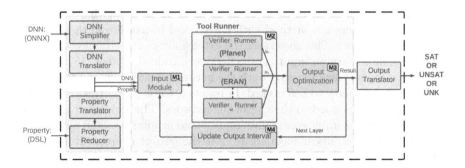

Fig. 2. The Framework Architecture

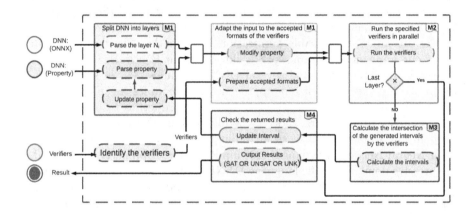

Fig. 3. Approach Workflow: Verification Process

We should mention here that our source code is made available online in a repository[1] along with the executed benchmarks. All the experiments were run on a server with Intel(R) Core(TM) i7-5500U CPU@2.4GHzx4 Processor, 15.5G Memory, and 64-bit Ubuntu 20.40.4 LTS.

It is noteworthy that our implemented framework is general in two ways: (1) it can be applied to verify any DNN, regardless of its application input specification format and its property description; and (2) it can integrate any DNN verifier engine provided that it is implemented in the DNNV framework, benefiting from any future improvement in terms of verification technology.

---

[1] https://figshare.com/s/73fd6b2c6d84a60c08c3.

4   Experimental Results and Evaluation

In this section, we aim to evaluate a number of criteria on our approach to demonstrate its usefulness. In particular, we investigate the following research questions:

- **RQ1:** Is our approach applicable to real-life case studies?
- **RQ2:** Does our approach present an improvement with respect to the integrated techniques?
- **RQ3:** How well does the proposed approach perform compared to relevant existing techniques in terms of robustness results?
- **RQ4:** How efficient is the proposed approach in terms of verification execution time?

To answer the above questions, we evaluated our approach using the ACAS Xu family of DNNs for airborne collision avoidance [24]. The Airborne Collision Avoidance System (ACAS) data set, as released by [25] is a neural network based advisory system recommending horizontal manoeuvres for an aircraft in order to avoid collisions with other aircrafts, based on sensor measurements. This benchmark is largely used in the literature and is considered as a reference for formal verification of DNNs [33].

RQ1 (Applicability of the Approach): In this RQ, we investigate whether our approach can effectively be applied to a real-life case study. To this aim, we use the neural networks available in the ACAS Xu dataset[2]. Such networks are provided by the DNNV framework. We consider the neural network N_1_1 composed of an input layer taking five inputs, an output layer generating five outputs, and six hidden layers, each containing 50 neurons activated with ReLU. We focus in particular on the verification of the property ϕ_5 presented in the benchmark of ACAS Xu. ϕ_5, is a property expressing that : *If the intruder is near and approaching from the left, the network advises "strong right"*. Table 1, gives the results obtained by applying the verification of the N_1_1 using our framework as well as using well-known existing techniques. The results in Table 1 from each verifier may indicate SAT, UNSAT, or Unknown (UNK). If the result is SAT, then a violation of the property was found. The output result UNSAT means that the property was proven to hold and UNK is issued when the verifier is incomplete and cannot prove whether the property holds or not. In this experiment, our framework is first compared to the ERAN and Planet verifiers, taken individually. Then, we compare it to the BaB [8] and Marabou [26] verifiers. We can observe that the verification of the property ϕ_5 on the ACAS N_1_1 deep neural network, is not solved by BaB and ERAN verifiers. While Marabou and Planet determine the satisfaction of the property, our approach shows better efficiency in terms of execution time.

---

[2] https://github.com/dlshriver/dnnv-benchmarks/.

Table 1. The execution of our method on the ACAS Xu benchmark and a comparison with existing techniques.

	SAT	UNSAT	UNK	Time (s)
Proposed Method	✓			43.09
BaB			✓	21.44
Marabou		✓		54.94
ERAN			✓	11.69
Planet		✓		156.79

Answer to RQ 1

Our approach is applicable to a real-life DNN, which indicates its usefulness when applying it in practice.

RQ2 (Precision Analysis): We focus here on the improvements introduced by our method with respect to existing integrated techniques, namely ERAN and Planet. We study the precision of the intervals computed by our methods in comparison with the two mentioned techniques (ERAN and Planet) and at the level of each neuron. Figure 4 presents the intervals computed by the different techniques over a set of randomly chosen neurons from the N_1_1 neural network of the ACAS Xu Benchmark. As described in detail in Sect. 2, we can observe that for all neurons, the computed interval of our method is more precise than both integrated methods.

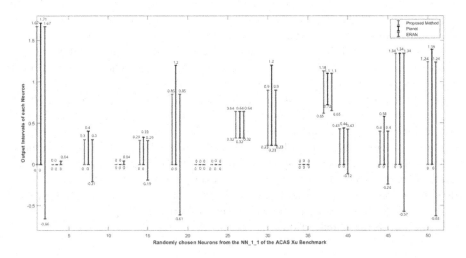

Fig. 4. Computing intervals of randomly chosen neurons of the N_1_1 neural network of the ACAS Xu benchmark.

Answer to RQ 2

Our approach significantly improves the precision of the propagated intervals compared to the integrated and parallelized methods, namely ERAN and Planet.

RQ3 (Robustness Analysis): Under this RQ, we focus on the capability of our method to decide about some given verification problem related to some given DNN. For this purpose, we consider 21 different DNNs extracted from the available ACAS Xu benchmark. Similarly, we use different well-known verifiers, namely Planet, Marabou, ERAN and Verinet [20], on these considered benchmarks. Table 2 reports the obtained results with our method as well as with the considered verification tools. In particular, we represent the number of solved verification problems, respectively. It should be noted that the number of solvable problems is 21 for four of the studied techniques including our method. In fact, only Verinet and ERAN failed to solve the whole 21 verification problems. Namely, while Verinet solved 17 verification problems over the 21 considered, ERAN verifier was able to solve only 5 DNNs verification problems.

Table 2. Comparison of the proposed method against Planet, Marabou, Verinet and Eran.

	SAT	UNSAT	UNK
Proposed Method	0	21	0
Planet	0	21	0
Marabou	0	21	0
Verinet	0	18	3
ERAN	0	5	16

Answer to RQ 3

Our approach successfully resolved all experimented verification problems, and was able to make decisions even in the cases where other verifiers, such as Verinet or ERAN, have failed.

RQ4 (Verification Time): Under this RQ, we compare the performance of our framework with some existing verification techniques in terms of the average verification time. We first compare our approach to the integrated techniques, namely ERAN and Planet. Figure 5 reports the time taken by each of the studied tools to decide about the verification of the DNNs presented in RQ3 (which correspond to a set of 21 DNNs with various sizes of the ACAS Xu benchmark). One can observe that our method systematically surpasses Planet in verification time. Despite ERAN being faster for certain DNN verification problems, one can note that it is limited to the verification problems that ERAN it cannot resolve.

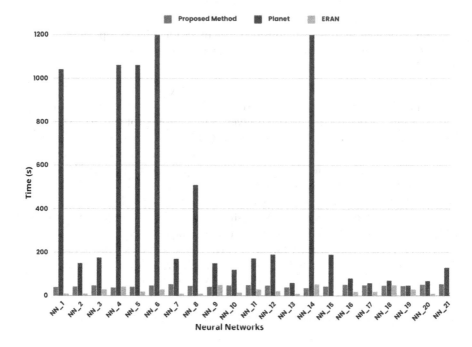

Fig. 5. Comparison of the verification time of our method to ERAN and Planet verifiers for solving a set of DNNs verification problems.

In Fig. 6, we compare the execution time of our approach to Marabou and Verinet verifiers. It is evident that our method significantly outperforms existing techniques in the majority of DNN cases. Notably, our approach shows remarkable superiority over the Verinet verifier for the $\{NN\_7, NN\_11$ and $NN\_13\}$ neural networks. In these cases, our method demonstrates a speed advantage of more than four times compared to Verinet. Compared to Marabou, our method consistently delivers results more quickly, especially in the instances $\{NN\_3, NN\_10, NN\_11$ and $NN\_12\}$.

Answer to RQ 4

Our method clearly surpasses other DNN verifiers, specifically Verinet and Marabou in terms of verification time across all verification problems. Furthermore, in the majority of data sets, the performance difference is significantly pronounced, attesting the effectiveness of our method.

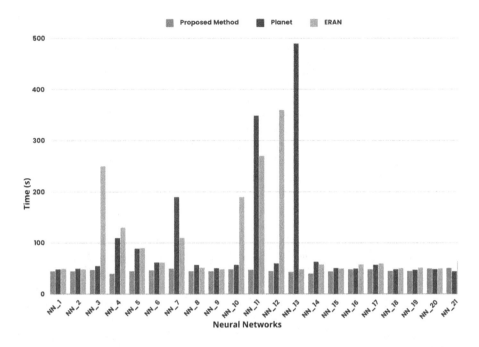

Fig. 6. Comparison of the verification time of our method w.r.t. Verinet and Marabou verifiers.

5   Related Work

In this section, we first provide an overview of existing and closely related works in the context of Neural Networks Verification (NNV) problem. Then, we focus on the verification approaches related to safety and robustness properties.

5.1   Formal Verification of Deep Neural Networks

Several techniques have been developed to provide guarantees for DNNs. Neural network verification approaches are proposed to check properties in neural networks [53,56], e.g., safety, adversarial robustness [54], and aim at providing formal guarantees to DNNs. Most of the contributions proposed in the literature focus only on some specific DNN property and consider restrictions of DNNs such as in terms of activation functions. The works in [22,37] deal specifically with Binarized (deep) NNs. In [19], authors propose verification approaches specifically designed for DNNs with ReLUs activation functions only. Other approaches, such as those in [7], [?] focus on the verification of DNNs composed of ReLUs with MaxPool nodes. In comparison to these approaches, our approach addresses the verification of DNNs without imposing restrictions on their activation functions. Specifically, we combine diverse incomplete verification methods and tailor existing approaches to verify DNNs with arbitrary, bounded, multi-variate, linear, and non-linear activation.

5.2 Safety and Robustness Verification of Deep Neural Networks

Several safety issues of DNNs have been identified in recent years [18,21], leading to the investigation of diverse techniques for certifying the safety and robustness of DNNs [51]. First attempts regarding the verification of safety and robustness of DNNs have been developed to provide rigorous guarantees. For example, the work presented in [17] offered the first automated approach for verifying robustness of DNNs using abstract interpretation. The subsequent works in [31,46,47] incorporated specialized transfer functions, abstract domains and a novel symbolic-propagation technique. Another interesting approach focusing on the safety verification of DNNs is Reluplex [25], which proposes a technique to investigate safety properties in Neural Networks containing linear functions and ReLU activation units. This approach as well as other approaches [28] consider Reluplex, as a Satisfiability Modulo Theories (SMT) solver, integrating a splitting framework [2] and are limited to the verification of ReLU nodes. Even though such satisfiability-based approaches offer a more compact encoding and exact methods, the resulting verification problem remains challenging to solve [41].

Recently, the authors in [50] and in [35] introduced some techniques that are based on abstract interpretation to certify dependency fairness for DNNs with ReLU activation functions. Their methods employ backward analysis, where they compute the network's output while abstracting the input space and conducting an intersection check. Despite these approaches perform an intersection check of several existing methods [12,31,47] in the same way as in the approach we discussed above, this latter adopts a forward propagation process and is not restricted to the ReLU activation function. In [48], a satisfiability modulo theories (SMT)-Based Model Checking method for safety verification is proposed and implemented in a tool. Even though the proposed approach implements different verification strategies (incremental and k-induction), the method still faces the primary limitation of SMT-based methods regarding scalability.

6 Conclusion

We presented a novel high-parallel approach for effectively combining over-approximation techniques used by incomplete verifiers. Our method is sufficiently general and can be easily improved, as any verifier can be directly integrated to improve precision and to speed up the verification process. In the present work, we instantiated our approach by implementing two well-known verifiers, that are based on completely different verification approaches, which allows us to get advantages of both methods and thus obtain better results. Our method offers a competitive performance on challenging data sets. Indeed, in the experiments, we demonstrated that the implemented instantiation is efficient in safety analysis of DNNs in the context of real-life case study networks and that it outperforms, in terms of execution time, several well-known verification techniques. In future work, we intend to implement further DNNs verifiers (other than ERAN and Planet) in our framework. It would also be straightforward to adapt our approach to integrate a backward analysis ([13,29]) in interval computation which may considerably refine the obtained results.

References

1. Anderson, G., Pailoor, S., Dillig, I., Chaudhuri, S.: Optimization and abstraction: a synergistic approach for analyzing neural network robustness. In: Proceedings of the 40th ACM SIGPLAN Conference on Programming Language Design and Implementation, pp. 731–744 (2019)
2. Barrett, C., Nieuwenhuis, R., Oliveras, A., Tinelli, C.: Splitting on demand in sat modulo theories. In: Logic for Programming, Artificial Intelligence, and Reasoning: 13th International Conference, LPAR 2006, Phnom Penh, Cambodia, 13–17 November 2006. Proceedings 13, pp. 512–526. Springer (2006)
3. Biere, A., Heule, M., van Maaren, H.: Handbook of satisfiability, vol. 185. IOS press (2009)
4. Bishop, C.M.: Neural Networks for Pattern Recognition. Oxford university press, Oxford (1995)
5. Boudardara, F., Boussif, A., Meyer, P.J., Ghazel, M.: Innabstract: an inn-based abstraction method for large-scale neural network verification. IEEE Trans. Neural Netw. Learn. Syst. 1–15 (2023). https://doi.org/10.1109/TNNLS.2023.3316551
6. Boudardara, F., Boussif, A., Meyer, P.J., Ghazel, M.: A review of abstraction methods towards verifying neural networks. ACM Trans. Embed. Comput. Syst. (2023). https://doi.org/10.1145/3617508
7. Bunel, R., Turkaslan, I., Torr, P.H., Kohli, P., Kumar, M.P.: Piecewise linear neural networks verification: a comparative study (2018)
8. Bunel, R.R., Turkaslan, I., Torr, P., Kohli, P., Mudigonda, P.K.: A unified view of piecewise linear neural network verification. Adv. Neural Inf. Process. Syst. **31** (2018)
9. Carlini, N., Wagner, D.: Towards evaluating the robustness of neural networks. In: 2017 IEEE Symposium on Security and Privacy (SP), pp. 39–57. IEEE (2017)
10. Chen, P.Y., Sharma, Y., Zhang, H., Yi, J., Hsieh, C.J.: Ead: elastic-net attacks to deep neural networks via adversarial examples. In: Proceedings of the AAAI Conference on Artificial Intelligence, vol. 32 (2018)
11. Cimatti, A., Griggio, A., Mover, S., Roveri, M., Tonetta, S.: Verification modulo theories. Form. Methods Syst. Des. **60**(3), 452–481 (2022)
12. Cousot, P., Cousot, R.: Static determination of dynamic properties of programs. In: Proceedings of the 2nd International Symposium on Programming, Paris, France, pp. 106–130. Dunod (1976)
13. Cousot, P., Halbwachs, N.: Automatic discovery of linear restraints among variables of a program. In: Proceedings of the 5th ACM SIGACT-SIGPLAN Symposium on Principles of Programming Languages, pp. 84–96 (1978)
14. Ehlers, R.: Formal verification of piece-wise linear feed-forward neural networks. In: Automated Technology for Verification and Analysis: 15th International Symposium, ATVA 2017, Pune, India, 3–6 October 2017, Proceedings 15, pp. 269–286. Springer (2017)

15. Ehlers, R.: Planet (2017). https://github.com/progirep/planet
16. Fan, Z., Wei, J., Zhu, G., Mo, J., Li, W.: Evolutionary neural architecture search for retinal vessel segmentation (2020). arXiv preprint arXiv:2001.06678
17. Gehr, T., Mirman, M., Drachsler-Cohen, D., Tsankov, P., Chaudhuri, S., Vechev, M.: Ai2: safety and robustness certification of neural networks with abstract interpretation. In: 2018 IEEE Symposium on Security and Privacy (SP), pp. 3–18. IEEE (2018)
18. Goodfellow, I., Shlens, J., Szegedy, C.: Explaining and harnessing adversarial examples. In: 3rd International Conference on Learning Representations, ICLR 2015, San Diego, CA, USA, 7–9 May 2015, Conference Track Proceedings, Y (2015)
19. Gopinath, D., Katz, G., Pasareanu, C.S., Barrett, C.: Deepsafe: a data-driven approach for checking adversarial robustness in neural networks. arXiv preprint arXiv:1710.00486 (2017)
20. Henriksen, P., Lomuscio, A.: Efficient neural network verification via adaptive refinement and adversarial search. In: ECAI 2020, pp. 2513–2520. IOS Press (2020)
21. Huang, X., Kwiatkowska, M., Wang, S., Wu, M.: Safety verification of deep neural networks. In: Computer Aided Verification: 29th International Conference, CAV 2017, Heidelberg, Germany, 24–28 July 2017, Proceedings, Part I 30, pp. 3–29. Springer (2017)
22. Jia, K., Rinard, M.: Efficient exact verification of binarized neural networks. Adv. Neural Inf. Process. Syst. **33**, 1782–1795 (2020)
23. Jin, T., et al.: Compiling onnx neural network models using mlir. arXiv preprint arXiv:2008.08272 (2020)
24. Julian, K.D., Lopez, J., Brush, J.S., Owen, M.P., Kochenderfer, M.J.: Policy compression for aircraft collision avoidance systems. In: 2016 IEEE/AIAA 35th Digital Avionics Systems Conference (DASC), pp. 1–10. IEEE (2016)
25. Katz, G., Barrett, C., Dill, D.L., Julian, K., Kochenderfer, M.J.: Reluplex: an efficient smt solver for verifying deep neural networks. In: Computer Aided Verification: 29th International Conference, CAV 2017, Heidelberg, Germany, 24–28 July 2017, Proceedings, Part I 30, pp. 97–117. Springer (2017)
26. Katz, G., et al.: The marabou framework for verification and analysis of deep neural networks. In: Computer Aided Verification: 31st International Conference, CAV 2019, New York City, NY, USA, 15–18 July 2019, Proceedings, Part I 31, pp. 443–452. Springer (2019)
27. Kriegman, S., Cheney, N., Corucci, F., Bongard, J.C.: A minimal developmental model can increase evolvability in soft robots. In: Proceedings of the Genetic and Evolutionary Computation Conference, pp. 131–138 (2017)
28. Kuper, L., Katz, G., Gottschlich, J., Julian, K., Barrett, C., Kochenderfer, M.: Toward scalable verification for safety-critical deep networks. arXiv preprint arXiv:1801.05950 (2018)
29. Lee, G., Park, H., Kim, N., Yu, J., Jo, S., Choi, K.: Acceleration of dnn backward propagation by selective computation of gradients. In: Proceedings of the 56th Annual Design Automation Conference 2019, pp. 1–6 (2019)
30. Leofante, F., Narodytska, N., Pulina, L., Tacchella, A.: Automated verification of neural networks: advances, challenges and perspectives. arXiv preprint arXiv:1805.09938 (2018)
31. Li, J., Liu, J., Yang, P., Chen, L., Huang, X., Zhang, L.: Analyzing deep neural networks with symbolic propagation: towards higher precision and faster verification. In: Static Analysis: 26th International Symposium, SAS 2019, Porto, Portugal, 8–11 October 2019, Proceedings 26, pp. 296–319. Springer (2019)

32. Li, L., Xie, T., Li, B.: SOK: certified robustness for deep neural networks. In: 2023 IEEE Symposium on Security and Privacy (SP), pp. 1289–1310. IEEE (2023)
33. Liu, C., Arnon, T., Lazarus, C., Strong, C., Barrett, C., Kochenderfer, M.J., et al.: Algorithms for verifying deep neural networks. Found. Trends® Optim. 4(3-4), 244–404 (2021)
34. Lundberg, S.M., Lee, S.I.: A unified approach to interpreting model predictions. Adv. Neural Inf. Process. Syst. **30** (2017)
35. Mazzucato, D., Urban, C.: Reduced products of abstract domains for fairness certification of neural networks. In: Static Analysis: 28th International Symposium, SAS 2021, Chicago, IL, USA, 17–19 October 2021, Proceedings 28, pp. 308–322. Springer (2021)
36. Müller, C., Serre, F., Singh, G., Püschel, M., Vechev, M.: Scaling polyhedral neural network verification on gpus. Proc. Mach. Learn. Syst. **3**, 733–746 (2021)
37. Narodytska, N., Kasiviswanathan, S., Ryzhyk, L., Sagiv, M., Walsh, T.: Verifying properties of binarized deep neural networks. In: Proceedings of the AAAI Conference on Artificial Intelligence, vol. 32 (2018)
38. Parker, A., Nitschke, G.: Autonomous intersection driving with neuro-evolution. In: Proceedings of the Genetic and Evolutionary Computation Conference Companion, pp. 133–134 (2017)
39. Pei, K., Cao, Y., Yang, J., Jana, S.: Deepxplore: automated whitebox testing of deep learning systems. In: Proceedings of the 26th Symposium on Operating Systems Principles, pp. 1–18 (2017)
40. Pulina, L., Tacchella, A.: An abstraction-refinement approach to verification of artificial neural networks. In: Computer Aided Verification: 22nd International Conference, CAV 2010, Edinburgh, UK, 15–19 July 2010. Proceedings 22, pp. 243–257. Springer (2010)
41. Pulina, L., Tacchella, A.: Challenging smt solvers to verify neural networks. AI Commun. **25**(2), 117–135 (2012)
42. Ruan, W., Huang, X., Kwiatkowska, M.: Reachability analysis of deep neural networks with provable guarantees. arXiv preprint arXiv:1805.02242 (2018)
43. Shriver, D., Elbaum, S., Dwyer, M.B.: DNNV: a framework for deep neural network verification. In: International Conference on Computer Aided Verification, pp. 137–150. Springer (2021)
44. Shriver, D., Elbaum, S., Dwyer, M.B.: DNNV framework (2021). https://github.com/dlshriver/DNNV
45. Silver, D., et al.: Mastering the game of go with deep neural networks and tree search. Nature **529**(7587), 484–489 (2016)
46. Singh, G., Gehr, T., Mirman, M., Püschel, M., Vechev, M.: Fast and effective robustness certification. Adv. Neural Inf. Process. Syst. **31** (2018)
47. Singh, G., Gehr, T., Püschel, M., Vechev, M.: An abstract domain for certifying neural networks. Proc. ACM Program. Lang. **3**(POPL), 1–30 (2019)
48. Song, X., et al.: Qnnverifier: a tool for verifying neural networks using smt-based model checking. arXiv preprint arXiv:2111.13110 (2021)
49. Tjeng, V., Xiao, K., Tedrake, R.: Evaluating robustness of neural networks with mixed integer programming. arXiv preprint arXiv:1711.07356 (2017)
50. Urban, C., Christakis, M., Wüstholz, V., Zhang, F.: Perfectly parallel fairness certification of neural networks. Proc. ACM Program. Lang. **4**(OOPSLA), 1–30 (2020)
51. Xie, X., Zhang, F., Hu, X., Ma, L.: Deepgemini: verifying dependency fairness for deep neural network. In: Proceedings of the AAAI Conference on Artificial Intelligence, vol. 37, pp. 15251–15259 (2023)

52. Yuan, X., He, P., Zhu, Q., Li, X.: Adversarial examples: attacks and defenses for deep learning. IEEE Trans. Neural Netw. Learn. Syst. **30**(9), 2805–2824 (2019)
53. Zakrzewski, R.R.: Verification of a trained neural network accuracy. In: IJCNN'01. International Joint Conference on Neural Networks. Proceedings (Cat. No. 01CH37222), vol. 3, pp. 1657–1662. IEEE (2001)
54. Zhang, C., Zhang, K., Li, Y.: A causal view on robustness of neural networks. Adv. Neural Inf. Process. Syst. **33**, 289–301 (2020)
55. Zhang, J.M., Harman, M., Ma, L., Liu, Y.: Machine learning testing: survey, landscapes and horizons. IEEE Trans. Softw. Eng. **48**(1), 1–36 (2020)
56. Zheng, Z., Hong, P.: Robust detection of adversarial attacks by modeling the intrinsic properties of deep neural networks. Adv. Neural Inf. Process. Syst. **31** (2018)

Monitoring of Neural Network Classifiers Using Neuron Activation Paths

Fateh Boudardara[ORCID], Abderraouf Boussif$^{(\boxtimes)}$, Pierre-Jean Meyer,
and Mohamed Ghazel

Univ. Gustave Eiffel, COSYS-ESTAS, 20 rue ÉlisÉe Reclus,
59666 Villeneuve d'Ascq, France
{fateh.boudardara,abderraouf.boussif,pierre-jean.meyer,
mohamed.ghazel}@univ-eiffel.fr

Abstract. To be deployed in safety critical applications, neural network (NN) systems require to be verified during the development phase and then monitored during the runtime phase. The latter phase is essential to closely supervise the performance and the behavior of NNs, particularly when used for safety-related tasks. This paper presents a novel approach for monitoring NN classifiers through real-time supervision of the model's behavior and decisions, to detect potential anomalies. The approach is based on the concept of *Neuron Activation Paths* (NAPath), which allows extracting relevant activated/inactivated paths that link the inputs to the outputs of the network and significantly influence the NN's classification decision. The main idea is to characterize paths for each class using training data, i.e., from the training data set, we group the images of the same class together. Then, for each group of images, we identify their common active and inactive paths, respectively. The sets of active and inactive paths constitute a NAPath, which is used as a signature to feature the corresponding class. The monitoring system then uses these NAPaths online to continuously check whether the paths activated by the image fit the NAPath characterization associated with its classification, as returned by the network. The monitoring system raises alarms if an abnormal decision of the network is detected. We evaluated our approach on a benchmark of neural networks pre-trained on the MNIST data set.

Keywords: Neural network (NN) classifiers · NN monitoring · Neural activation patterns · Neural Activation paths

1 Introduction

Neural networks (NNs) are one of the most successfully used techniques in artificial intelligence-based systems [9]. The ability of NNs to generalize the input-output relationship of a training data set allows its application to tackle various complex problems, such as image classification and object detection and recognition [16,18]. Nowadays, academia and industry are showing more and more interest in applying this technique in some safety-critical domains, such as autonomous transportation systems [3, 20]. Considering the safety requirements pertaining to these systems, the question of validating and certifying NN systems becomes central.

Test-based verification (testing for short), formal verification, and runtime monitoring are three key verification activities for ensuring the safe and reliable deployment of NN systems. Testing involves running the trained model on a set of data to measure its performance and validate it with respect to a set of (representative) test cases [9]. Formal verification involves using mathematical techniques to verify and provide formal guarantees that the model satisfies a set of desired properties [4, 5, 7, 12]. While testing and formal verification are performed during the system design phase, monitoring is an ongoing runtime activity performed during the system operational phase. It involves real-time tracking of the inputs, the performances, and the behavior of the model [6].

In this paper, we propose a monitoring approach for NN image classifiers with the ReLU activation function. The proposed approach is used to supervise and control the network's outputs with respect to the input images, towards detecting misclassified images and adding a level of confidence to the NN decision. The approach relies on the concept of neuron activation pathway (NAPath), which we introduce as part of the contribution. NAPath is used to identify relevant activation paths for each class in a NN. A path is defined as a sequence of neurons of the same type of activation (active or inactive) linking the input of the NN to its output. For a NN with a *Relu* activation function, NAPath extracts learned features of the network when it processes images that belong to the same class. We define a feature as a set of paths on the network that are similarly activated or inactivated for the selected images. This work is inspired by the Neuron Activation Pattern (NAP) concept discussed in [8]. While a NAP is a tuple of two sets: active and inactive neurons, we define a NAPath as a tuple $NAPath = (\mathcal{A}, \mathcal{D})$, with:

1. $\mathcal{A}$ being the set of paths that are active for most of the selected images.
2. $\mathcal{D}$ is the set of paths that are inactive for most of the selected images.

The first step of our approach involves identifying active and inactive neurons within the neural network for a set of samples, for each class c. Specifically, a neuron is deemed active for class c if its output value is strictly positive for a considered percentage of input images of this class. Similarly, a neuron is considered as inactive if its output is equal to zero for a considered percentage of samples of this class. Once the neurons have been labeled as active or inactive, the next step involves constructing paths that are exclusively constituted of active or inactive neurons. In essence, an active (resp. inactive) path represents a sequence of active (resp. inactive) neurons linking the input layer to the output layer. These paths are then used to build the NAPath for the given set of images. The main intuition consists in assuming that the inputs belonging to the same class tend to behave similarly and activate the same paths. Therefore, a NAPath can be viewed as a feature associated with that specific class c.

We construct a set of NAPaths, where each NAPath corresponds to a specific class of images. Leveraging these NAPaths, we propose an online monitoring process for image classifiers when they are applied to new unseen images. Our NN monitor relies on the premise that an image x, whose classification output by the network N is class c (denoted as $N(x) = c$), should generate active and inactive paths similar to the NAPath pre-computed for class c ($NAPath_c$). Therefore, for an arbitrary image x, the network's classification $N(x) = c$ and the NAPath generated by this image x in the network (denoted as $NAPath_x$), the monitor processes this data and compares them to the pre-computed NAPath associated with each class, and can raise two different types of alarms:

1. *Misclassification detection*: if $NAPath_x$ is highly similar to the NAPath associated with a class c' other than the network's classification (class c) of this input, i.e., $N(x) \neq c$, the monitor raises an alarm and suggests a re-classification of this image.
2. *Novelty detection*: if $NAPath_x$ does not share any similar paths with any of the pre-computed NAPaths, the monitor raises an alarm that this input does not fit any feature of any class; thus, it is considered as a novel (or out-of-distribution) sample.

To evaluate the effectiveness of our approach, we performed a series of experiments on neural networks trained for digit classification on the MNIST dataset [15]. The experimental results show how the proposed approach enhances efficiently and the reliability of the classification decision made by the network. The use of NAPaths for runtime monitoring provides more confident and trustworthy predictions. Based on our findings, we believe that our approach shows great promise and can pave the way for further research in the area of monitoring image classifiers.

The remaining of this paper is organized as follows: Sect. 2 provides definitions and notations related to NNs and introduces the NAPath concept. Section 3 presents the proposed monitoring method. The experiments' setups and the obtained results are given in Sect. 4. Finally, in Sect. 5 we provide a review of related works before concluding the paper in Sect. 6.

2 Preliminary Concepts

2.1 Neural Networks

In this paper, we consider feed-forward neural networks with *Relu* activation function, and we refer to them as neural networks (NNs). A NN is a set of interconnected neurons, also called nodes, organized in layers. The neurons of layer l_i are connected to all neurons of layer l_{i+1} via weighted edges. The weights of layer l_i are organized as a matrix $W_i \in \mathbb{R}^{|l_i| \times |l_{i-1}|}$. Each layer has a vector bias $b_i \in \mathbb{R}^{|l_i|}$. Using these notations, NNs can be seen as a function $f : \mathbb{R}^n \to \mathbb{R}^m$ that is defined recursively as:

$$\begin{cases} f(x) = v_L(x) \\ v_i(x) = W_i \times \sigma(v_{i-1}(x)) + b_i \\ v_0(x) = x \end{cases} \quad (1)$$

where L is the number of layer of N and σ is a non-linear activation function, which represents the *Relu* function $\sigma(x) = \max(x, 0)$ in this work.

For an image classification problem of m classes, f maps an input-image $x \in \mathbb{D}_x{}^1$ to an output $y \in \mathbb{R}^m$, where $y_i = f_i(x)$ is the score of the ith class, and the element of the highest score $(c = \operatorname*{argmax}_{1 \le i \le m}(f_i(x)))$ is considered as the predicted class for the image x. We write $f(x) = c$ or $N(x) = c$ where there is no ambiguity.

2.2 Neuron Activation Patterns (NAP)

To provide the necessary background for our proposed approach, we first recall the concept of Neuron Activation Pattern (NAP) [8]. A NAP is a representation of the activation levels of neurons in a neural network in response to a given input or a set of inputs, indicating which neurons (from the hidden layers) are active or inactive. It is easier to explain this concept in the case of the *Relu* function, since it is a piece-wise linear function (with two linear regions).

Definition 1. *Let N be a network with Relu (denoted Relu-NN), and let S be the set of its hidden neurons. The set of all active (resp. inactive) neurons on the network N, for an input x, is denoted as A (resp. D) and defined such that:*

$$\begin{cases} A = \{n \in S : n(x) > 0\} \\ D = \{n \in S : n(x) = 0\} \end{cases} \quad (2)$$

In Definition 1, $n(x)$ denotes the output value of a neuron $n \in S$ when the network has x as input. For a *Relu*-NN, a NAP of an input x on N (denoted $NAP(x, N)$) is defined as the set of its corresponding active and inactive neurons, i.e., $NAP(x, N) = (A, D)$.

For a set of inputs X_c such that $\forall x \in X_c : N(x) = c$, we define its associated *NAP* as the common NAP between all inputs:

$$\begin{cases} A_c = \{n \in S : \forall x \in X_c, n(x) > 0\} \\ D_c = \{n \in S : \forall x \in X_c, n(x) = 0\} \end{cases} \quad (3)$$

For a set X_c considered as a representative set of inputs of class c, then its NAP calculated using Eq. 3 represents the NAP corresponding to this class, which is denoted as $NAP_c = (A_c, D_c)$.

---

[1] E.g.: $\mathbb{D}_x = \mathbb{R}^{n_1 \times n_2}$ for grayscale images, or $\mathbb{D}_x = \mathbb{R}^n$ if the image is transformed to a vector.

2.3   Neuron Activation Paths (NAPath)

As mentioned in the introduction, the NAPath is built upon the concept of NAP; however, instead of solely focusing on the activation levels of individual neurons, it represents learned features through paths. Specifically, a path is a sequence of neurons that connects the input and output layers, passing through all hidden layers. This concept provides a more comprehensive view of the network's learned features, as it allows us to maintain the relation between neurons of different layers. By following the paths, we can better understand the sequence of neural activations that leads to a classification decision.

Formally, a path on a network N of L hidden layers is a set of neurons $P = \{n_1, \ldots, n_L\}$ such that n_k is a neuron of layer l_k for $1 \leq k \leq L$. In our work, we define two types of paths:

1. **Active path:** For an input x and a network N of L layers, an active path is a set of neurons $P = \{n_1, \ldots, n_L\}$ such that for all k: $1 \leq k \leq L$, we have $n_k \in l_k$ and $n_k(x) > 0$.
2. **Inactive path:** For an input x and a network N of L layers, an inactive path is a set of neurons $P = \{n_1, \ldots, n_L\}$ such that for all k: $1 \leq k \leq L$, we have $n_k \in l_k$ and $n_k(x) = 0$.

Figure 1 presents an example of a network with marked active and inactive paths for the input $x = 1$.

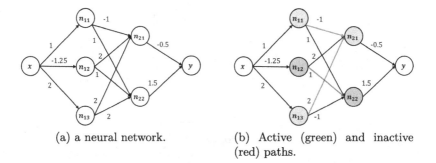

(a) a neural network.

(b) Active (green) and inactive (red) paths.

Fig. 1. NAPath computation process for an input $x = 1$ on a neural network (Color figure online)

Definition 2. *The NAPath of an input x using a network N, denoted as $NAPath(x, N)$, is the tuple $(\mathcal{A}, \mathcal{D})$ where $\mathcal{A}$ is the set of all active paths and $\mathcal{D}$ is the set of all inactive paths. Formally, we write: $NAPath(x, N) = (\mathcal{A}, \mathcal{D})$.*

To maintain consistency with the definition of NAPs, in Definition 2 we used the notation $\mathcal{A}$ and $\mathcal{D}$ to denote the set of active and inactive paths, respectively. When there is no ambiguity, we omit the argument N and write $NAPath(x) = NAPath_x = (\mathcal{A}, \mathcal{D})$.

Remark 1. It is worth noting that the NAP of an individual input x, denoted as $NAP(N, x) = (A, D)$, is a partition of the set of all neurons S of the network N, such that $A \cap D = \emptyset$ and $A \cup D = S$. However, the NAP of a class c generated using a set of images and denoted as $NAP_c = (A_c, D_c)$ only forms a subset of S, i.e., $A_c \cup D_c \subseteq S$. This is due to the fact that NAP_c is an intersection of the NAPs of the selected images. On the other hand, a NAPath of the same input is a subset of paths of N, and consequently, the set of participating neurons (the neurons in $\mathcal{A}$ and $\mathcal{D}$) is a subset of S. This is due to the fact that some paths of the network may be neither active nor inactive.

3   Monitoring with NAPath

In this section, we present our NAPath-based approach for runtime monitoring of NN image classifiers. The approach consists in firstly (i) building offline the monitor using the NAPath concept, and then (ii) using the monitor in runtime operation (in parallel to the NN model). The first phase, which we call it *NAPathing*, is devoted to compute the NAPaths, and the second phase, namely monitoring, is responsible for supervising the classification decision of the network during runtime. The general structure of the monitoring process is presented in Fig. 2.

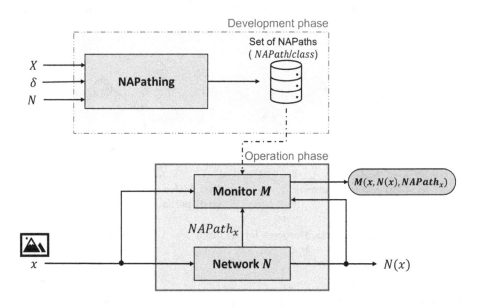

Fig. 2. The general structure of the monitoring system.

3.1   NAPathing Phase

This phase is performed during the development phase of the monitor, its objective is to compute the set of NAPaths, i.e., a NAPath for each image class. For this purpose, this phase involves computing the set of active and inactive paths for each class using the training set. The following three parameters are required for this phase:

1. The network N.
2. The set of inputs X from which the NAPaths will be computed, e.g., the training set used to obtain N.
3. A parameter δ (called precision parameter) specifying the threshold of activations or inactivations required for a path to be considered as active or inactive, for a given class, respectively.

The paths' mining is an important step. First, we partition the set X into subsets such that each subset corresponds to one class. Then, for a set X_c representing a class c, we start by filtering this set by eliminating inputs that are misclassified by the network N. Next, we choose a precision parameter δ, used to determine the NAPath (i.e., activated and inactivated paths) for a given class c. The next step consists in assuring that the NAPath is valid; this is performed by checking that the sets of active and inactive paths are not empty. If the NAPath is valid, it is saved as the NAPath of class c ($NAPath_c$), otherwise, the value of δ is updated to generated a new NAPath. The NAPathing phase is performed during the development phase of the monitor. Once the set of NAPaths are computed and validated, it is saved and can be used during the monitoring phase. The main steps of this process are presented in Fig. 3.

3.2   Monitoring Phase

During the operational phase of the system, the NN monitor is executed in parallel with the network N to supervise its decisions in real-time. In addition to the stored pre-calculated NAPaths, the monitor receives in real-time the input-image x with its corresponding output y issued by the NN, i.e.: $N(x) = y$ and the NAPath ($NAPath_x$) computed on-the-fly. Next, the monitor measures the similarity between $NAPath_x$ and the pre-computed NAPaths. This involves comparing the set of active and inactive paths of $NAPath_x$ to those of each pre-calculated NAPath. Two particular cases can be observed:

1. **Novelty detection:** the $NAPath_x$ has no similar NAPath within the set of pre-computed NAPaths; thus, the monitor raises a novelty alarm indicating that this image is new to the NN and may be an out-of-distribution input.
2. **Misclassification detection:** the $NAPath_x$ is found to have a high similarity with one of the $NAPath_c$ pre-computed during the development phase for class c. In this case, we check whether the classification decision from the network ($N(x) = y$) is consistent with the NAPath similarity to class c detected by the monitor.
   (a) $y = c$: this strengthens the classification decision and confirms that the input image shares similar features with the other images of the same class, represented by $NAPath_c$.

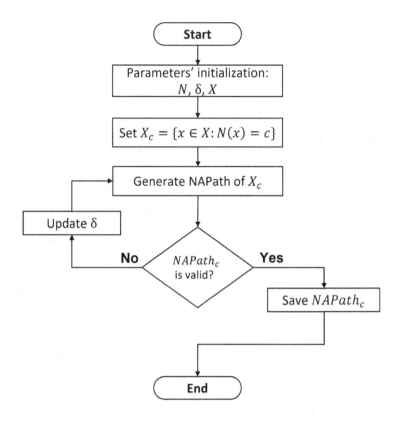

Fig. 3. The flowchart of the NAPath mining process

(b) $y \neq c$: since $NAPath_x$ and $NAPath_c$ have the highest similarity degree, it is expected that x belongs to class c. Therefore, our monitoring system will raise an alarm informing that the classification decision needs to be checked. Furthermore, the monitor suggests a re-classification of the input based on its NAPath, recommending that this image should be of class c instead of class y.

The main steps of the monitoring phase are illustrated in Fig. 4.

In order to determine the similarity degree between a path of a class c denoted by $NAPath_c = (\mathcal{A}_c, \mathcal{D}_c)$, and the corresponding NAPath of an input x: $NAPath_x = (\mathcal{A}_x, \mathcal{D}_x)$, we define a function $sim : NAPath \times NAPath \rightarrow \mathbb{R}^+$ as follows:

$$sim(NAPath_c, NAPath_x) = p \times \frac{|\mathcal{A}_c \cap \mathcal{A}_x|}{|\mathcal{A}_c|} + (1-p) \times \frac{|\mathcal{D}_c \cap \mathcal{D}_x|}{|\mathcal{D}_c|}$$

where $|\cdot|$ is the cardinality of a set and the parameter $p \in [0,1]$ is used to control the rate of active (and inactive) paths that contribute to calculating

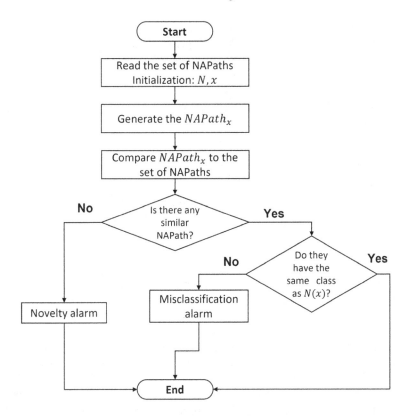

Fig. 4. The flowchart of the monitoring procedure using NAPaths

the similarity degree. In the context of the proposed approach, two NAPaths are considered similar if they have a high degree of overlap in terms of their paths. By adjusting the value of p, we can gain insights into which type of paths have more importance in the similarity degree's calculation. For instance, when p approaches 1, it indicates that similar NAPaths share many identical active paths and few inactive paths. Notice that the parameter p can be approximated empirically from the evaluation of the training and testing data.

4   Experiments and Results

To evaluate the effectiveness of our NN monitoring approach, we conducted a series of experiments on a pre-trained neural network on the MNIST dataset used in VNNCOMP 2021 [1]. The MNIST is a popular benchmark dataset in the field of machine learning and computer vision. It is a collection of handwritten digits ranging from 0 to 9, each digit represented as a 28x28 grayscale image. The dataset consists of 60,000 training images (around 6000 images per class) and 10,000 test images. The NN used in this section consists of an input layer of size

784, followed by 4 hidden layers with 256 *Relu* neurons for each layer, and an output layer of size 10 representing the 10 possible classes (digits 0 to 9).

For each class in the MNIST dataset, we applied our NAPathing method to generate the corresponding NAPath, using images from the training set. To further evaluate the performance of our approach, we analyzed the number of inputs that exhibit the NAPath of the corresponding class and the size of NAPaths for various values of the parameter δ (0.8, 0.85, 0.90, 0.95). In our experiments, we observed that the number of inactive paths was consistently large across all classes. Therefore, to represent the size of the NAPath, we focused solely on the active paths.

The results of our analysis are presented in Figs. 5 and 6. We observe that the number of inputs involved in the computation of NAPaths increases by increasing the value of δ, which leads to build NAPaths that are able to cover larger number of inputs. However, this decreases the size of the NAPaths (active paths). This is because increasing δ results in the inclusion of more inputs in the construction of the NAPath. Since the NAPath of a class is formed by the intersection of NAPaths of participating inputs, adding more inputs reduces the size of the common NAPath.

These results suggest that the value of the control parameter δ can be adjusted to control the sensitivity of the NAPath approach, enabling a trade-off between the coverage and the size of the NAPath. Notably, we have observed that the pre-trained network [1] misclassifies a significant portion of the training images for classes 3, 5, 6, and 7. As a result, we can see that the number of covered inputs and active paths corresponding to these classes is considerably low. Note that this behavior is due to the used benchmark taken from, and is not related to the performances of our approach.

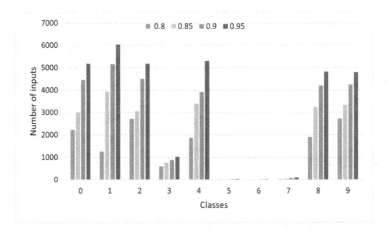

Fig. 5. The number of inputs generating the same NAPath for different values of δ.

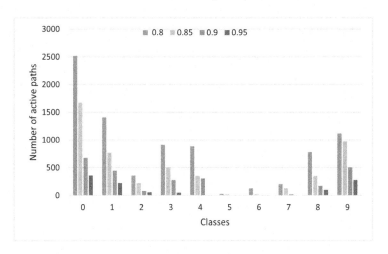

Fig. 6. The number of active paths for different values of δ.

In the second set of experiments, we investigate the impact of the monitoring control parameter p by using different values of $p : \{0.0, 0.1, \cdots, 1.0\}$. We set $\delta = 0.9$, and we generate NAPaths for each class using its corresponding training data. To assess the monitoring system's performance, we use the NAPaths set we previously computed, and for each value of p, we evaluate the monitoring precision in terms of the rate of no alarms[2] (*true negative*), correct alarms (*true positive*), false alarms (*false positive*), missed alarms (*false negative)*, and additionally, the rate of correctly re-classified inputs proposed by the monitor.

We conducted experiments on the MNIST testing set, which includes a total of 6112 images evenly distributed among the six selected classes: 0, 1, 2, 4, 8, 9. Figures 7 and 8 illustrate the monitoring performance for different values of p. The results demonstrate that the monitoring system reaches its best performance with respect to most of the metrics when the value of p is low, i.e., the rate of inactive paths participating in the calculation of the similarity degree is higher than the rate of active paths. The percentage of true negatives (correctly classified and no alarm is triggered) is almost stable and very close to 100%. Accordingly, the rate of false alarms (raised alarms for correctly classified images) is almost zero. For the other metrics, while the rate of correct raised alarms for misclassified images slightly decreases, the rate of correct reclassification generally increases by increasing the value of p. It means that for higher values of p, the monitor raises fewer alarms, but the re-classification of the misclassified images is more precise. The rate of missed alarms is generally between 24% and 26%. It increases slightly when the value of p is increasing, and then

---

[2] The term *alarm* refers to an output from the monitor indicating a discrepancy between the classifier's decision and the one expected by the monitor.

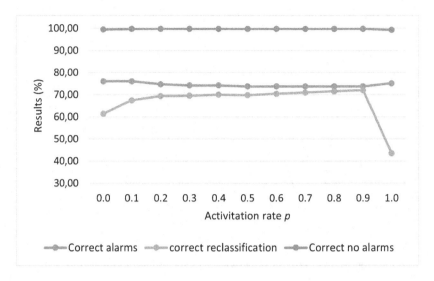

Fig. 7. Monitoring performance on different values of the parameter p - Correct alarms and correct reclass.

decreases when p is greater than 0.9. Moreover, the performance of the monitoring system is significantly reduced when only active paths or inactive paths are used in the similarity computation. This is demonstrated by the case where $p = 0$ or $p = 1$, where the rate of correct reclassification is notably lower.

We can conclude that tuning the parameter p can affect the monitoring performance. Generally, the lower the value of p, the more alarms are raised by the monitor, hence less missed alarms and more correct alarms, but less precision (less correct re-classification). Therefore, a small value of p ($p \leq 0.3$) to include more inactive paths tends to provide better performance of the monitoring system. For re-classification purposes, the system performs better when p is close to 0.9. Further research is needed to determine the optimal values of p for different datasets and network architectures.

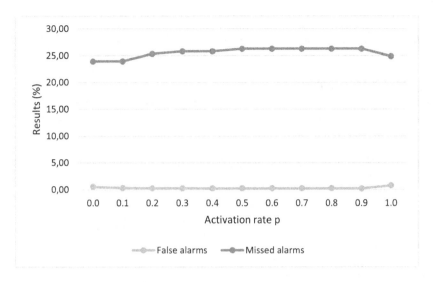

Fig. 8. Monitoring performance on different values of the parameter p - False and missed alarms

5   Related Works

In this section, we present and discuss the approaches related or close to our contribution.

Cheng et al. [6] proposed a runtime monitoring based on activation patterns. First, they build activation patterns from training data using Binary Decision Diagrams (BDD). During monitoring, in addition to making a classification decision using the neural network, the monitor checks whether the activation patterns of the input are close (using Hamming distance) to one of the pre-built NAPs. If no similar NAP is found, the system raises a warning that the classification decision should be re-checked. The effectiveness of this approach is constrained by the performance of BDDs, which have several limitations, including restrictions on the number of variables they can handle. Recently, Geng et al. [8] proposed a type of specifications called *neural representation as specification*. They introduced a new formula of the robustness property by adding a new constraint using NAPs. The specification states that all inputs following a NAP will never be misclassified. The authors used Marabou verifier [13] to support the new formula of robustness. Additionally, in case the property is violated, the authors claimed that the generated counter-examples are more realistic.

The problem of detecting novel inputs, which is called novelty or out-of-distribution problem, has been studied for many years, and many methods have been proposed [19, 22]. One of the most promising approaches involves analyzing the activation patterns of hidden neurons. Henzinger et al. [11] proposed a monitoring method for neural networks based on abstraction. The method involves constructing box abstractions by over-approximating the output of selected hidden layers using the training data. During the monitoring phase, the system checks whether the values of these layers lie within the range of the calculated intervals or boxes. If they are outside the calculated boxes, the corresponding input is considered as a novelty, and a warning is issued. Hashemi et al. [10] introduced a method by modelling the neuron's activations as a Gaussian model. During runtime, this model is used as an out-of-distribution detector. In recent work, Olber et al. [17] extended NAPs to extract activation patterns on convolution layers, and then used these patterns to detect out-of-distribution image samples on CNNs.

NAPs have also been applied in various studies for explainability evaluation. For instance, Bauerle et al. [2] leveraged the activation values of neurons to analyze and extract learned features. They then identified groups of similar NAPs that could be used to visually interpret the learned features within a layer. While Krug et al. [14] utilized NAPs for interpreting CNN models used in speech recognition, Stano et al. [21] proposed a method that involves encoding the behavior of neurons using a Gaussian Mixture Model (GMM) when exposed to a set of inputs from the same class. The resulting GMM is then used to explain the classification decision made by the network.

6   Conclusion

The present work proposes a novel NN monitoring approach based on the concept on Neural Activation Paths (NAPath). The approach allows for analyzing the behavior of hidden neurons in response to a set of inputs belonging to the same class, and then computes paths (both active and inactive) that link the input layer to the output layer of the network. To do so, we construct a set of NAPaths, where each NAPath is associated to an image class. These NAPaths are subsequently used to monitor the classification decision, whereby a novelty detection alarm is issued if the NAPath has no similar NAPath from the set of pre-computed NAPaths, or a misclassification alarm is issued if an input's predicted class is different of the class of the most similar NAPath to the one of this input. In the latter, the monitor suggests a new classification of this input with respect to its computed NAPath.

To assess the effectiveness of our proposed NAPath approach, we conducted an experimental study on the MNIST benchmark, which included tuning various parameters. Our experiments demonstrated that NAPath can efficiently be used as a tool for monitoring neural network, and it can significantly enhance their reliability and trustworthiness.

In future work, we plan to expand the capabilities of our proposed NAPath approach by incorporating support for a wider range of network architectures and activation functions. We also aim to conduct more comprehensive evaluations of our NAPath-based method by testing its performance on a variety of benchmarks with different architectures and applying it to real-world models. We also intend to conduct a comparative study with NAP-based monitoring approaches to further validate the effectiveness of NAPath. Furthermore, as NAPath has the potential to provide explanations and interpretations of network decisions, we plan to conduct further experiments in this direction.

References

1. Bak, S.: VNN Neural network verification competition 2021 (vnn6comp 2021) (2021). https://github.com/stanleybak/vnncomp2021/tree/main/benchmarks/mnistfc/mnist-net_256x4.onnx
2. Bäuerle, A., Jönsson, D., Ropinski, T.: Neural activation patterns (NAPs): visual explainability of learned concepts. arXiv preprint arXiv:2206.10611 (2022)
3. Bojarski, M., et al.: End to end learning for self-driving cars. arXiv preprint (2016)
4. Boudardara, F., Boussif, A., Meyer, P.J., Ghazel, M.: Innabstract: an inn-based abstraction method for large-scale neural network verification. IEEE Trans. Neural Netw. Learn. Syst. 1–15 (2023). https://doi.org/10.1109/TNNLS.2023.3316551
5. Boudardara, F., Boussif, A., Meyer, P.J., Ghazel, M.: A review of abstraction methods toward verifying neural networks. ACM Trans. Embed. Comput. Syst. **23**(4), 1–19 (2024)
6. Cheng, C.H., Nührenberg, G., Yasuoka, H.: Runtime monitoring neuron activation patterns. In: 2019 Design, Automation & Test in Europe Conference & Exhibition (DATE), pp. 300–303. IEEE (2019)
7. Gehr, T., Mirman, M., Drachsler-Cohen, D., Tsankov, P., Chaudhuri, S., Vechev, M.: Ai2: safety and robustness certification of neural networks with abstract interpretation. In: 2018 IEEE Symposium on Security and Privacy (SP), pp. 3–18. IEEE (2018)
8. Geng, C., Le, N., Xu, X., Wang, Z., Gurfinkel, A., Si, X.: Toward reliable neural specifications. arXiv preprint arXiv:2210.16114 (2022)
9. Goodfellow, I., Bengio, Y., Courville, A.: Deep Learning. MIT press, Cambridge (2016)
10. Hashemi, V., Křetínský, J., Mohr, S., Seferis, E.: Gaussian-based runtime detection of out-of-distribution inputs for neural networks. In: Runtime Verification: 21st International Conference, RV 2021, Virtual Event, 11–14 October 2021, Proceedings, pp. 254–264. Springer (2021)
11. Henzinger, T.A., Lukina, A., Schilling, C.: Outside the box: abstraction-based monitoring of neural networks. In: 24th European Conference on Artificial Intelligence-ECAI 2020, pp. 2433–2440 (2020)
12. Katz, G., Barrett, C., Dill, D.L., Julian, K., Kochenderfer, M.J.: Reluplex: an efficient SMT solver for verifying deep neural networks. In: International Conference on Computer Aided Verification, pp. 97–117. Springer (2017)
13. Katz, G., et al.: The Marabou framework for verification and analysis of deep neural networks. In: International Conference on Computer Aided Verification, pp. 443–452. Springer (2019)
14. Krug, A., Knaebel, R., Stober, S.: Neuron activation profiles for interpreting convolutional speech recognition models. In: NeurIPS Workshop on Interpretability and Robustness in Audio, Speech, and Language (IRASL) (2018)
15. LeCun, Y.: The MNIST database of handwritten digits (1998). http://yann.lecun.com/exdb/mnist/
16. Liu, W., Wang, Z., Liu, X., Zeng, N., Liu, Y., Alsaadi, F.E.: A survey of deep neural network architectures and their applications. Neurocomputing **234**, 11–26 (2017)

17. Olber, B., Radlak, K., Popowicz, A., Szczepankiewicz, M., Chachula, K.: Detection of out-of-distribution samples using binary neuron activation patterns. arXiv preprint arXiv:2212.14268 (2022)
18. Pathak, A.R., Pandey, M., Rautaray, S.: Application of deep learning for object detection. Procedia Comput. Sci. **132**, 1706–1717 (2018)
19. Pimentel, M.A., Clifton, D.A., Clifton, L., Tarassenko, L.: A review of novelty detection. Signal Process. **99**, 215–249 (2014)
20. Ristić-Durrant, D., Franke, M., Michels, K.: A review of vision-based on-board obstacle detection and distance estimation in railways. Sensors **21**(10), 3452 (2021)
21. Stano, M., Benesova, W., Martak, L.S.: Explaining predictions of deep neural classifier via activation analysis. arXiv preprint arXiv:2012.02248 (2020)
22. Yang, J., Zhou, K., Li, Y., Liu, Z.: Generalized out-of-distribution detection: a survey. arXiv preprint arXiv:2110.11334 (2021)

Formal Security Analysis of Deep Neural Network Architecture

Marwa Zeroual[1,2]([✉]), Brahim Hamid[2], Morayo Adedjouma[1],
and Jason Jaskolka[3]

[1] Université Paris-Saclay, CEA, List, 91120 Palaiseau, France
{marwa.zeroual,morayo.adedjouma}@cea.fr
[2] IRIT, Université de Toulouse, CNRS, UT2 118 Route de Narbonne,
31062 Toulouse Cedex 9, France
brahim.hamid@irit.fr
[3] Systems and Computer Engineering, Carleton University, Ottawa, ON, Canada
jason.jaskolka@carleton.ca

Abstract. Neural networks have been successfully adopted in many security-critical systems. Neural network verification is gaining more interest, since these models can be attacked and fooled in several different ways. In this paper, we propose a formal approach to verify some security properties of neural networks. The overall approach goes through three steps: (1) specify security objectives as properties of a modeled neural network in a technology-independent specification language; (2) implement the developed model in a suitable tooled language for analysis; and (3) suggest a set of security requirements necessary to fulfill the targeted security objectives. We use first-order logic and modal logic as abstract and technology independent formalism and Alloy as a tooled language. To validate our work, we explore a set of representative security objectives from the Confidentiality, Integrity, and Availability classification in a use case from the unmanned aircraft domain.

Keywords: Deep Neural Networks · formal methods · model checking · neural network architecture · security analysis

1 Introduction

Deep Neural Networks (DNN) have found many applications in safety and security-critical domains such as automotive systems, health care, and air traffic control systems. Much of the recent work in deep learning has indeed focused on proposing different architectures for different learning tasks. The DNN architecture involves the distribution of neurons through different layers and different connections linking them. Looking for high-performing DNN architectures might be sought at the expense of security properties which opens up new avenues for potential threats. Moreover, most of the tools used for DNN development do not provide any security controls at compilation time, making the developers deal with unexpected run-time errors and uncertainties. DNN are known to be

© The Author(s), under exclusive license to Springer Nature Switzerland AG 2025
B. Ben Hedia et al. (Eds.): VECoS 2024, LNCS 15466, pp. 97–112, 2025.
https://doi.org/10.1007/978-3-031-85356-2_7

vulnerable to a wide range of security threats, including adversarial examples, data poisoning, model extraction, and Trojan attacks [4,6].

DNN architectures represent attractive targets for adversaries who aim to change the behavior of the DNN by exploiting vulnerabilities due to misconceptions. The security analysis of DNN architecture helps detect some security issues related to the architecture alteration. One of the issues that can be caused by altering the architecture is modifying a trained model to change its behavior to gain unauthorized access to sensitive information [18]. Another way is to add a hidden functionality or a "backdoor" to a neural network triggered by a specific input or condition [13]. However, analyzing the security of DNN architecture is challenging because of their complexity (i.e., large size DNN can have millions of parameters and it is hard to understand the affect of each parameter) and their lack of transparency (i.e., the relationships between the input and output can be difficult to interpret).

The proposed approach is a form of parameterized model checking. We begin by providing an informal description of the security objectives that need to be achieved by the DNN. We then propose a logical specification that uses an abstract system computing model to define the DNN and its security objectives. Afterward, we construct a model of the DNN using the Alloy language. This model provides a simple and discrete representation of the DNN's structure and behavior. We specify the security objectives as properties of the modeled DNN and then check the model for interactions that violate the security properties. Finally, we elicit a set of security requirements as properties of the modeled DNN to restrict its operation and achieve the corresponding objectives. The paper's contributions are: a metamodel that describes the structure and behavior of the DNN, a formalization based on first-order and modal logic of the security objectives, an approach for eliciting security requirements necessary to achieve the security objectives, and a demonstration of the approach through a case study.

The remainder of this paper is organized as follows. Section 2 describes the DNN metamodel. After, Sect. 3 provides the computing model and the formalization of objectives using first-order and modal logic. Then, Sect. 4 presents the implementation of our approach using Alloy. Section 5 provides an illustrative example that models neural networks used for collision avoidance. Section 6 reviews related works. Finally, Sect. 7 concludes this paper.

2   Deep Neural Network Metamodel

This section delves into the concept of DNN, providing a clear definition and a practical example to illustrate their fundamental principles.

2.1   Defintion of DNN

Among DNN goals, a DNN aims to extract some mapping relation from training data. This relation will later enable matching, as best as possible, new data inputs to the correct output, namely for classification and regression tasks. The processing node in DNN is called a neuron. A neuron processes some received data and forwards it to neurons in the next layer. A DNN comprises one input layer, one output layer, and one or more hidden layers. In this work, we will focus only on Feedforward Neural Network (FNN), those in which the information flows through the network in a single direction, from the input to the output layer, without looping back.

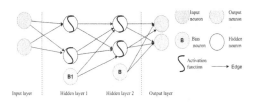

Fig. 1. Example of DNN architecture

To illustrate a DNN, we consider a simple example in Fig. 1. An input neuron corresponds to one feature of the input to classify. An output neuron corresponds to one class label. A bias neuron adds a constant value to neurons in the next layer. The value is called bias and is used with the weight's product sum and neuron inputs to produce an output. A hidden neuron accepts input data, performs calculations, and produces output. An edge is a weighted link to connect neurons in successive layers. Weights increase or decrease the impact of the neuron's inputs on its output. An activation function transforms the neuron's output before passing it to the next layer.

2.2 The Metamodel

We build a metamodel providing concepts to describe DNN using two different views: the structural view, to capture the functional architecture of a DNN in terms of neurons, layers, and other structural aspects, and the scenario view, which builds upon the logical view, describing the behavioral aspects of a DNN. A previous DNN structure metamodel is presented in [12]. In our vision, we enrich the metamodel with the scenario view where we use the message passing paradigm to describe communication between neurons. We mimic the way that communication occurs in the human brain, i.e., neurons communicate by exchanging electrical impulses, and these communication artifacts are passed from one neuron to the next in a distributed manner. In addition, we keep the layered structure of the DNN. In what follows, we detail the principal classes of our metamodel, as described with UML notations in Fig. 2.

– *Layer.* A Layer is a set of neurons that are organized and connected to perform specific computations.

- *Neuron.* A Neuron is a unit processing and transmitting information. We define four types of neurons:
  - *InputNeuron.* It receives input data and passes it through the network. Each input neuron represents a single feature in the input data.
  - *HiddenNeuron.* It is responsible for extracting features and representations from the data. The hidden neurons perform complex computations to transform the input data into a meaningful representation.
  - *BiasNeuron.* It is used to offset the output of other neurons. Bias Neurons add a constant value to the output of other neurons and can be used to adjust the output to better fit the data.
  - *OutputNeuron.* It produces the network's prediction or classification. The output neurons generate the final result based on the computations performed by the hidden neurons.
- *Edge.* An Edge specifies a link that enables communication between Neurons by allowing the exchange of messages.
- *Weight.* A Weight of an edge represents the strength of the connection between two neurons.
- *Message.* A message represents an exchange between a sender Neuron, which produces it, and a receiver Neuron, which consumes it.
- *Payload.* A Payload defines the data exchanged in messages. We recognize one particular type of payload:
  - *Bias.* A Bias is the constant value added by bias neurons.

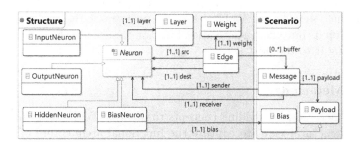

Fig. 2. DNN architecture metamodel

3 Logical Specification of Security Properties

In this section, we present the computing model based on first-order logic and modal logic as a formalism that is abstract and technology-independent. Then, we describe a set of security properties to specify security objectives from the CIA (CIA stands for Confidentiality, Integrity and Availability) triad.

3.1   Abstract System Computing Model

After defining the DNN metamodel, we define the following domain to capture the notion of both legitimate and illegitimate actions done by neurons: sending messages (e.g., inject), receiving messages (e.g., intercept), and processing the inputs received from other neurons (e.g., process). We define these concepts on top of the basic communication primitives (e.g., send, receive, and activate):

Sets:

- $\mathcal{N}$ is the set of neurons, it is partitioned by the following subsets:
  - $\mathcal{IN}$ is the set of input neurons.
  - $\mathcal{HN}$ is the set of hidden neurons.
  - $\mathcal{ON}$ is the set of output neurons.
  - $\mathcal{BN}$ is the set of bias neurons with the following predicate:
    - $has\_bias(n, b)$ indicates that $b \in \mathcal{B}$ is the bias of the neuron $n \in \mathcal{BN}$
- $\mathcal{W}$ is the set of weights
- $\mathcal{E}$ is the set of edges with the following predicates:
  - $has\_dest(e, n)$ indicates that the neuron $n \in \mathcal{N}$ is the destination of the edge $e \in \mathcal{E}$
  - $has\_weight(e, w)$ indicates that the weight $w \in \mathcal{W}$ is the weight of the edge $e \in \mathcal{E}$
- $\mathcal{P}$ is the set of message payloads, it is extended by the set:
  - $\mathcal{B}$ is the set of biases.
- $\mathcal{M}$ is the set of messages with the following predicates:
  - $has\_receiver(m, r)$ indicates that the recipient of $m \in \mathcal{M}$ is $r \in \mathcal{N}$, where r may not be the intended receiver of m
- $\mathcal{A}$ is the set of actions
  - $inject(n, m)$ denotes that neuron $n \in \mathcal{N}$ adds message $m \in \mathcal{M}$ into the DNN.
  - $intercept(n, m)$ denotes that neuron $n \in \mathcal{N}$ gets message m from the DNN.
  - $get\_weight(n, e, w)$ denotes that neuron $n \in \mathcal{N}$ gets the weight $w \in \mathcal{W}$ from edge $e \in \mathcal{E}$, where w is not necessarily the true weight
  - $get\_payload(n, m, p)$ denotes that neuron $n \in \mathcal{N}$ gets the payload $p \in \mathcal{P}$ from message $m \in \mathcal{M}$, where p is not necessarily the true payload

Modalities:

- $\mathbb{E}_n(a)$ is a predicate indicating that action $a \in \mathcal{A}$ is **enabled** for neuron $n \in \mathcal{N}$
- $\mathbb{F}(a)$ is a predicate indicating that action $a \in \mathcal{A}$ will **finally** occur, i.e., sometimes strictly in the future.
- $\mathbb{F}^-(a)$ is a predicate indicating that action $a \in \mathcal{A}$ occurred **antecedently**, i.e., sometimes strictly in the past.

3.2 Confidentiality

Confidentiality denotes the property that information is not made available or disclosed to unauthorized individuals, entities, or processes [1]. In the context of a DNN, confidentiality means that there is no disclosure or unauthorized access to the architecture and parameters of the network, the training data, or any other sensitive information that could be used to recreate or compromise the DNN [9]. Therefore, we consider weight confidentiality as a representative property of the confidentiality property. It can be identified by verifying whether an edge weight is known only by its destination neuron. For edge $e \in \mathcal{E}$, we denote this representative property as $WeightConfidentiality(e)$ which is specified for all weights $w \in \mathcal{W}$, and all disjoint neurons $n_1, n_2 \in \mathcal{N}$ as:

$$has\_dest(e, n_1) \; \wedge \; has\_weight(e, w) \Rightarrow \neg \mathbb{F}(get\_weight(n_2, e, w)) \qquad (1)$$

The violation of the property indicates the presence of a threat that refers to a leak of the parameter values (weight of the edges) of the DNN. This DNN leakage could occur because of human error or contraction with a third party with a too low security level [5].

3.3 Integrity

Integrity refers to the accuracy and completeness of the information [1]. In the context of a DNN, the integrity property means that the DNN structure and data can be modified only by authorized parties [3,11]. Therefore, bias integrity is a representative property of the integrity property. It can be identified by verifying whether the payload sent by a bias neuron, in a message, is the accurate (authentic) bias related to the sender neuron. For bias neuron $n \in \mathcal{BN}$, we denote this representative property as $BiasNeuronIntegrity(n)$ which is specified for all messages $m \in \mathcal{M}$, all biases $b \in \mathcal{B}$, and all edges $e \in \mathcal{E}$ as:

$$\mathbb{F}^-(inject(n, m)) \; \wedge \; \mathbb{E}_{n_2}(get\_payload(n_2, m, b)) \Rightarrow has\_bias(n, b) \qquad (2)$$

The violation of the integrity property indicates the presence of a threat that refers to a modification of some parameter values (bias neuron) which alter the DNN behavior and functionality.

3.4 Availability

Availability denotes the property of a system function of being accessible and usable on demand by an authorized entity [1]. In the context of a DNN, availability means that the DNN is accessible and returns an output for every input [15]. Therefore, we define edge availability as a representative property of availability property. It can be identified by verifying whether a message sent through this edge will reach its destination. For edge $e \in \mathcal{E}$, we denote this representative property as $EdgeAvailability(e)$ which is specified for all messages $m \in \mathcal{M}$, all payloads $p \in \mathcal{P}$, and all distinct neurons $n, ns \in \mathcal{N}$ as:

$$has\_dest(e, nd) \; \wedge \; inject(ns, m) \; \wedge \; has\_receiver(m, nd) \Rightarrow \mathbb{F}(intercept(nd, m))$$
$$(3)$$

The violation of the property indicates the presence of a threat that might refer to a denial of service caused by DNN input data whose format is inappropriate. The threat can arise if a malicious user of the DNN creates an input (a sponge example) specifically designed to increase the model's computation time, potentially leading to a denial of service [15].

4   Implementation in Alloy

In this section, we present the implementation of the DNN architectural (structural and behavioral) model, as well as the security objectives in Alloy [8].

Remember that during the logical specification, we associated each security objective category with a representative property such that the violation of the specified property indicates the not satisfaction of the objective. Thus, we define an appropriate security requirement as a predicate to codify a security mechanism to constrain the system's operation and guarantee the satisfaction of the corresponding security objective.

4.1   Overview of Alloy

Alloy is a lightweight formal modeling language based on first-order relational logic. An Alloy model comprises a set of signatures, each defining a set of atoms. Atoms may have fields that define relations between atoms. There are several ways to specify constraints in the model. *Facts* should always hold. *Predicates* are defined in the form of parameterized formulas that can be used elsewhere. and as *Assertions* are intended to follow from the facts of a model. We can instruct Alloy Analyzer to verify whether the property *prop* of the system design holds, with the command: **check** *prop* **for** n, which would exhaustively explore every model instance within a scope of n, (n represents the number of atoms typed by each signature). If the property does not hold, the analyzer generates a counterexample we can visualize. The absence of counterexamples guarantees that the property holds in the modeled system within the specified scope. As claimed in [8], most counterexamples are found in a reasonably small scope. *A complete presentation of our Alloy metamodel, the full specification of the other constructs (e.g., communication primitives, etc.), and the security properties are available online via* https://gitlab.com/semcoproject/semcofdt/mlbs/dnn/alloy.

4.2   DNN Architecture and Communication Model in Alloy

Structural Model. The mapping of the metamodel elements is straightforward. We map neuron, edge, weight, layer, message, payload, and bias to their namesake types in Alloy. Thus, we represent them as a set of Alloy signatures as depicted in Listing 1.1. The associations between classes of the metamodel are mapped to their namesake fields. Field types and cardinalities are respecting the relations in the metamodel.

```
1  abstract sig Neuron{ layer : one Layer }       sig Layer { }
2  sig InputNeuron extends Neuron { }  sig OutputNeuron extends Neuron { }
3  sig HiddenNeuron extends Neuron { }
4  sig BiasNeuron extends Neuron { bias : one Bias }
5  sig Payload { }     sig Bias extends Payload{ }    sig Weight { }
6  sig Edge { src: one Neuron,          dest: one Neuron,
7      buffer : set Msg -> Tick,        weight: one Weight }
```

Listing 1.1: DNN structure metamodel in Alloy

We add additional constraints on these signatures using facts such as: (1) edges linking neurons from two adjacent layers, (2) input neurons situated only in the first layer, (3) bias neurons can be the destination of any edge.

Behavioral Model. During the execution of a DNN, the input data is passed through the input layer and then propagated in messages through the hidden layers of the network, where it is transformed and processed by the artificial neurons. Finally, the processed data is passed through the output layer, which produces the prediction or decision made by the DNN. To model the described behavior, we model time as a sequence of steps, where two successive time points define a step. These time points represent the instants at which actions occur during the execution of the DNN. By using time as a parameter, we can express the occurrences of actions at specific instants in the sequence of steps. In Alloy, the ordering module provides a way to model time by defining a total ordering over a set of time points referred to as Ticks. At each discrete Tick, we can determine which layer is active (i.e., its neurons are either sending, receiving, or activating data). We can also determine the messages sent, received, and visible to each neuron. A neuron might have one available payload (all messages sent by this neuron will have this available payload). Listing 1.2 depicts the communication primitives used for the behavior.

```
1  abstract sig Msg {          sender: one Neuron,
2      receiver: one Neuron,   payload: one Payload,
3      sent: one Tick,         received: Neuron -> lone Tick }
4  sig Tick { available: Neuron -> one Payload,
5      active : one Layer,     sentMsg: Neuron -> Msg,
6      visible: Neuron ->  Msg, receivedMsg: Neuron -> Msg }
7  /* Communication primitives */
8  pred Neuron.activate[d:Payload, t:Tick] {
9      some m:Msg { m.payload = d     d in t.available[this] }   }
10 pred Neuron.send[c:Neuron,d:Payload, t:Tick] {
11     some m:Msg { m.receiver = c    m.payload = d          m.sent = t }}
12 pred Neuron.receive[c:Neuron,d:Payload,t:Tick] {
13     some m:Msg { m.sender = c    m.payload = d     m.received[this] = t }}
```

Listing 1.2: DNN behavior metamodel in Alloy

We encode the set of actions described in Sect. 3.1 considering the notion of execution steps as follows: Each action $act(param_1, \ldots, param_n) \in \mathcal{A}$ is transformed to $act(param_1, \ldots, param_n, t)$ denoting the execution step $t \in \mathcal{T}$ when it occurs, and where $\mathcal{T}$ is the sequence of execution steps. For example, $inject(n, m)$ is transformed to $inject(n, m, t)$, indicating that a sender $n \in \mathcal{N}$ adds a message $m \in \mathcal{M}$ into the DNN at step $t \in \mathcal{T}$.

The *Msg* and *Edge* concepts are then extended with a set of attributes defined on the basis of these actions and their corresponding steps that should be logged when they occur. Listing 1.3 depicts the presentation of the new concepts called *MsgConstraint* and *EdgeConstraint* in Alloy.

```
1  sig MsgConstraint extends Msg { get_pld: Neuron -> Tick,} { all n:Neuron, t:Tick |
       get_pld.t=n => some m:Msg, s:Neuron | get_pld[n,m,s,t] }
2  sig EdgeConstraint extends Edge {get_weight: Neuron -> Tick,}{
3    all n:Neuron, t:Tick | get_weight.t = n => some e:Edge, w: weight | get_weight[n
       ,e,w,t] }
```

Listing 1.3: Message data and example of action in Alloy

4.3 Security Objectives in Alloy

In this section, we model the objective categories presented in Sect. 3 in Alloy, using constructions such as predicate, assertion, and fact. Remember that during the logical specification, we associated each security objective category with a representative property such that the violation of the specified property indicates the not satisfaction of the objective. Therefore, each security objective is associated with a security property defined as a predicate to map the logical definition of the corresponding security property to the Alloy model describing the targeted DNN architecture (e.g., WeightConfidentiality). Then, the Alloy analyzer detects the violation of a security objective as a result of the violation of its representative property through an assertion finding a counterexample (e.g., confidentialityNotHold). Thus, we define an appropriate security policy as a predicate (e.g., ConfRequirement) to codify a security mechanism to constrain the system's operation and guarantee the satisfaction of the corresponding security objective.

Confidentiality. The confidentiality property is defined as a predicate according to the logical specification of the confidentiality (see Eq. 1) and the computing model.

```
1  pred WeightConfidentiality[e:Edge] {
2    all w:Weight, t:Tick, disjoint n1,n2:Neuron |
3      e.dest=n_1 and e.weight=w => not get_weight[n_2,e,w,t]}
4  assert confidentialityNotHold { all e:Edge| WeightConfidentiality[e] }
```

Listing 1.4: Weight Confidentiality

Alloy Analyzer detects the violation of the weight confidentiality property by finding a counterexample, as a violation of the *confidentialityNotHold* assertion defined in Listing 1.4. Then, we proceed by defining a security requirement as a predicate (*ConfRequirement*) to realize the confidentiality objective. The idea is to ensure that only the neurons that are allowed to get the weight of an edge can get it, as depicted in Listing 1.5.

```
1  pred ConfRequirement[e:Edge]{
2    all n:Neuron, t:Tick, w:Weight| E_get_weight[n,e,w,t] <=> e.dest=n }
3  assert confidentialityHold { all e:Edge | ConfRequirement[e] }
```

Listing 1.5: Confidentiality requirement

The satisfaction of the *confidentialityHold* assertion allows the fulfillment of the corresponding security requirement to realize the objective of weight confidentiality.

Integrity. The integrity property is defined in this respect as a predicate according to the logical specification of the integrity property (see Eq. 2) and the computing model.

```
1  pred BiasNeuronIntegrity[n:BiasNeuron]{
2     all b:bias, m:Message, n2:Neuron |
3     injected[n,m,t] and E_get_pld[n2,m,b,t] => has_bias[n,b]}
4  assert integrityNotHold  { all n: BiasNeuron| BiasNeuronIntegrity[n] }
```
Listing 1.6: Bias Neuron Integrity

Alloy Analyzer detects the violation of the integrity property by finding a counterexample, as a violation of the assertion *integrityNotHold* defined in Listing 1.6. Then, we proceed by defining a security requirement as a predicate (*IntegRequirement*) to realize the integrity objective. The idea is to ensure that the message that was sent by a bias neuron is sent wih the accurate payload which is the bias of the neuron sender (Listing 1.7).

```
1  pred IntegRequirement[n: BiasNeuron]  { all m: Msg, t:Tick |
2  injected[m,n,t] and has_src[m,n] => n.bias = m.payload}
3  assert integrityNotHold { all bn: BiasNeuron |  BiasNeuronIntegrity[bn]}
```
Listing 1.7: Integrity requirement

The satisfaction of the assertion *integrityNotHold* property allows the fulfillment of the corresponding security requirement to realize the objective of bias neuron integrity.

Availability. The availability property is defined as a predicate according to the logical specification of the availability property (see Eq. 3) and the computing model.

```
1  pred EdgeAvailability [e:Edge] {
2     all m:Msg,  t:Tick | let nd=e.dest , t2:t.nexts |
3     inject [ns,m,t] and m.receiver=nd => intercept[nd,m,t2]}
4  assert availabilityNotHold { all e:Edge |  EdgeAvailability[e] }
```
Listing 1.8: Edge Availability

Alloy Analyzer detects the violation of the edge availability property by finding a counterexample, as a violation of the assertion *AvailabilityNotHold* defined in Listing 1.8. Then, we proceed by defining a security requirement as a predicate (*AvailRequirement*) to realize the availability objective. The idea is to ensure that the message sent remains in the edge's buffer until its reception by the destination neuron. (Listing 1.9).

```
1  pred AvailRequirement[e:Edge] {
2     all m: message | let nd=e.dest, t2:t.nexts | m in e.buffer
3     => intercept[nd,m,t2] and not (m in e.buffer.t2.nexts)}
4  assert availabilityHold  { all e:Edge | AvailRequirement[e]}
```
Listing 1.9: Availability requirement

The satisfaction of the assertion *availabilityHold* allows the fulfillment of the corresponding security requirement to realize the objective of edge availability.

4.4   Large Architectural DNN Models

The challenge of state space explosion is a significant issue in formal verification. In our work, we encounter the problem of the Alloy Analyzer's capacity being exceeded when specifying the entire DNN architecture as a single model. To overcome this, we propose decomposing the layered architecture model into sub-models of pairs of adjacent layers, where neurons from one layer are only connected to neurons in the following layer. The layerwise decomposition as a means to partially alleviate this issue has been proposed in [7]. We adopt it for the verification of each of the proposed security properties. Therefore, in all what follows, we assume that the formal tool allows us to verify a security property in a model composed of two DNN adjacent layers. Considering the definitions of the proposed security properties provided so far, we will proceed by induction.

Proposition 1. *Given a DNN with n layers $L_1, L_2, \ldots, L_n$, if a security property p holds between each pair of adjacent layers (L_i, L_{i+1}) for $1 \leq i < n$, then the security property p holds for the entire DNN, and vice versa.*

Proof. We prove by induction.

Base Case. For $n = 2$: we consider a DNN composed of two layers. We use the proposed Alloy formal specification and verification language and its associated Alloy Analyzer tool to verify a security property p on the two layers L_1, L_2
 - *Case 1:* A security property p holds in the sub-model composed of the two adjacent layers, thus, the security property holds in the entire DNN.
 - *Case 2:* A security property p does not hold in the sub-model composed of the two adjacent layers, thus, the security property does not hold in the entire DNN.

Inductive Hypothesis. Assume that for a DNN with k layers $L_1, L_2, \ldots, L_k$, Proposition 1 is true.

Inductive Case. We show that for a DNN with $k+1$ layers $L_1, L_2, \ldots, L_{k+1}$, Proposition 1 is true. Consider the DNN with the first k layers $L_1, L_2, \ldots, L_k$. By the induction hypothesis, the security property p holds for the entire sub-DNN composed of these k layers. Now we use the proposed Alloy formal specification and verification language and its associated Alloy Analyzer tool to verify the security property p in the sub-model composed of the last two layers L_k and L_{k+1}.
 - *Case 1:* The security property p holds in the sub-model composed of the two last adjacent layers (L_k and L_{k+1}), and thus, the security property holds in the entire DNN.
 - *Case 2:* The security property p does not hold in the two last adjacent layers, thus, the security property does not hold for the entire DNN.

5   Case Study

We illustrate our contributions through an example of a use case scenario from ACAS Xu [10] used for collision avoidance in unmanned aircraft systems (drones).

5.1   Use Case Description

We consider encounters between just two drones: the ownship and the intruder [10] (Fig. 3). The ownship is equipped with ACAS Xu using the DNN showed in Fig. 4.

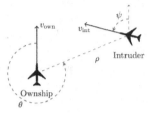

Fig. 3. ACAS Xu system

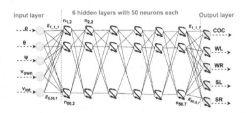

Fig. 4. ACAS Xu neural network

ACAS Xu, uses as inputs, various parameters related to the state of the ownship and the intruder, such as the distance between them (ψ), their velocities, respectively (v_{own}, v_{intr}), the angle to the intruder (θ), and the heading of the intruder (ψ). This information is used to predict a set of recommended actions to avoid a collision. The first option is to do nothing, also known as the "Clean of Conflict" (COC) option. However, we also have the option to make a weak adjustment by turning left (WL) or right (WR). Additionally, we can make a strong adjustment by turning left (SL) or right (SR).

5.2   Modelling of the DNN Architecture

```
1   sig rho, theta, psi, v_int, v_own extends InputNeuron{}
2   sig n_1,2, n_2,2, n_3,2, n_4,2, .....n_49,2, n_50,2 extends HiddenNeuron{}
3   sig W_1,1,1, W_1,2,1, .....W_1,49,1, W_1,50,1, ...W_5,49,1, W_5,50,1 extends Weight{}
4   sig E_1,1,1 extends Edge{}{weight= W_1,1,1 and src=ρ and dest=n_1,2}
5   .......
6   sig E_5,50,1 extends Edge{}{weight= W_5,50,1, src=rho and dest=n_50,2}
```

Listing 1.10: Excerpt describing the two first layers of ACAS Xu DNN

A model specifying the entire DNN architecture will exceed the analyzer's capacity. We propose decomposing the model into different sub-models: i.e., pairs of adjacent layers. Thus, there are no dependencies between neurons belonging to non-adjacent layers. We assume that verifying all the sub-models will verify the complete model. For the sake of brevity, we will present results for checking the sub model composed by the input layer and the first hidden layer as described in Listing 1.10. We start by defining the neurons types and the edges using our DNN metamodel. Line 1 specifies the input neurons. Line 2 specifies the hidden neurons of the first layer where neuron $n_{i,j}$ is the ith neuron in the jth layer. Next, line 3 specifies the weights where weight $W_{x,y,z}$ is associated with the edge $E_{x,y,z}$. Similarly, lines 4-6 specify the weighted edges linking between different neurons where the edge $E_{x,y,z}$ is linking the xth neuron from the zth layer to the yth neuron from the following layer.

5.3   Analysis

```
1   assert WeightConfidentialityE_{1,1,1} {
2       WeightConfidentiality.holds[E_{1,1,1}]}
3   check WeightConfidentialityE_{1,1,1} for 5
4   assert WeightConfidentialityE_{1,2,1} {
5       WeightConfidentiality.holds[E_{1,2,1}]}
6   check WeightConfidentialityE_{1,2,1} for 5
7   ..........
8   assert EdgeAvailabilityE_{1,1,1} {
9       EdgeAvailability.holds[E_{1,1,1}]}
10  check EdgeAvailabilityE_{1,1,1} for 5
```

Listing 1.11: Instructing the DNN looking for security requirements

In the next step, we focus on finding security requirements that will allow DNN developers to develop secure DNN. We will check the objectives of the concrete architecture. The objectives to check are the confidentiality of the weight of edges linking the DNN and the availability of the edges. As this DNN does not contain bias neurons, we cannot check the integrity property. In Listing 1.11, we specify assertions required to check the objectives on the relevant and concerned parts of the DNN architecture. The properties are verified on local parts of the DNN (one edge per assertion) using the function holds. For brevity seeks, we will show an excerpt of the assertions we need to check to verify the security of the DNN. Lines 1-3 assert and check the weight confidentiality objective concerning the edge $E_{1,1,1}$. Next, we assert and check the confidentiality of the adjacent edge $E_{1,1,2}$ edge until we verify all edges. Similarly, we assert and check the availability of edges, starting with the edge $E_{1,1,1}$ as depicted in lines 8-10.

We show in Fig. 5, a model where the confidentiality is violated regarding the Edge $E_{1,1,1}$.

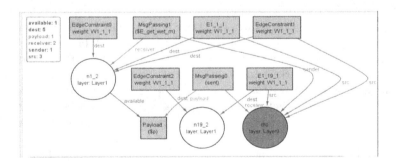

Fig. 5. Counterexample: Violation of edge confidentiality

Consequently, we can reuse the previously developed security requirement *ConfRequirement* in order to mitigate the violations and realize the objective. If an adversary recovers the weights of edges from a DNN, it might steal the functionality of the DNN and create a new DNN model with the same functionality. Thus, the attacker can learn more about the original DNN and potentially create malicious queries to deceive it. Moreover, the analysis results, performed on an abstract model, are used to guide an implementation-level analysis that checks a concrete DNN for the presence of a vulnerability. By the end, the final verification shows no more violations, meaning that the set of suggested security requirements are complete regarding the identified objectives and that added requirements do not violate any of the other properties that DNNs have come to rely on.

6   Related Works

While many methods are proposed for verifying DNN operating in the presence of maliciously crafted inputs, methods for verifying faults presented in the DNN architecture itself still need to be explored.

Regarding the security verification of DNN, Wang et al. [17] note that using Satisfiability Modulo Theories to analyze the security of DNNs can be time-consuming. They propose to use symbolic intervals to verify the presence or absence of adversarial examples by determining if the DNN returns an output within a given interval after several propagations through its layers. Later in another work [16], they combine *symbolic linear relaxation* and *directed constraint refinement* to provide a formal guarantee that no adversarial examples exist. Moreover, Baluta et al. [2] focus on determining the number of adversarial examples a given neural network may have. They also quantified the inputs with Trojan triggers the DNN might detect. All these works aim at bounding the worst-case value of output when its input is perturbed within a specified range. They verify trained and non-deployed DNN models. However, they only cover input-output verification without preceding it with a structure verification.

Work done by Pineyro et al. [14] focuses on structure verification. They define the DNN model structure by simply providing three components: (1) layers that are responsible for the processing operations done by DNN; (2) the input shape that represents the structure of the data that the DNN will be fed with; and (3) the output shape, which represents the expected shape of the predictions of the DNN. Similar to our work, it just takes care of the structural definition, leaving the computational part of the problem to the external frameworks once the model is compiled. Nonetheless, they are limited to type-based security problems: it verifies if the types defined in input and output shapes are compatible with types required by layers. This limitation facilitates the integration of their library TensorSafe into the development tools, namely Tensor Flow. Our formalization allows us to describe more security properties covering multiple concepts of the DNN structure. However, it might be constraining when integrating the approach results into the development tools.

7   Conclusion

In this work, we present an approach for formally verifying the security objectives of DNN. We define a formal computing model that allows us to formalize the DNN architecture and some security properties. According to this computing model, the violation of the property indicates the non-fulfillment of the security objective, which requires adding more security requirements. We use the DNN from ACAS Xu as a case study to showcase how the approach can be applied to verify the security properties related to DNN architecture. The approach returns the security requirements related to DNN architecture.

In our future work, we plan to provide a tool support for more automation developing a Domain Specific Languages (DSL) for the DNN architecture description and model transformation to generate formal Alloy model. We would also like to study the integration of our analysis results into the development tool of DNN. Indeed, we will consider other security properties related neural networks such as backdooring and adversarial examples.

References

1. ISO-IEC. information technology - security techniques - information security management systems - overview and vocabulary. *IEC*, 2018
2. Baluta, T., Shen, S., Shinde, S., Meel, K.S., Saxena, P.: Quantitative verification of neural networks and its security applications. In: Proceedings of the 2019 ACM SIGSAC Conference on Computer and Communications Security, pp. 1249–1264, 2019
3. Botta, M., Cavagnino, D., Esposito, R.: Neunac: a novel fragile watermarking algorithm for integrity protection of neural networks. Inf. Sci. **576**, 228–241 (2021)
4. Carlini, N., Wagner, D.: Towards evaluating the robustness of neural networks. In: 2017 IEEE Symposium on Security and Privacy, pp. 39–57. IEEE (2017)
5. Caroline, B., et al.: Securing machine learning algorithms (2021)
6. Hanif, M.A., Khalid, F., Putra, R.V.W., Rehman, S., Shafique, M.: Robust machine learning systems: reliability and security for deep neural networks. In: 2018 IEEE 24th International Symposium on On-Line Testing And Robust System Design, pp. 257–260. IEEE, 2018
7. Xiaowei Huang, Marta Kwiatkowska, Sen Wang, and Min Wu. Safety verification of deep neural networks. In: Computer Aided Verification: 29th International Conference, CAV 2017, Heidelberg, Germany, 24–28 July 2017, Proceedings, Part I 30, pages 3–29. Springer, 2017
8. Jackson, D.: Software Abstractions: Logic, Language, and Analysis. MIT press, Cambridge (2012)
9. Joud, R., Moëllic, P.-A., Bernhard, R., Rigaud, J.B.: A review of confidentiality threats against embedded neural network models. In: 2021 IEEE 7th World Forum on Internet of Things, pp. 610–615. IEEE (2021)
10. Katz, G., Barrett, C., Dill, D.L., Julian, K., Kochenderfer, M.J.: Reluplex: an efficient SMT solver for verifying deep neural networks. In: Computer Aided Verification: 29th International Conference, CAV 2017, Heidelberg, Germany, 24–28 July 2017, Proceedings, Part I 30, pp. 97–117. Springer, 2017
11. Kumar, R.S.S., Brien, D.O., Albert, K., Viljöen, S., Snover, J.: Failure modes in machine learning systems. arXiv preprint arXiv:1911.11034, 2019
12. Lechevalier, D., Hudak, S., Ak, R., Lee, Y.T., Foufou, S.: A neural network metamodel and its application for manufacturing. In: 2015 IEEE International Conference on Big Data (Big Data), pp. 1428–1435. IEEE, 2015
13. Li, S., Xue, M., Zhao, B.Z.H., Zhu, H., Zhang, X.: Invisible backdoor attacks against deep neural networks. arXiv preprint arXiv:1909.02742, 2019

14. Piñeyro, L., Pardo, A., Viera, M.: Structure verification of deep neural networks at compilation time using dependent types. In: Proceedings of the XXIII Brazilian Symposium on Programming Languages, pp. 46–53, 2019
15. Shumailov, I., Zhao, Y., Bates, D., Papernot, N., Mullins, R., Anderson, R.: Sponge examples: energy-latency attacks on neural networks. In: 2021 IEEE European Symposium on Security and Privacy (EuroS&P), pp. 212–231. IEEE, 2021
16. Wang, S., Pei, K., Whitehouse, J., Yang, J., Jana, S.: Efficient formal safety analysis of neural networks. Adv. Neural Inf. Process. Syst. **31** (2018)
17. Wang, S., Pei, K., Whitehouse, J., Yang, J., Jana, S.: Formal security analysis of neural networks using symbolic intervals. In: 27th USENIX Security Symposium (USENIX Security 18), pp. 1599–1614, 2018
18. Yeom, S.-K., et al.: Pruning by explaining: a novel criterion for deep neural network pruning. Pattern Recogn. **115**, 107899 (2021)

MDE in the Era of Generative AI

Ahmed Alaoui Mdaghri[1], Meriem Ouederni[2(✉)], and Lotfi Chaari[2]

[1] University of Nantes, Nantes, France
ahmed.alaoui-mdaghri@etu.univ-nantes.fr
[2] Toulouse INP, University of Toulouse, IRIT, Toulouse, France
{meriem.ouederni,lotfi.chaari}@irit.fr

Abstract. Domain-Specific Languages (DSLs) play a vital role in software development, enabling the concise expression of domain-specific concepts and requirements. In this study, we propose a novel approach leveraging Large Language Models (LLMs) to assist the DSLs modelling starting from natural language description. Our solution is a proof of concept where Model Driven Engineering (MDE) is revisited taking advantage from the power of generative AI. Starting from human friendly description and domain modelling language document type, LLM-based system extracts relevant domain knowledge and builds the corresponding DSL model. Such a model is then validated through an iterative process. We applied our proposal to several case studies from different application domains including software engineering, healthcare, and finance. Furthermore, we consider a wide range of existing LLMs usually adapted for code generation. We also study the effectiveness of our solution through multi-criteria experimental evaluation. Lastly, the results demonstrate the feasibility and efficiency of our LLM driven MDE for DSL development, and then advancing domain-specific modelling practices. By doing so, we would enable the developer to save time and effort for further tasks such as functional properties' verification. A demo as well as a web application for our developed solution are available online via the following link https://alaouimdaghriahmed.github.io/demo-ecore-gen/.

Keywords: OMG MDA · MDE · DSL · LLM · Generative AI

1 Introduction

Generative AI (GenAI) is revolutionizing our everyday personal and professional life. It uses sophisticated algorithms to understand contextual knowledge, grammar, and style in order to produce coherent and meaningful output. This is done based on patterns and examples that Gen AI has been trained on. Here, we are particularly interested in Large Language Models (LLMs) which are specific models of GenAI. They rely on prompt engineering and are trained on considerable amounts of text data and learn their statistical properties. In such a context, we focus on the intrinsic link between Software Engineering (SE) and GenAI, and particularly LLMs driven engineering. While the application of GenAI recognize several good impacts, there still many open issues to be studied when

B. Ben Hedia et al. (Eds.): VECoS 2024, LNCS 15466, pp. 113–127, 2025.
https://doi.org/10.1007/978-3-031-85356-2_8

developing new software systems. For instance, it is well recognised to achieve general-purpose languages generation using LLMs. However, LLMs are still not well adapted for generating Domain Specific Languages (DSLs).

DSLs are languages designed for specific application domains. They offer substantial gains in expressiveness and ease of use compared with general-purpose programming languages (GPS, *e.g.* Java, Python, C, etc.) in their domain of application. DSL development is hard, requiring both domain knowledge and language development expertise. However few people could have both.

DSLs can be well developed following Model Driven Engineering (MDE from OMG MDA[1]) methodology. By doing so, both developers and domain experts focus on abstract models rather than actual system code. Here domain experts are the future users and are not usually programmers. Both language expert and domain expert cooperate together for developing a DSL following MDE techniques. Such cooperation enables better understanding of each other, ambiguity resolution and bugs could be detected at early development stage. Hence, this would ease DSL building and also increase software reliability.

The abstract syntax of a DSL is typically defined by a meta-model, which serves as the foundation for establishing the language's structure and rules. To achieve this, a modeling language like Ecore (based on EMOF standard[2]) is suitable and is tool supported within the Eclipse Modeling Framework (EMF).

In the era of LLMs, domain experts find themselves equipped with a potent tool for expression, *i.e.* natural language. Thus, applying LLMs would bridge the gap between both domain and developer experts. However, generating a meta-model from a natural language description faces two challenges. First, the intricate and specific syntax of languages like Ecore can be difficult to manage accurately, especially when the LLMs has not been trained on it. Second, even when the syntax is learnt after giving its technical knowledge into prompting step, the resulting artifacts might be erroneous *w.r.t* that syntax, and/or hold semantics ambiguities. The later issue might arise mainly due to the unclear/incomplete description given to the prompt.

In this paper, we explore the application of LLMs (and LLMs agents) for assisting MDE in order to build new DSLs rather than generating general-purpose languages. We suggest a full process including the syntactic verification and its automatic fix. We also propose human interactive method to fix semantics ambiguity. We apply our approach to several real-world use cases and perform analytic study on given results to validate our process. Our ultimate goal is twofold: *i)* define a new systematic LLM driven MDE methodology, and thus *ii)* provide users with good quality "assistance" in order to ease and improve the DSL design and development cycle. The current work is different from classical code-generation oriented LLMs (starCoder and other similar purpose models). Although such LLMs are not heavy to be manipulated (including 1 to 15 billions of parameters), they remain more adapted for GPL code engineering. To achieve our goal, namely, assisting DSL development following OMG MDA principles, we

---

[1] http://www.omg.org/mda/.
[2] https://www.omg.org/spec/MOF/2.4.1/PDF/.

need to use additional APIs and LLMs agents to perform advanced and complex software tasks.

The remainder of the paper is structured as follows. The Sect. 2 briefly discusses related research work. Next, Sect. 3 outlines our LLM-Driven MDE process. Section 4 presents all details about tool support as well well conducted experiments. We synthesize in Sect. 5 several lessons learned from our work. Finally, Sect. 6 sums up this work and gives some promising perspectives.

2   Related Work

In this section, we review previous research that is closely related to our work. The recent review given in [4] details several existing work in the application of LLMs for code engineering, ranging from general-purpose generation, summarizing, understanding, comment generation, to example recommendation, etc. To the best of our knowledge, there is no similar work addressing MDE engineering using LLMs for modelling new DSLs as recommended by OMG MDA. In the following, we first explore earlier approaches that uses Natural Language Processing (*i.e.* NLP) techniques for DSL generation, highlighting the foundational methods and their contributions. We, then briefly explore LLMs where NLP are highly augmented with intensive data and calculus techniques. Later, introduce LLM agents from the literature since we believe that they are potential candidate to achieve DSL modelling following somehow standardized process.

2.1   LLM for DSL Generation

DSL building is well known as a laborious task and it is remains not fully automated due to its complexity. There exists several approaches working on DSL development, and this is following different methodologies. For example, some approach such as [1,12] use of NLP or ML techniques for domain modelling. The authors of [1] propose an approach where they use model extraction rules with complementary rules from the information retrieval literature to extract a domain model. However, the work given by Saini et al. [12] combine both NLP and ML techniques to automatically extract models with higher accuracy.

Recent work such as Netz et al. [9] uses LLMs to generate a DSL, called CD4A, from natural language describing informal requirements. Here, CD4A relies on UML to define class diagrams in a Java-like syntax. The CD4A model is then used to generate a web application. Jha et al. [5] aimed to fix LLM hallucination, *i.e.* LLMs can sometimes produce outputs that sound confident but are completely incorrect. This approach relies on formal methods and iterative prompting to improve result correctness.

A lot of other work focused on text-to-SQL tasks and achieved good results using fine-tuning, Retrieval Augmented Generation [6] or even In Context-Learning. For instance, Sun et al. [13] propose an SQL code-based generation following few-shot prompting and instruction fine-tuning. Our work proceeds quite similarly such that we combine, *e.g.*, iterative prompting and fine-tuning for passing incremental input, and to better check and fix errors. However, our approach is generic and applies for modelling any DSL following MDA spirit.

2.2 LLM Agents

Although LLMs have not yet reached human levels of problem-solving ability, their achievements are still impressive. Many of these models are pre-trained on massive datasets and then fine-tuned for specific problem-solving or coding tasks. However, LLMs often face challenges with complex tasks. This is primarily why LLM agents were introduced. LLM agents are all systems that use LLMs as their engine and can perform actions on their environment based on observations. We state here some agents from the literature *w.r.t* their use case :

- Reflection: The idea is to give back the LLM output itself as an input with a self correct instruction. Madaan et al. [7] introduces Self-Refine, an approach for improving initial outputs from LLMs through iterative feedback and refinement
- Tool Usage: LLM agents can use various tools and APIs to perform tasks that require specific functionalities, such as web searches, calculations, or data retrieval. In a very recent paper, Patil et al. [10] addresses the challenge of effectively using tools via API calls with LLMs. This work relies on Gorilla, a fine-tuned LLaMA-based model, which demonstrates improved performance in writing API calls and mitigates hallucination issues commonly encountered when prompting LLMs directly.
- Task Planning: it consists of decomposing a problem into easier and manageable sub problems. Existing approaches such as the one presented by Wei et al. [15] apply task planning throughout chain-of-thoughts prompting in order to improve LLMs ability to perform complex reasoning tasks.

In our research, we investigate and integrate multiple agents to address challenges encountered in DSL design. This approach builds on the work of Qian et al. [11], who decompose complex problems into smaller sub-problems that can be tackled by various AI agents. Typically, an LLM is tasked with dividing the problem and managing the outputs from these AI agents.

3   LLM Driven Engineering

Traditional MDE focuses on creating and exploiting domain models, which serve as the primary artifacts of the engineering process. This classical approach emphasizes the systematic use of models as the main drivers of information exchange, system design, and implementation.

LLM-driven Engineering, on the other hand, leverages the capabilities of LLMs to drive the engineering process based on prompting of natural language description and possibly additional inputs. In our proposal, we considered the following LLMs pillars:

- **Natural Language Usage**: LLMs provide a natural language interface for defining and describing system requirements, designs, and implementations. This reduces the barrier to entry, enabling a broader range of stakeholders to participate in the engineering process.
- **Automatic Code Generation**: LLMs can generate code directly from natural language descriptions, bypassing the need for intermediate abstract models. This can accelerate development and reduce the overhead associated with model creation and transformation.
- **Contextual Understanding**: LLMs possess the ability to understand and incorporate context from a wide range of sources, including documentation, prior interactions, and example data. This enhances their ability to generate relevant and contextually appropriate solutions.

3.1 Achieved Goals

Based on the aforementioned LLMs' pillars, our solution is able to empower model-driven engineering. Through innovative approaches and careful design considerations, our solution ensures the following meaningfully advantages:

- **Automation of DSL Generation:** Our solution automates the process of model generation from human given description, reducing the need for manual intervention and speeding up the development cycle. By leveraging LLMs, we empower domain experts to describe their requirements in natural language. In addition, we equip the developer with language model to alleviate the complexity of design task.
- **Automation of LLM Output Validation:** Thanks to the use of AI agent collaboration, we are able to solve inconsistencies in our LLM output by iterative prompting and passing the errors back to the LLM until getting correct output *w.r.t.* some correctness procedure.
- **Enhanced Productivity and Efficiency:** By streamlining the DSL generation process, our solution enhances productivity and efficiency in software development, enabling rapid prototyping and iteration of domain-specific models. The automation of validation and refinement tasks reduces manual effort and accelerates the delivery of high-quality DSLs.

3.2 A New DSL Modelling Process

Our LLM-driven MDE for DSL development is sketched on Fig. 1 where each enumerated step is detailed below. The proposed process aims at generating a meta-model written in Ecore language (formatted *w.r.t* serialised XMI format [3]), and this is performed based on two inputs: a Natural Language Description and an Ecore technical description. The result is validated using a syntactic parser based on agentic reasoning to handle ambiguous or incomplete requests. By doing so, we ensure accuracy and completeness of generated models.

Notice that we use two different LLM agents' families (see left-side and right-side of Fig. 1) depending of our usage needs. One main reason for doing so is that our generation module (on the left-side) is fine-tuned after the generation task, which is not the case for the right-side agents. Another reason is relative to the used inputs and tools. The left-side one is equipped with document parsing and web search while the right-side one needs a syntactic validator.

1. **Specific Prompt:** Our solution starts with an input prompt holding two parameters: *i)* the Natural Language Description (NLD) of a future DSL including user requirements and semantics' constraints; and *ii)* document type definition on a specific modelling language which rigorously gives all technical and syntactic rules that must be satisfied by generated output. For illustration, in the current work, this stands for Ecore definition file passed as second prompt parameter. This is needed because LLMs are not initially trained on such kind of modelling languages. Regarding prompting method, we combine many techniques, namely, grammar prompting [14], COT [15] and tool use [16]. Notice that by doing so, we increase prompting quality taking benefit from different methodologies. We illustrate our prompt template on Fig. 2a.

2. **Output Generation:** The LLM processes the input prompt to generate the serialized result (in XMI format) by LLM inference. Considering Ecore meta-model as target output, the inference consists in: first, parsing Ecore language markers and extracting relevant concepts, entities, attributes, and relationships, and then build structural model $w.r.t$ the Ecore syntax. Notice that, the inference step could use some components needed for complementary tasks, *e.g.* document parsing.

3. **Model Validation:** Initially, a meta-model is "one-shot" generated (see the right arrow "$\longrightarrow$" going from step 1 to step 2) based on both input parameters mentioned in the initial step 1. This model is then parsed using the domain grammar to check syntactic errors. If no errors are found, the validation process needs human intervention for semantics' checking. He/shed will be asked to provide more clarifications on missing/ambiguous semantics' related features. If this is validated then the validated process terminates and then step 4 on Fig. 1 could be performed. However, if syntactic errors raise, the algorithm incrementally fixes each of them thanks to LLM agents and following iterative prompting. For each increment (*i.e.* repeating step 3), both raised error and its corresponding meta-model are passed once again into a LLM using the prompt as shown on Fig. 2b. The LLM is then prompted to fix detected errors. The meta-model is updated with the suggested corrections, and the verification is restarted. This validation cycle ends up once the meta-model is free from syntactic errors. Regarding the process modelled in Fig. 1, we formalize our syntactic validation method in Algorithm 1.

Regarding semantics' quality and/or precision, this is left to domain expert appreciation. Our current goal is to assist both domain and developer experts. Domain expert could add some precision to be taken into consideration during the iterative prompting to improve and complete the previously generated result. This would be also helpful for our ambiguity resolution as explained further in step 5.

4. **Database Storage for Use Cases:** Validated outputs are stored in a database for further analysis and fine-tuning of the LLM. This repository of use cases facilitates iterative refinement of the generation process, enabling continuous improvement based on feedback and real-world application scenarios.

5. **Ambiguity Resolution:** In cases where the generated model fails the validation step[3] or encounters unresolved ambiguity (*e.g.* non-explicable issue), our solution re-prompt the LLM with the occurred error and possibly additional description from the user, enabling it to revisit and refine its understanding of the domain context. Additionally, access to external tools such as API search calls and documentation enhances the LLM's understanding and resolution of ambiguous requests.

6. **Fine-tuning and model improvements:** After correcting the generate model based on iterative reasoning and additional inputs, the validated results get stored, after gathering enough validated models, we can use them to fine-tune our LLMs.

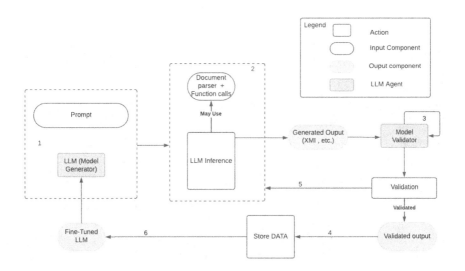

Fig. 1. LLM-guided DSL Building Process

---

[3] There is a maximum iteration number concluded by learning from most examples.

Algorithm 1 Function GenMM(NLD, Ecore_DT): returns MM

Input: NLD	▷ Natural Language Description text
Input: Ecore_DT	▷ Ecore Document Type
Output: MM	▷ MM is Valid

Valid ⟵ False
MM ⟵ ∅
while NOT Valid **do**   ▷ Generate the MM from NLD and EDT
        Parse MM using **Ecore_DT** to check syntactic errors
        if no syntactic errors found **then**
                Valid ⟵ True
        else
                Get the list of syntactic errors (from pyecore use)
                for each error in the list **do**
                        Input MM and the error to the LLM
                        Ask the LLM to fix the error
                        Update the MM with the fix
                end for
        end if
end while
Return MM

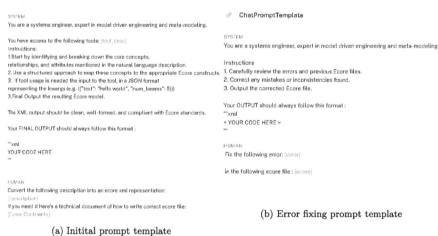

(a) Initial prompt template

(b) Error fixing prompt template

Fig. 2. Prompt templates.

4   Tool Support

This section provides a comprehensive overview of the implementation details of our study, including the used models and the specific use cases to which they were applied. We will delve into the technical aspects of the system. Additionally, we will present the various models selected for this research, elucidating their roles and functionalities within our framework. Lastly, we will describe one use case in detail, highlighting the practical applications and the outcomes observed.

4.1   Implementation

In order to implement our approach, we have started by studying several existing LLMs. We summarize in Table 1 the most significant ones for our purposes while providing more details on the model weights, if they are open source and how they have been used. Other models were utilized in our study, and they will be discussed subsequently with an analysis of the reasons for not considering them viable options. Notice that both weights and contextual window columns stand for the amount of, respectively, the trainable LLM's parameters, and the tokens we can pass to an LLM without loosing track of its context [8]. Referenced Hugging-Chat-API[4] is an open source project to access the HuggingFace Chat[5] granting access to the latest models in a production environment. Grid5000[6] is is a large-scale and flexible test-bed for experiment-driven research in all areas of computer science. We used Grid5000 to run lighter models and the Hugging-Chat-API to use already deployed heavier models.

Table 1. Available Large Language Models characteristics.

Name	Owner	Model Weights	Inference Endpoint	Open-Source	Context Window
GPT-4 Omni	OpenAI	–	OpenAI API	No	128K
GPT-4 Turbo	OpenAI	8 × 220 billion parameters	OpenAI API	No	128K
GPT-3.5 Turbo	OpenAI	175 billion parameters	OpenAI API	No	16K
LLaMA3-70B	Meta	70 billion parameters	Grid5000	Yes	8K
LLaMA3-8B	Meta	8 billion parameters	HuggingChat API	Yes	8K
LLaMA2-7B	Meta	7 billion parametes	Grid5000	Yes	32K
Mixtral-8x7B	Mistral AI	8 × 7 billion parameters	HuggingChat API	Yes	32K
Mistral-7B	Mistral AI	7 billion parameters	Grid5000	Yes	8K
Gemma-7B	Google	7 billion parameters	HuggingChat API	Yes	8K
Gemma-2B	Google	2 billion parameters	Grid5000	Yes	8K
C4AI-Command-r	C4AI	104 billion parameters	HuggingChat API	Yes	128K

Our main use case involved the generation and validation of Ecore models using Pyecore for parsing the generated artifacts. We provided detailed management of these artifacts through several key steps. First, a natural language description was used as a prompt parameter to generate a model using a LLM. Second, a technical Ecore description was employed as a prompt parameter to give the language model better insight into writing syntactically correct Ecore

---

[4] https://github.com/Soulter/hugging-chat-api.
[5] https://huggingface.co/chat.
[6] https://www.grid5000.fr/w/Grid5000:Home.

files. Third, we developed a model validator using Pyecore[7] as a library for parsing our produced models and metamodels with Python. The errors identified
during this process were utilized in conjunction with iterative prompting (see
step 3 in Sect. 3) as presented in Algorithm 1.

4.2 Experimentation

We applied our approach to several real-world use cases gathered from the literature. Table 2 cites some of them for illustration. During the experimentation,
we collected both the natural language description and the corresponding DSL
meta-model. We then applied our approach to generate the Ecore meta-model
for each use case. Lastly, we systematically compared our result with the one
given by the correspondent reference (mentioned Table 2). We noticed that our
generated output is identical to the existing result for all examples.

Table 2. Some Checked use cases.

Use Case	Reference
SimplePDL	https://eclipse.dev/atl/usecases/SimplePDL2Tina/
FSM	http://melange.inria.fr/defining-an-executable-dsl/
Website Phone friendly	https://olegoaer.developpez.com/tutos/model/xtext/wdl/
GemRBACCTX	https://orbilu.uni.lu/bitstream/10993/22759/1/codaspy2016.pdf
MontiArc	https://github.com/MontiCore/montiarc/blob/develop/languages/MontiArc.md

We now illustrate how our approach does work throughout one use case called
SimplePDL [2]. This stands for a DSL which describes software developpement
process. Here, we initially provide the LLM prompt with its natural language
description as well as the Ecore document type, and we get as an output the
corresponding meta-model in Ecore format. Figure 3 shows the graphical diagram
of the meta-model.

Later, we proceed as follows. The first one-shot output will be passed to
our verification module and checks whether it is correct. For instance, when we
applied GPT4-Turbo for this DSL, we found the following error: **"Namespace
prefix xsi for type on eClassifiers is not defined, line 3, column 55
(SIMPLEPDL0.ecore, line 3)"**. After error fix, the output is re-parsed again
and another error is then found, namely, **"Unknown eType in eClassifier"**.
Similarly, the erroneous output is fixed and checked again. At this level, no more
errors are detected. It concludes that in two iterations we have an error free Ecore
file.

---

[7] https://github.com/pyecore/pyecore.

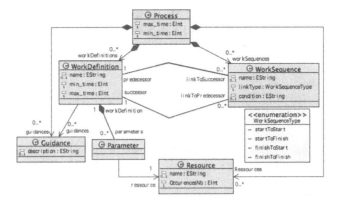

Fig. 3. SimplePDL metamodel.

5   Learned Lessons

In order to evaluate the proposed method, namely, LLM-driven domain specific modelling, we discuss in this section some analytic studies we carried out for this purpose. We systematically comment on our implementation details, describe usage and validation of our meta-model, and present qualitative results. The analysis presented in the remainder of this paper is stored in a preliminary dataset available online[8].

5.1   Syntactic Error Frequency by Error Category

The syntactic errors generated by different LLMs (mentioned on Fig. 5) were categorized into the most frequent types where "Other" category is left for less common errors:

- Invalid comment: this category includes errors related to the use of unsupported tags in XMI.
- Start tag: This category encompasses errors occurring at the beginning of the file.
- Wrong declaration: This category includes errors involving the use of incorrect types or attributes.
- Other: This category comprises miscellaneous errors, including empty files or unsupported syntax.

Figure 4 illustrates the overall occurrence (denoted frequency) of errors categorized as "Invalid Comment," "Other," "Start Tag," and "Wrong Declaration". This plot reveals that "Invalid Comment" is the most common error type, respectively followed by "Other", "Start Tag", and "Wrong Declaration". More precisely, almost half encountered errors belong to the "Invalid Comment" category.

---

[8] https://huggingface.co/datasets/VeryMadSoul/Errors.

This is due to a confusion made by LLMs between XML [3] tags and Ecore serialization (*i.e.* XMI tags). In order to fix detected issues we rely on our iterative prompting method (see Sect. 5.3).

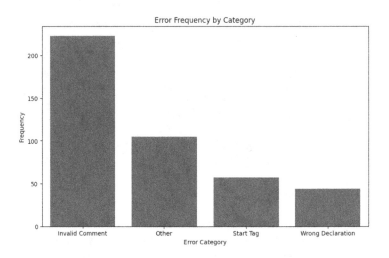

Fig. 4. Error distribution by category.

5.2 Syntactic Error Category Distribution by LLMs

The plot, shown in Fig. 5, presents the error category distribution for each LLMs being evaluated. LLMs with very low application frequency do not enable us to generate well-formed Ecore code, *i.e.* no possible parse *w.r.t* standard syntax. In other words, those LLMs would generate code in XML rather than XMI format with the prevalent error being "Start Tag" or "Empty File". From the plot, it is clear that "GPT-4.0", "Llama-3-70B" and "Mixtral-8x7B" models have a high frequency of "Invalid Comment" errors, while the other models exhibit relatively fewer instances of other error categories, such as "Other", "Start Tag", and "Wrong Declaration".

5.3 Distribution of Use Case Resolutions for Each LLM

Table 3 summarizes the distribution of use case resolutions for each LLMs. These statistics were collected based on the resolution rate of one use case (*i.e.* SimplePDL) for which we repeated our full process given in Fig. 1 40 times. This aims at evaluate the LLMs efficiency. Notice since this task is time and resources consuming, we have been limited to fix the execution repetition to 40 times.

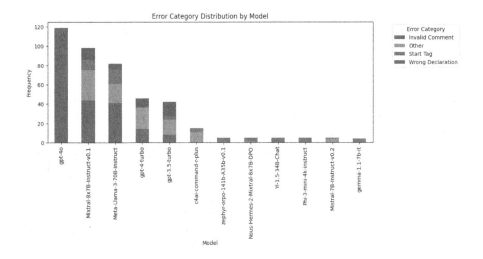

Fig. 5. Error Category Distribution by each of Checked LLMs.

Table 3. Success rate of the same task using different contexts, evaluated over 40 times.

Model	Context provided	Correct output
GPT-4o	Zero-shot	0
	Our one-shot prompt	2
	Our iterative prompting	32
meta-llama/Meta-Llama-3-70B-Instruct	Zero-shot	0
	Our on-shot prompt	21
	Our iterative prompting	30
mistralai/Mixtral-8x7B-Instruct-v0.1	Zero-shot	0
	Our one-shot Prompt	8
	Our iterative prompting	18

It makes sense to have a 0% correct output for zero-shot context as this work aims to solve exactly that, we also saw that the number of low correct outputs using our prompt for GPT-4o is due to generating comment tags that aren't supported while most of these mistakes would be correct, in 8 cases the model could not resolve the issue. Meta-Llama-3 being the best at generating correct ecore format using only the technical file we provide, still noticing an increase using iterative prompting. Even in the case of Mixtral-8x7B the results tend to improve using iterative prompting

Similar to GTP-4o, the other OPENAI's models tend to perform better at error resolution but not at one shot generation. In terms of the type of error committed, they tend to generated a bit more diverse errors, entailing a further hypothesis, that GPT-4o has seen more XML syntax in its training data.

6 Conclusion

The rapid growth of LLMs enabled remarkable achievements for SE, including the ability to perform several code tasks based on text-only descriptions. For instance, it is possible to transform, add comments, think on and summarize code. In this paper, we tackled the DSLs' development following OMG MDA principles, *i.e.* starting with the design of meta-model for a future DSL. The result does respect a required output format and it is generated based on two input parameters: human-friendly description and modelling language document type. However, the one-shot generation results often contain syntactic and semantics errors. We applied an iterative prompting approach and LLM agents to solve these issues. Detected errors are given back as input for the iterative process until correctness achievement. We checked our suggested process on several real-world case studies and performed an analytic study in order to show the advantages and actual LLMs limits to be dealt with in the future.

To sum up, while we believe that LLMs are potentially revolutionising software development, little attention in the literature is given to Model Based Software Engineering (MBSE). We also notice that there still have relevant questionable limitations to be addressed in term of insufficient training on specific languages, explicability, reliability, scalability, and resources consumption. Those challenges once dealt with, LLMs would be insightful assistant for model-based software engineering.

Acknowledgement. This work is supported and funded by IBCO-CIMI research project (2021–2024). It is also partially supported by FOR program coordinated by ANITI, CRIAQ, IRT Saint Exupery, and IVADO.

References

1. Arora, C., Sabetzadeh, M., Briand, L., Zimmer, F.: Extracting domain models from natural-language requirements: approach and industrial evaluation. In: Proceedings of the ACM/IEEE 19th International Conference on Model Driven Engineering Languages and Systems, pp. 250–260. ACM, Saint-malo France (October 2016). https://doi.org/10.1145/2976767.2976769,
2. Combemale, B., Garoche, P.L., Crégut, X., Thirioux, X., Vernadat, F.: Towards a formal verification of process model's properties - SimplePDL and TOCL case study. In: INSTICC (ed.) 9th International Conference on Enterprise Information Systems, pp. 80–89. INSTICC, Funchal, Madeira, Portugal (June 2007). https://hal.science/hal-00160807
3. Grose, T.J., Doney, G.C., Brodsky, S.A.: Mastering XMI: Java Programming with XMI, XML and UML, vol. 21. John Wiley & Sons, Hoboken (2002)
4. Hou, X., et al.: Large Language Models for Software Engineering: A Systematic Literature Review (March 2024). arXiv:2308.10620 [cs]

5. Jha, S., Jha, S.K., Lincoln, P., Bastian, N.D., Velasquez, A., Neema, S.: Dehalluci-
    nating large language models using formal methods guided iterative prompting. In:
    2023 IEEE International Conference on Assured Autonomy (ICAA), pp. 149–152
    (June 2023). https://doi.org/10.1109/ICAA58325.2023.00029, https://ieeexplore.
    ieee.org/document/10207581
6. Lewis, P., et al.: Retrieval-augmented generation for knowledge-intensive nlp
    tasks. In: Larochelle, H., Ranzato, M., Hadsell, R., Balcan, M., Lin, H. (eds.)
    Advances in Neural Information Processing Systems, vol. 33, pp. 9459–9474.
    Curran Associates, Inc. (2020). https://proceedings.neurips.cc/paper_files/paper/
    2020/file/6b493230205f780e1bc26945df7481e5-Paper.pdf
7. Madaan, A., et al.: Self-Refine: Iterative Refinement with Self-Feedback (May
    2023).https://doi.org/10.48550/arXiv.2303.17651, arXiv:2303.17651 [cs]
8. Minaee, S., et al.: Large language models: a survey (2024). https://arxiv.org/abs/
    2402.06196
9. Netz, L., Michael, J., Rumpe, B.: From Natural Language to Web Applications:
    Using Large Language Models for Model-Driven Software Engineering, pp. 179–
    195. Gesellschaft fúr Informatik e.V. (2024). https://dl.gi.de/handle/20.500.12116/
    43620
10. Patil, S.G., Zhang, T., Wang, X., Gonzalez, J.E.: Gorilla: Large Language Model
    Connected with Massive APIs (May 2023). https://doi.org/10.48550/arXiv.2305.
    15334, arXiv:2305.15334 [cs]
11. Qian, C., et al.: Communicative Agents for Software Development, December 2023.
    arXiv:2307.07924 [cs]
12. Saini, R.: Artificial intelligence empowered domain modelling bot. In: Proceedings
    of the 23rd ACM/IEEE International Conference on Model Driven Engineering
    Languages and Systems: Companion Proceedings, pp. 1–6. ACM, Virtual Event
    Canada (October 2020). https://doi.org/10.1145/3417990.3419486
13. Sun, R., et al.: SQL-PaLM: Improved Large Language Model Adaptation for Text-
    to-SQL (June 2023). http://arxiv.org/abs/2306.00739, arXiv:2306.00739 [cs]
14. Wang, B., Wang, Z., Wang, X., Cao, Y., Saurous, R.A., Kim, Y.: Grammar
    Prompting for Domain-Specific Language Generation with Large Language Models
    (November 2023). arXiv:2305.19234 [cs]
15. Wei, J., et al.: Chain-of-Thought Prompting Elicits Reasoning in Large
    Language Models (January 2023). https://doi.org/10.48550/arXiv.2201.11903,
    arXiv:2201.11903 [cs]
16. Yang, Z., et al.: MM-REACT: Prompting ChatGPT for Multimodal Rea-
    soning and Action (March 2023). https://doi.org/10.48550/arXiv.2303.11381,
    arXiv:2303.11381 [cs]

Intrusion Detection Using an Enhancement Bi-LSTM Recurrent Neural Network Model

Nour Elhouda Oueslati[1]([✉]), Hichem Mrabet[1], and Abderrazak Jemai[2]

[1] Faculty of Sciences of Tunis, University of Tunis El Manar, Tunis, Tunisia
{nourelhouda.oueslati,hichem.mrabet}@fst.utm.tn
[2] National Institute of Applied Sciences and Technology, Tunis, Tunisia
abderrazak.jemai@insat.tn

Abstract. Malicious intrusions are constant threats to networks, intrusion detection systems (IDS) have been developed to identify and classify these attacks to prevent them from occurring. However, the accuracy and efficiency of these systems are still not satisfactory. Currently, the actual detection accuracy of some detection models is relatively low. Most earlier research approaches relied on regular neural networks, which had low accuracy. The IDS works well while machine learning (ML) and especially deep learning (DL) algorithms are employed to identify and prevent various threats. To solve these problems, an enhancing Bidirectional long short-term memory (Bi-LSTM) model has been proposed in this paper. To train our model, the up-to-date publicly available NSL-KDD dataset is introduced, which is a widely used benchmark dataset in the field of intrusion detection. We have performed 10-fold cross-validation to demonstrate the unbiasedness of the results. Furthermore, we compare the enhancing Bi-LSTM model with existing classifiers. Our proposed model achieves impressive results in terms of accuracy up to 97,93%.

Keywords: Machine Learning (ML) · Deep Learning (DL) · Intrusion Detection Systems (IDS) · Bidirectional Long Short-Term Memory · Cybersecurity

1 Introduction

In recent years, network infiltration has rapidly spread, resulting in the invasion of personal privacy and becoming the primary assault platform [1]. Security flaws have also surfaced. Network infections, eavesdropping, and malicious attacks are on the rise, making network security a top priority for society and government departments. However, detecting breaches in huge datasets can be difficult. There are many sophisticated uses of the developing networks, including smart homes, cities, grids, gadgets, and objects, as well as e-commerce, e-banking, and e-government. Intrusion detection is an important part of a comprehensive cybersecurity strategy. It detects intrusions effectively by monitoring the condition and activity of the defence system. As a result, it can detect unauthorised or anomalous network activity [2]. It is described as "network security devices that monitor network traffic to find unexpected patterns" [3]. Intrusion detection seeks to discover potential security breaches and notify security personnel so that they can take immediate action to prevent additional damage. There are several types of IDS (intrusion detection systems) that can be employed, including host-based and network-based IDS. Host-based IDS analyses activity on a particular device or server, whereas network-based IDS monitors all network traffic on a specific segment. In fact, network traffic can be divided into two types (normal and malignant). Furthermore, network traffic can be divided into five types: normal, DoS (Denial of Service attacks), R2L (Root to Local attacks), U2R (User to Root attacks), and Probe. Thus, intrusion detection can be viewed as a classification problem. Intrusion detection accuracy can be significantly increased by boosting classifier performance in efficiently recognising malicious traffic. Most previous research methods relied on conventional neural networks, which had limited accuracy. The IDS works best when machine learning (ML) [4] and, particularly, deep learning (DL) algorithms [5] are used to detect and prevent various threats. Artificial intelligence technology is constantly evolving, and many types of machine learning or deep learning have been applied to intrusion detection systems [6]. However, it still has several drawbacks, such as the necessity for a large number of training samples, the time required, and the reliance on feature selection. Several deep learning models have been studied, built, and tested to improve intrusion detection and efficiency. In this research, we propose an intrusion detection method based on an improved Bi-LSTM model.

Contribution. Our major contributions in the under contention research study are enlisted as follows:

- A new taxonomy of Machine Learning by domain is proposed
- A new taxonomy of Deep Learning by domain is proposed
- An enhancing Bi-LSTM model is proposed
- 10-fold cross-validation is conducted in this research to show the unbiasedness of our results.
- We evaluate our proposed model with an NSL-KDD Dataset, the experimental results show that the performance of the enhancing BLSTM is better than the existing literature

Organization. The remaining paper is designed as follows. Section 2 A taxonomy of Machine Learning and Deep Learning. In Sect. 3, the methodology, proposed model, dataset description, and other details are elaborated. Section 4 presents the experimental setup. The results is discussed in detail in Sect. 5. Finally, we conclude the paper in Sect. 6.

2   A Taxonomy of Machine Learning and Deep Learning

Learning is essentially the ability to enhance task performance over time; this was the rationale for the existence of machine learning. Machine learning is a word that refers to a variety of algorithms. The purpose of these algorithms is to develop and enhance task execution in the same way that humans can. Over the years, a tremendous amount of work has been done to improve the performance of these algorithms; these advances allow these algorithms to be used in a variety of human life elements and real-world situations. Machine learning algorithms are classified based on the type of input rather than how the output is produced [21]. Supervised algorithms rely on data that is labelled with the appropriate output. The unsupervised algorithm examines an array of unlabeled knowledge to identify patterns [7].

In reinforcement learning, the right output is not available from the start. In any instance, in a trial-and-error style, the projected output can be evaluated using a positive or negative reward to indicate how good or bad the output [8]. Machine learning has various limits, the most difficult of which is dealing with novel issues that require a large amount of labelled data. The solution to the preceding problem is to determine the feature of the data input before running the machine learning algorithm. The aforementioned technique may result in a significant level of bottleneck because humans have a limited ability to discern data features.

Deep learning solves this constraint by identifying features and representations directly from raw data. The term "deep" alludes to the hierarchy of distinguishing features as well as the ability to learn directly from raw data. Deep learning techniques consist of numerous layers known as hidden layers, which can offer the model with feature extraction and learning methods [9]. Deep learning has numerous implementations. The goal of these implementations differs, as they require modifying or rearranging the hidden layers. These solutions can include either forwarding or reverse processing. The feedforward neural network is the foundation for all deep learning implementations; it consists of an input layer, hidden layers, and an output layer. Each feed-forward layer contains a certain number of perceptrons that accept input data, weights, and a bias value. That output will be created in accordance with the activation function. In the feed-forward neural network, there is errorcalculated using values from the output layer. The purpose is to reduce mistakes by adjusting the parameters (bias and weights) [9].

Recurrent neural networks (RNN) [10] use the same concept as feed-forward neural networks; the difference is that RNN use the concept of "data memory." Data memory involves storing the value of distinct layers' outputs and passing it to prior layers via cross-sequence steps (see [11]). There is also an RNN expansion known as Long Short-term Memory (LSTM) [12]. LSTM employs a gating strategy. In LSTM, a hidden state is created from paste outputs. The gate uses the input and concealed state as parameters in the activation function to construct.

Convolutional Neural Network (CNN) is the primary implementation of deep learning when the input is multidimensional and cannot be handled by regular neural networks [13].

2.1 A Taxonomy of Machine Learning by Domain

Table 1 presents a new taxonomy of ML who is divided as a function of supervised learning, unsupervised learning, and reinforcement learning. In supervised learning we presented these algorithms: '- Hidden Markov Model (HMM)', 'Markov Random Fields', 'Naive Bayes (NB)', 'Latent Dirichlet Allocation (LDA)', 'Belief Network', 'Linear Regression', 'Logistic Regression', 'Artificial Neural Network (ANN)', 'Support Vector Machine (SVM)', 'Maximum Entropy', 'Decision Tree', 'Conditional Random Field (CRF)', and 'Random Forest (RF)' with their domains.

In unsupervised learning, we presented these algorithms: 'K-means Clustering', 'Spectral Clustering', 'Hierarchical Clustering', 'Expectation Maximization (EM)', 'Principal Component Analysis (PCA)', and 'Linear Discriminant Analysis (LDA)' with their domains.

In addition, in reinforcement learning, we presented these algorithms: 'Iterative Value (Value Iteration)', 'Iterative Policy (Policy Iteration)', 'Q-Learning', 'SARSA', 'XCS (eXtended Classifier System)', 'Stochastic Gradient Descent (SGD)', and 'Genetic Algorithm' with their domains.

2.2 A Taxonomy of Deep Learning by Domain

Table 2 presents a new taxonomy of DL who is divided as a function of supervised learning, unsupervised learning, and reinforcement learning. In supervised learning, we presented these algorithms: 'MLP (Multi-Layer Perceptron)', 'CNN (Convolutional Neural Network)', and 'RNN (Recurrent Neural Network)' with their domains.

In unsupervised learning, we presented these algorithms: 'GAN (Generative Adversarial Network)', 'AE (Autoencoder)', 'SOM (Self-Organizing Map)', 'RBM (Restricted Boltzmann Machine)', and 'DBN (Deep Belief Network)' with their domains. In addition, in reinforcement learning we presented this algorithm: 'Deep Reinforcement Learning (DRL)' with his domain.

3 Methodology

This research work aims to propose an enhancement Bi-LSTM model for intrusion detection. This part of the paper describes the proposed work methodology, i.e., background on Bi-LSTM, the proposed model, dataset description, and preprocessing.

3.1 Background on Bi-LSTM

LSTM

Is a specific sort of recurrent neural network. This architecture is specifically designed to handle the problem of vanishing and exploding gradients. Furthermore, this form of network is better at preserving long-distance connections

Table 1. A taxonomy of Machine Learning by domain

Machine Learning (ML)		
	Name	*Domain*
Supervised Learning)	- Hidden Markov Model (HMM):	- time-series analysis and speech recognition
	- Markov Random Fields:	- computer vision for tasks such as image segmentation, object recognition, and image reconstruction
	- Naive Bayes (NB):	- text classification, spam filtering, and sentiment analysis
	- Latent Dirichlet Allocation (LDA):	- topic modeling in natural language processing
	- Belief Network:	- artificial intelligence for probabilistic reasoning
	- Linear Regression:	- statistics and machine learning for predicting a continuous outcome
	- Logistic Regression:	- binary classification problems, i.e., medical diagnosis, marketing analytics, and credit scoring
	- Artificial Neural Network (ANN):	- image and speech recognition, natural language processing, and autonomous systems
	- Support Vector Machine (SVM):	- classification and regression tasks
	- Maximum Entropy:	- natural language processing, information retrieval, and text classification tasks
	- Decision Tree:	- classification and regression tasks, including finance, healthcare, and marketing
	- Conditional Random Field (CRF):	- structured prediction tasks such as image segmentation, natural language processing, and sequence labeling
	- Random Forest (RF):	- ensemble learning in classification and regression tasks
Unsupervised Learning)	- K-means Clustering:	- data analysis and pattern recognition
	- Spectral Clustering:	- image segmentation, social network analysis, and community detection
	- Hierarchical Clustering:	- biology for taxonomy, in finance for portfolio analysis, and in social sciences for similarity analysis among individuals or groups
	- Expectation Maximization (EM):	- statistics for estimating parameters of probabilistic models
	- Principal Component Analysis (PCA):	- image processing, signal processing, and finance for dimensionality reduction and feature extraction
	- Linear Discriminant Analysis (LDA):	- machine learning for feature extraction and dimensionality reduction, particularly in face recognition, pattern recognition, and bioinformatics
Reinforcement Learning)	- Iterative Value (Value Iteration):	- robotics, game playing, and autonomous systems
	- Iterative Policy (Policy Iteration):	- control systems, game playing, and optimization problems
	- Q-Learning:	- robotics, game playing, and control systems
	- SARSA:	- robotic control, game playing, and adaptive systems
	- XCS (eXtended Classifier System):	- evolving rule sets for complex control problems and autonomous systems
	- Stochastic Gradient Descent (SGD):	- computer vision, natural language processing, and speech recognition
	- Genetic Algorithm:	- optimization and search problems

and recognising the relationship between values at the start and end of a sequence [14].

The LSTM model introduces expressions, namely gates.

Table 2. A taxonomy of Deep Learning by domain

	Deep Learning (ML)	
	Name	*Domain*
Supervised Learning)	- MLP (Multi-Layer Perceptron):	- both structured and unstructured data
	- CNN (Convolutional Neural Network):	- processing grid-like data, such as images and videos
	- RNN (Recurrent Neural Network):	- sequence data, i.e., natural language processing (NLP), speech recognition, and time series analysis
Unsupervised Learning)	- GAN (Generative Adversarial Network):	- image generation, style transfer, and data augmentation
	- AE (Autoencoder):	- image denoising, feature learning, and data compression
	- SOM (Self-Organizing Map):	- clustering and visualization of high-dimensional data
	- RBM (Restricted Boltzmann Machine):	- dimensionality reduction, classification, collaborative filtering, feature learning, and topic modelling
	- DBN (Deep Belief Network):	- speech recognition and image classification
Reinforcement Learning)	- Deep Reinforcement Learning (DRL)	- Games, Robotics, Autonomous Systems, Resource Management and Simulated Environments

In actuality, there are three kinds of gates:

- The forget gate determines how much information the memory cell will acquire from the memory cell in the previous phase.
- The update (input) gate determines whether the memory cell will be updated. It also controls how much information the present memory cell receives from a potential new memory cell.
- The output gate determines the value of the following concealed state.

Mathematically, we define an LSTM block as:

$$\Gamma_u = \sigma(W_{uu}a^{<t-1>} + W_{ux}x^{<t>} + b_u)$$
$$\Gamma_f = \sigma(W_{ff}a^{<t-1>} + W_{fx}x^{<t>} + b_f)$$
$$\Gamma_o = \sigma(W_{oo}a^{<t-1>} + W_{ox}x^{<t>} + b_o)$$
$$\hat{c}^{<t>} = tanh(W_{cc}a^{<t-1>} + W_{cx}x^{<t>} + b_c)$$
$$c^{<t>} = \Gamma_u \odot \hat{c}^{<t>} + \Gamma_f \odot c^{<t-1>}$$
$$a^{<t>} = \Gamma_o \odot \tanh(c^{<t>}), \tag{1}$$

W and b are weight matrices and vectors, t is the current iteration of the recurrent network, Γ_u is the update gate, Γ_f is the forget gate, Γ_o is the output gate, $\hat{c}^{<t>}$ is the potential value of the memory cell, $c^{<t>}$ is the current value of the memory cell, and $a^{<t>}$ is the output value or hidden state. The architecture of the LSTM block can be shown as:

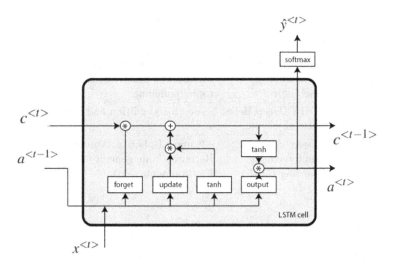

Fig. 1. The architecture of the LSTM block

Bidirectional LSTM

Bidirectional LSTM (Bi-LSTM) is a recurrent neural network designed primarily for natural language processing. Unlike regular LSTM, the input travels in both directions, and it can use data from both sides. It's also an effective tool for modelling the sequential interdependence of words and sentences in both sides of the sequence [14].

In short, Bi-LSTM adds an additional LSTM layer that reverses the direction of information flow. In a nutshell, it means that the input sequence flows backward via the additional LSTM layer. Then we aggregate the outputs of both

LSTM layers in a variety of ways, including average, sum, multiplication, and concatenation.

To illustrate, the unrolled BiLSTM is presented in the figure below:

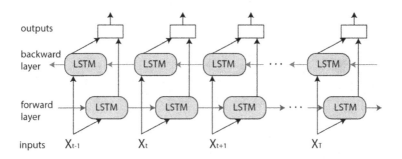

Fig. 2. The architecture of Bi-LSTM

Advantages

This style of architecture offers numerous advantages in real-world problems, particularly in NLP. The major reason is that each component of an input sequence contains information from both the past and the present. As a result, Bi-LSTM can create more relevant output by integrating LSTM layers in both directions.

3.2 Proposed Model

The proposed model is tested and trained with low false positive (FP) and greater detection accuracy.

The model consists of different layers, i.e., one Input layer with 200 neurons, one Bi-LSTM layer possessing 100 neurons with "Tanh" activation function, 0,3 dropout, and two dense layers possessing 100 and 50 neurons with "Relu" activation function. We have used Softmax as an activation function in the output layer with 05 neurons. To achieve efficient results, we have performed the experimentation till ten epochs with batch sizes of 32. For experimentation, we have used Google Colaboratory is a hosted Jupyter Notebook service that requires no setup to use and provides free access to computing resources, with the processing of T4 GPU for improved performance.

Furthermore, the proposed work utilized Keras framework with the backend of TensorFlow for Python. Figure 3 illustrate the architecture of enhancing Bi-LSTM model and Table 3 describe the different layers. To effectively learn the relationship between future and past information using deep learning method, forward and backward information must be processed concurrently. Meanwhile, ordinary LSTMs did not learn from reverse order processing. The BiLSTM may process input sequences in two ways: forward from past to future and backward from future to past. This technique combines two hidden states from two LSTM models while retaining information from the past and future, resulting in better long-term learning dependencies and model's accuracy. The system consists of an input layer, a BiLSTM layer which contains LSTM backward layer, an LSTM forward layer, and 2 Dense layer.

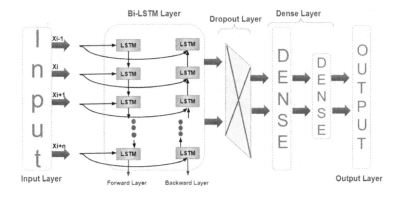

Fig. 3. The architecture of enhancing Bi-LSTM model

Table 3. Bi-LSTM model description

layers	Neurons	AF	Epochs	Optimizer	Batch-size
Input Layer (1)	200	–			
Bi-LSTM Layer (1)	100	Tanh			
Dropout Layer(1)	0,3	–	10	Adamax	32
Dense Layer (2)	100, 50	ReLu			
Output Layer (1)	05	Softmax			

3.3 Dataset

The NSL-KDD dataset represents a refined version of the KDDcup99 dataset [15]. The NSL-KDD dataset contains a significant amount of data. Many scholars carried out diverse analysis on the NSL-KDD dataset, employing different tools and approaches. Nonetheless, their unifying goal was to develop effective IDS. A full NSL-KDD dataset analysis utilising several machine learning approaches was carried out using the WEKA tool and discussed in [16]. Handling large amounts of data, such as those in the NSL-KDD dataset, and accelerating IDS performance is a tough task [17].

Three important modifications were conducted on the KDD dataset.

- Remove unnecessary records so the classifier can produce an unbiased result.
- A suitable number of entries are included in the test and training datasets. These records are reasonable, allowing for experiments on the entire set.
- The number of selected records from each challenging level group is inversely proportional to the original KDD dataset's record percentages.

The attacks replicated in our studies can be classed into one of four groups [15], as shown below:

- Denial of service (DoS): A DoS attack occurs when an attacker prohibits legitimate users from accessing the network by consuming memory or computer resources. This renders the system incapable of processing valid requests. DoS attacks include 'neptune', 'back', 'land', 'pod', 'smurf', 'teardrop', 'mailbomb', 'apache2', 'processtable', 'udpstorm' and 'worm'.
- Probing attack (PROBE): This sort of attack involves an attacker bypassing security and obtaining data from networked machines. PROBE assaults involve 'ipsweep', 'nmap', 'portsweep', 'satan', 'mscan' and 'saint'.
- Remote-to-local attack (R2L): An attacker who does not own an account exploits machine vulnerabilities to get local access to a genuine user account. Common R2L attacks include 'ftp_write', 'guess_passwd', 'imap', 'multihop', 'phf', 'spy', 'warezclient', 'warezmaster', 'sendmail', 'named', 'snmpgetattack', 'snmpguess', 'xlock', 'xsnoop' and 'httptunnel'.
- Users-to-root attack (U2R): This sort of attack occurs when an attacker gains access to the system by using a genuine user account. It is able to obtain access to the system's root component by exploiting existing system vulnerabilities. Examples of U2R attacks include 'buffer_overflow', 'loadmodule', 'perl', 'rootkit', 'ps', 'sqlattack' and 'xterm'.

We considered five classes: Normal, DoS, Probe, R2L, and U2R. In greater detail, there are 11 attack types for denial of service (DoS), 6 for probing (Probe), 15 for unauthorized access from a remote computer (R2L), and 7 for unauthorized access to the local super user (U2R). Table 4 summarises the NSL-KDD datasets utilized in this study to test and train the created IDS. This table displays the percentage of certain records and the amount of data components in the whole collection. Figure 4 and Fig. 5 show the shape of dataset for train and test, respectively.

3.4   Dataset Preprocessing

In the proposed model, pre-processing involves the following main tasks:

Categorical Value Handling: The dataset includes categorical features like 'protocol_type', 'service', and 'flag'. These category values are retrieved, and a function preprocess_dataset is developed to encode them using LabelEncoder and one-hot encoding with OneHotEncoder.

One-Hot Encoding: The categorical values are one-hot encoded, resulting in binary columns for each category. This phase helps to convert categorical features into a format that machine learning models can understand.

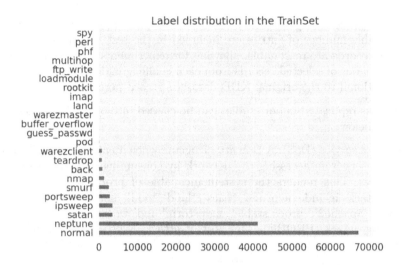

Fig. 4. Shape of Dataset for Train

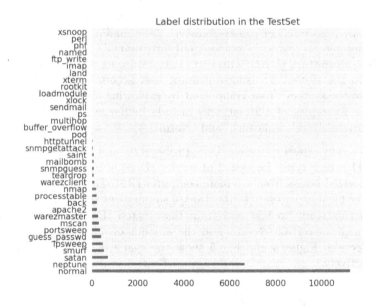

Fig. 5. Shape of Dataset for Test

Concatenation and Dropping Columns: To combine the one-hot encoded categorical columns with the original dataset, concatenation and dropping columns are used. The original category columns ('protocol_type', 'service', and 'flag') are then removed from the dataset after being replaced with their one-hot encoded equivalents.

Table 4. Dataset description, NSL-KDD

NSL-KDD Dataset	Records	Normal	DoS	Probe	U2R	U2R
NSL-KDD Train	125973	67343	45927	11656	52	995
	%	53.46	36.45	9.25	0.04	0.79
NSL-KDD Test	22543	9711	7458	2421	200	2754
	%	43.08	33.08	10.74	0.89	12.22

Label Encoding: The variable 'labels' is label-encoded, mapping assault kinds to numerical values. This is essential for training a machine learning model since it requires numerical labels.

Normalization involves applying Min-Max scaling to normalise the features. This guarantees that all characteristics are on a similar scale, preventing any one feature from dominating the learning process.

Train-Test Split: The dataset is separated into training and testing sets. The features (X_train_scaled, X_test_scaled) and labels (y_train, y_test) are properly separated. Furthermore, a subset of the training set is divided into training and validation sets (X_train_final, X_val, y_train_final, y_val) for model training and evaluation.

In summary, the preparation methods are intended to convert the raw NSL-KDD dataset into a format appropriate for deep learning models. This involves managing categorical variables, one-hot encoding, label encoding, normalisation, and proper dataset partitioning for training and testing.

4   Experimental Setup

4.1   Standard Evaluation Metrics

In multi-classification, to asses the detection effectiveness of the model on the unbalanced dataset in a more reasonable manner, each index is compututed using a weigted average technique based on the number of samples in each category. Each indicator's formula is presented in Eqs. (2) to (6)

$$TruePositiveRate = \frac{TP}{TP+FN} \tag{2}$$

$$FalsePositiveRate = \frac{FP}{TN+FP} \tag{3}$$

$$TrueNegativeRate = \frac{TN}{FP+TN} \tag{4}$$

$$FalseNegativeRate = \frac{FN}{TP+FN} \tag{5}$$

$$Accuracy = \frac{TP+TN}{TP+FP+TN+FN} \tag{6}$$

5   Results and Discussion

5.1   Cross-Validation

Cross-validation is a technique for determining the performance and generalizability of a deep learning model. In a 10-fold cross-validation, the dataset is divided into ten equal sections (folds), and the model is trained and assessed ten times, each time utilising a different fold as the test set and the remaining nine folds for training. The accuracy for each fold is printed, and the average accuracy across all folds is displayed at the end. Table 5 depicts a thorough description of each fold.

Table 5. 10-fold cross validation results

Parameter: Accuracy %

(1)	(2)	(3)	(4)	(5)	(6)	(7)	(8)	(9)	(10)
95.80	96.66	97.54	97.99	98.26	98.43	98.46	98.65	98.66	98.82

5.2   Proposed Model Compared with Existing Literature

To show the efficiency of our proposed model, i.e., enhancing BLSTM, we used other deep learning models in this work for the purpose of comparison. These models in [18,19] and [20] are trained in NSL-KDD, NVD& SARD, and UNSW-NB15 datasets with the same metrics of evaluation.

Table 6 shows the complete architecture of these models. Furthermore, wa have also made the comparison of our proposed model with existing benchmark algorithms. The proposed model, i.e., enhancing BLSTM, delivers better results in evaluation metric, i.e., accuracy.

Table 6. Proposed model compared with existing literature

Ref	Approach	Dataset	Algorithm	10-fold	Accuracy
Our model	Our model	NSL-KDD	Bi-LSTM	$\checkmark$	97.93%
[18]	technical review and comparative analysis of machine learning techniques for intrusion detection systems in MANET(Mobile Ad Hoc Network)	NSL-KDD	BLSTM	–	84.03%
[19]	Explainable Software Vulnerability Detection based on Attention-based Bidirectional Recurrent Neural Networks	NVD and SARD	ABLSTM	–	96.70%
[20]	LBDMIDS: LSTM-based Deep Learning Model for Intrusion Detection Systems for IoT Networks	UNSW-NB15	BLSTM	–	96.41%

6   Conclusion

In this paper, an enhancing BLSTM Recurrent Neural Network (named Bi-LSTM) is proposed for the intrusion detection of malware and cyberattacks, i.e., DDoS, Probe, R2L, and U2R. The results of our proposed model are compared with three other algorithms that are trained and evaluated on the different datasets, including NSL-KDD, NVD&SARD, and UNSW-NB15. Furthermore, the results are evident, that the proposed model beats the results of these three models. The performance advantages of the model are verified by comparing the evaluation metric of accuracy. The proposed model achieved 97.93% accuracy which is relatively better than the existing literature.

References

1. Manzoor, I., Kumar, N.: A feature reduced intrusion detection system using ANN classifier. Expert Syst. Appl. **88**, 249–257 (2017)
2. Thapa, S., Mailewa, A.: The role of intrusion detection/prevention systems in modern computer networks: a review. In: Proceedings of the Conference: Midwest Instruction and Computing Symposium (MICS), 3–4 April 2020, vol. 53, pp. 1–14 (2020)
3. Patgiri, R., Varshney, U., Akutota, T., Kunde, R.: An investigation on intrusion detection system using machine learning. In: Proceedings of the 2018 IEEE Symposium Series on Computational Intelligence (SSCI), Bangalore, India, 18–21 November 2018, pp. 1684–1691 (2018)
4. Matherly, J., Hewlett, W., Xu, Z., Meshi, Y., Weinberger, Y.: Machine learning in cyber-security-problems, challenges and data sets. arXiv preprint arXiv:1812.07858 (2018)
5. Ghumro, A., Memon, A.K., Memon, I., Simming, I.A.: A review of mitigation of attacks in IoT using deep learning models. Quaid-E-Awam Univ. Res. J. Eng. Sci. Technol. Nawabshah **18**(1), 36–42 (2020)
6. Liu, H., Lang, B.: Machine learning and deep learning methods for intrusion detection systems: a survey. Appl. Sci. **9**, 4396 (2019)
7. Alabadi, M., Celik, Y.: Anomaly detection for cyber-security based on convolution neural network: a survey. In: 2020 International Congress on Human-Computer Interaction, Optimization and Robotic Applications (HORA) 26 June 2020, pp. 1–14. IEEE (2020)
8. Samie, F., Bauer, L., Henkel, J.: From cloud down to things: an overview of machine learning in Internet of Things. IEEE Internet Things J. **6**(3), 4921–4934 (2019)
9. Schmidhuber, J.: Deep learning in neural networks: an overview. Neural Netw. **61**, 85–117 (2015)
10. Amit, I., Matherly, J., Hewlett, W., Xu, Z., Meshi, Y., Weinberger, Y.: Machine learning in cyber-security-problems, challenges and data sets. arXiv preprint arXiv:1812.07858 (2018)
11. Rumelhart, D.E., Hinton, G.E., Williams, R.J.: Learning representations by back-propagating errors. Nature **323**(6088), 533–536 (1986)
12. Hochreiter, S., Schmidhuber, J.: Long short term memory. Neural Comput. **9**(8), 17351780 (1997)

13. Fukushima, K.: Neocognitron: a self-organizing neural network model for a mechanism of pattern recognition unaffected by shift in position. Biol. Cybern. **36**(4), 193–202 (1980)
14. Zvornicanin, E.: Differences between bidirectional and unidirectional LSTM. Baeldung on Computer Science (1997)
15. Dhanabal, L., Shantharajah, S.P.: A study on NSL-KDD dataset for intrusion detection system based on classification algorithms. Int. J. Adv. Res. Comput. Commun. Eng. **4**, 446–452 (2015)
16. Malathi, A., Revathi, S.: A detailed analysis on NSL-KDD dataset using various machine learning techniques for intrusion detection. Int. J. Eng. Res. Technol. **2**(12), 1848–1853 (2013)
17. Aljawarneh, S., Aldwairi, M., Yassein, M.B.: Anomaly-based intrusion detection system through feature selection analysis and building hybrid efficient model. J. Comput. Sci. **1**(25), 152–60 (2018)
18. Laqtib, S., El Yassini, K., Hasnaoui, M.L.: A technical review and comparative analysis of machine learning techniques for intrusion detection systems in MANET. Int. J. Electr. Comput. Eng. **10**(3), 2701 (2020)
19. Mao, Y., Li, Y., Sun, J., Chen, Y.: Explainable software vulnerability detection based on attention-based bidirectional recurrent neural networks. In: IEEE International Conference on Big Data (Big Data), pp. 4651–4656. IEEE (2020)
20. Saurabh, K., et al.: LBDMIDS: LSTM based deep learning model for intrusion detection systems for IoT networks. In: IEEE World AI IoT Congress (AIIoT), pp. 753–759. IEEE (2022)
21. Oueslati, N.E., Mrabet, H., Jemai, A.: A survey on intrusion detection systems for IoT networks based on long short-term memory. In: Mosbah, M., et al. (eds.) Advances in Model and Data Engineering in the Digitalization Era. MEDI 2023. Communications in Computer and Information Science, vol. 2071. Springer, Cham (2024)

A Formal Approach for Verifying and Validating Security Objectives in Software Architecture

Loïc Thierry[1,2]($\boxtimes$), Brahim Hamid[1]🆔, and Jason Jaskolka[2]🆔

[1] IRIT, Université de Toulouse, CNRS, UT2 118 Route de Narbonne,
31062 Toulouse Cedex 9, France
{loic.thierry,brahim.hamid}@irit.fr
[2] Systems and Computer Engineering, Carleton University,
1125 Colonel By Drive, Ottawa, ON K1S 5B6, Canada
jason.jaskolka@carleton.ca

Abstract. The design and analysis of security in distributed computing systems raises numerous questions on the tools available for modeling and verification. Particularly, it is difficult to ensure the correctness when using different validation processes in software architecture design. Assuring cross-platform validation manually is labor intensive, expertise dependent, and error prone. This paper proposes an approach for the design and analysis of secure software architecture in the context of a component-port-connector architecture model and message passing communication. We use the Event-B formal method to create the software architecture model and security in successive steps using the refinement process. We also use proof obligations to verify the security of the successive software architecture models. Furthermore, we use the ProB model-checker and animator for the model validation.

Keywords: formal methods · model-driven engineering · component-based software architecture · security objectives · Event-B · ProB

1 Introduction

System and software security engineering has become a crucial business aspect because organizations are completely dependent on computer-based systems and invest substantial resources in maintaining them [15]. Security flaws are not just detected in code from the standpoint of the system developer. They must be recognized early and at the highest levels of development, primarily during the architecture design stage, where their semantics are comprehended. Recently, there has been a shift in terms of software architecture design [13] to promote a combination of multiple software engineering paradigms, namely, Component-based Software Engineering (CBSE) [6], Model-Driven Engineering [19], and formal methods [14]. In the spirit of using multi-paradigms, many description

B. Ben Hedia et al. (Eds.): VECoS 2024, LNCS 15466, pp. 143–158, 2025.
https://doi.org/10.1007/978-3-031-85356-2_10

languages and formalisms for modeling complex distributed systems have been proposed in the literature. A significant proportion of these works have aimed at capturing the communication, concurrency, and some non-functional properties of the components that comprise a given system. However, empirical evidence shows that existing analysis techniques can be labor intensive [18], lack formal connection between the non-functional requirements (e.g., security concerns, objectives, threats, etc.) and solutions (e.g., policies, mechanisms, etc.), and lack automation [21]. As a result, security modeling and analysis and their automation must be considered during the development of model-based systems. To address these issues, we propose an approach for the verification and validation of security objectives at design-time, mainly during the software architecture design. In the context of our work, the security requirements are specified in terms of a set of desirable security objectives (i.e., positive statements). As opposed to this, the current practice to formulate security statements is given through expressing attacker capabilities to e.g. gain access to a protected data from a message observation (i.e., negative statements).

In our previous work [20], we studied different facets of the problem of communication paradigms specification and verification in the context of component-based software architecture. This prior work includes a metamodel and formal models in Event-B for the specification and analysis of various communication protocols. In this paper, we extend these ideas and present an approach for formally specifying and verifying security objectives for distributed systems architecture. We use formal methods for the precise specification and analysis of security architecture objectives as *properties* of a modeled system. Starting from an informal description of a security objective (i.e., from standards and classifications such as CIAAA[1]) in the context of component-based software architecture development, a logical specification of these properties is proposed using first-order logic and modal logic, followed by a more concrete specification of the software architecture model and security using Event-B [1]. We leverage the Event-B refinement process to create the software architecture model and security in successive steps. Finally, security mechanisms are applied as *constraints* of a modeled system to constrain the system operation and guarantee the corresponding objectives. Each of the successive software architecture models are verified using proof obligations, the ProB model-checker and animator is used for model validation.

The rest of the paper is organized as follows. Section 2 describes a metamodel for component-based software architecture properties and constraints. Section 3 presents the formalization of the component-based software architecture in Event-B. Section 4 describes the main contribution of the paper which consists of the formalization of security objectives and constraints in the context of the metamodel. Section 5 presents the verification and validation objectives and mechanisms using a concrete architecture as a refinement of the Event-B models. Section 6 presents a short summary of the related work. Finally, Sect. 7 concludes and outlines directions for future work.

---

[1] *Confidentiality, Integrity, Availability, Authenticity,* and *Authorization.*

2 Software Architecture Property/constraint Metamodel

We use the same software architecture metamodel presented in [20], referred to in this work as the CBSE metamodel. The metamodel allows us to describe architectural models in a component-port-connector fashion which are conceptually close to the industrial practice. The metamodel concepts are structured to capture both the functional architecture and behavior of the system.

We extend the CBSE metamodel with a new package named *PropertyConstraint*, as shown in Fig. 1, to incorporate security in software architecture models. This extension is defined around two primary concepts: *Property* and *Constraint*. Properties are what the system is expected to do, while constraints are the actual mechanisms put into place to make the system behave in a certain way. By making this distinction, we can see that constraints contribute to the satisfaction of properties. In the context of this work, security objectives and mechanisms are respectively properties and constraints. These properties and constraints are bundled in respective libraries to support their reuse. We also introduce the notion of *PropertyCategory* and *ContraintCategory* to group some properties and constraints that may not be implemented inside the same library but share some similarities (e.g., they all represent confidentiality objectives).

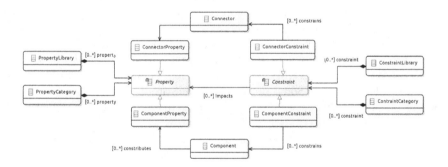

Fig. 1. Software architecture property/constraint metamodel

Example 1. Confidentiality is defined as a category (i.e., *PropertyCategory*) within the CIAAA library (i.e., *PropertyLibrary*), and *PayloadConfidentiality* (one of the properties studied in this paper) is defined as a property (i.e., *ConnectorProperty*) as part of this Confidentiality category. We also define *restrictivePayload* as a category (i.e., *ConstraintCategory*) within the access control library (i.e., *ConstraintLibrary*), and *restrictiveGetPld* (one of the constraints studied in this paper) is defined as a constraint (i.e., *ConnectorConstraint*).

3 Formalization in Event-B

In this section, we present the formalization of our software architecture and property and constraint metamodel using Event-B and its dedicated tool support

Rodin [2] and *ProB* [11]. We then provide the specification, verification, and validation of a representative set of security objectives and mechanisms.

3.1 Introduction to Event-B

Event-B is a formal modeling language heavily based on the set theory and first order logic. It is a simplification as well as an extension of the B formalism. Event-B uses an event/state-based approach [1]. The specification of the states is done by a group of sets that are manipulated by the events. When working with Event-B, we manipulate two parts: the contexts and the machines.

The *contexts* define the static part of the model. Event-B offers constructs such as Carrier sets that are general infinite sets. In addition, it provides constants. The properties of the sets and constants are defined as axioms. The *machines* define the behavioral aspect of the model. Event-B offers constructs such as (model) variables to represent the current state of the machine. These variables are then manipulated by the events through actions. These events have parameters (local variables) and guards that restrict when they can be triggered. Guards are predicates on the parameters. When an event is triggered, the corresponding actions are executed changing the state of the machine. In addition, the machines contain the variants and the invariants. These two constructs respectively define predicates that will always become true at one point and predicates that must be true at every state reached.

To support model analysis in Event-B, properties of the model are specified using invariants defined in the form of predicates using first order logic. The Event-B proof system works by automatically generating proof obligations whenever it is necessary. Some of the generated proof obligations may be discharged automatically. Others require interactive proof through explicit case analysis and/or hypothesis instantiation and rewriting.

Event-B is based on *correctness by construction* which uses an important concept known as *refinement*. Refinement enables model creation to be done in successive steps, starting from an abstract model and slowly adding more concrete elements, all while keeping the correctness of the properties previously proven.

3.2 Logical Specification

A distributed software system is modeled by a set of components. Components communicate and synchronize by sending and receiving messages. A computation program encodes the sequence of actions that components may perform. The actions of the program include modifying local variables, sending messages, and receiving messages to/from each component in the corresponding system architecture. In the context of engineering secure systems, we define the following domain to capture both legitimate and illegitimate message providers (e.g., *inject*) and message consumers (e.g., *intercept*) of the system messages.

Sets

– $\mathcal{C}$ is the set of components

- $\mathcal{D}$ is the set of message payloads
- $\mathcal{M}$ is the set of messages with the following predicates:
  - has_spld(m, d) indicates that $m \in \mathcal{M}$ contains a payload $d \in \mathcal{D}$
- $\mathcal{A}$ is the set of actions associated with a component $c \in \mathcal{C}$
  - inject(m) denotes that component $c \in \mathcal{C}$ adds message $m \in \mathcal{M}$ into the system
  - intercept(m) denotes that component $c \in \mathcal{C}$ gets message $m \in \mathcal{M}$ from the system
  - get_pld(m, d) denotes that component $c \in \mathcal{C}$ gets the payload $d \in \mathcal{D}$ from message $m \in \mathcal{M}$, where d is not necessarily the true payload (i.e., the payload that was initially injected)
  - set_pld(m, d) denotes that $c \in \mathcal{C}$ sets the payload $d \in \mathcal{D}$ in message $m \in \mathcal{M}$, where c is not necessarily the sender

Modalities

- $\mathbb{H}_c(a)$ is a predicate indicating that action $a \in \mathcal{A}$ **H**appens for component $c \in \mathcal{C}$
- $\mathbb{E}_c(a)$ is a predicate indicating that action $a \in \mathcal{A}$ is **E**nabled for component $c \in \mathcal{C}$
- $pred1 < pred2$ is a predicate indicating that all possible sequences of actions that contain a valid predicate $pred2$ also contain a valid predicate $pred1$ that **Precedes** $pred2$

Axioms

- $\forall\, m \in \mathcal{M}, \forall\, c_1 \in \mathcal{C}, \exists\, d \in \mathcal{D} \cdot \mathbb{H}_{c_1}(set\_pld(m, d)) < \mathbb{H}_{c_1}(inject(m))$ is an axiom that states if a component c_1 injected a message m, then c_1 should have set the payload of m before.
- $\forall\, m \in \mathcal{M}, \forall\, c \in \mathcal{C}, \forall\, d \in \mathcal{D} \cdot$
  $(\mathbb{H}_c(intercept(c, m)) \;\wedge\; has\_pld(m, d)) < \mathbb{E}_c(get\_pld(m, d))$ is an axiom that states if a component c is able to get the payload d of message m, then previously the component c intercepted the message m containing the payload d.

3.3   Interpretation in Event-B

We use the separation of the static (context/logical) and the dynamic (machine/scenario) views from both Event-B and the metamodel. Therefore, elements in the contexts represent the structural aspect of the metamodel and the elements in the machines represent the behavioral aspect. *A complete presentation of our Event-B modeling and analysis artefacts are available online via* https://gitlab.com/semcoproject/toc.

The mapping of the structural elements of the metamodel to Event-B with respect to the semantics given in the definition of the metamodel is straightforward (see Listing 3.1). Carrier sets are used to capture model elements' type (i.e., COMPONENT to represent the *COMPONENT* architectural concept). The architecture model of a system is then described through constant subsets of the corresponding carrier set. A component is connected to a connector through a number of ports. This is represented in the model as relations between the components, the ports, and connectors (Uses, Connects). These statements are specified using axioms, as depicted in Listing 3.1. This mapping is done manually following some simple transformation rules from the meta-model to the Event-B code ($class \Rightarrow set, attributes \Rightarrow relations$).

```
1   sets COMPONENT // Set of components
2        PORT // Set of ports
3        CONNECTOR // Set of connectors
4        PORTKIND // Set of the types of ports
5   constants Component // Finite set of system components
6             Port // Finite set of system ports
7             Connector // Finite set of system connectors
8             Uses // Connection of the port to the components
9             Connects // Connection of the connectors to the ports
10  axioms
11    @axmComp1 Component ⊆ COMPONENT
12    @axmPort1 Port ⊆ PORT
13    @axmConn1 Connector ⊆ CONNECTOR
14    @axmCompPort1 Uses ∈ Port → Component
15    ...
16  end
```

Listing 3.1. Context of the structural model

To model the behavior of the system, we introduce in our model two events to describe the Inject/Intercept primitives introduced in Sect. 3.2. Furthermore, to specify message passing communication (MPS) we add two new events: (1) *CreateMessage* to create a new communication artifact with attributes defining the MPS paradigm (e.g., *Payload, DataType*) and (2) *GetPayload* for a component to get the payload of a message it has received. An excerpt of the behavior of the *CBSE MPS Event-B model* is shown in Listing 3.2.

```
1   invariants
2     ...
3     @messagesHavePayload ∀ m · m ∈ message ⇒ m ∈ dom(artifactsPayloads)
4   events
5     event Inject extends Inject // Extends the same event from the previous machine
6       where
7         @messageParadigm ConnectorParadigm(conn) = MPS ⇔ a ∈ message
8         @portsRealizeData ConnectorParadigm(conn) = MPS ⇔ (Realizes(p) ∈ Data ∧ Realizes(c) ∈
            Data)
9         ...
10    end
11
12    event GetPayload
13      any m // message
14          messagePayload // payload
15          c // component
16      where
17        @mIsMessage m ∈ message
18        @mHasBeenReceived m ∈ artifactIntercepted
19        @mHasMessagePayloadAsPayload messagePayload = messagePayloads(m)
20        @clsReceiver  c = Uses(receiver(m))
21        @payloadNotAlreadyRead messagePayload ∉ ran(readPayload)
22      then
23        @act1 readPayload := readPayload ∪ {c ↦ messagePayload}
24    end
25  end
```

Listing 3.2. Machine of the CBSE using MPS

4 Formal Specification and Analysis of Security Objectives and Mechanisms

Our goal is to formally establish links between security objectives and their corresponding mechanisms, in the context of a component-port-connector architecture model and message passing communication, as visualized in Fig. 1. Our approach is composed of three steps. First, we define security objectives using first-order logic and modal logic, as an abstract and technology-independent formalism. Second, using Event-B as a formal language, we define security objectives and their related mechanisms as a refinement of the *CBSE MPS Event-B model* introduced earlier in Listing 3.2. Third, we verify and validate formally the security objectives, encoded as a properties in the model, and the mechanisms, encoded as a constraints in the model. For instance, a component behavior (resp. structure) *contributes* to the satisfaction of a model property, where a component constraint *constrains* a component behavior (resp. structure). This is also true for a connector. In the following, we use three examples of representative security objectives from the CIAAA classification to illustrate the approach.

4.1 A Representative Confidentiality Security Objective

According to the ISO/IEC 27000:2018 standard [9], *confidentiality* ensures that information is not made available or disclosed to unauthorized individuals, entities, or processes. In the context of message passing communications within software architectures, payload confidentiality allows a transmitted message to be received by other components, but only specific components can get the actual content of the payload. In other words, a payload is deemed confidential if a component c_3 receives a message m with a payload d sent by c_1 with c_2 as its intended destination, then c_3 will not be able to get the content of the payload d. Formally, this is expressed as:

$$\mathbb{E}_{c_3}(\text{get\_pld}(m,d)) \Rightarrow \neg(\mathbb{H}_{c_1}(\text{inject}(m)) \ \wedge \ \text{has\_rcv}(m,c_2) \ < \ \mathbb{E}_{c_3}(\text{get\_pld}(m,d)))$$

Here, $\mathbb{E}_{c_3}(\text{get\_pld}(m,d))$ is a predicate indicating that component $c_3 \in \mathcal{C}$ is able to get the payload $d \in \mathcal{D}$ from the message $m \in \mathcal{M}$ and $\neg(\mathbb{H}_{c_1}(\text{inject}(m)) \ \wedge \ \text{has\_rcv}(m,c_2) \ < \ \mathbb{E}_{c_3}(\text{get\_pld}(m,d)))$ is a predicate indicating that it is never the case at some past before that the component $c_1 \in \mathcal{C}$ sent message $m \in \mathcal{M}$ with a component $c_2 \in \mathcal{C}$ as the declared receiver. Therefore, the validity of the property *PayloadConfidentiality*(c_1, c_2) would show that the *PayloadConfidentiality* objective is fulfilled between c_1 and c_2 in the system.

Formal Specification and Analysis in Event-B. We build a new Event-B model named *CBSE MPS CIAAA Event-B model* as a refinement of the *CBSE MPS Event-B model*. Assuming a mechanism (i.e., constraint) as an abstract security solution called *restrictiveGetPayload* is deployed, then we show that the security objective (i.e., property) *PayloadConfidentiality* holds. The payload confidentiality property is represented in Event-B as an *Invariant* (see Listing 4.1) that states that if a payload has been read and the message containing this payload has been sent into a connector enforcing *restrictiveGetPld* then the component that reads the payload is the intended destination.

```
1   invariants
2     @payloadConfidentialityInv  ∀ p, conn, m ·
3         conn ∈ Connector
4         ∧ conn ↦ ConnectorPayloadConfidentiality ∈ ConnectorProperty
5         ∧ p ∈ ran(readPayload)
6         ∧ m ↦ p ∈ messagePayloads
7         ∧ connectorsUsed(m) = conn
8         ⇒ Uses( receiver (m)) = allowedGetPayload(m)
```

Listing 4.1. PayloadConfidentiality property invariant

For the invariant encoding the security objective to hold, we add a constraint in the model (security mechanism), as shown in Listing 4.2. This constraint is modeled in Event-B as a guard (line 3) in the *GetPayload* event: when the considered message exchange is realized through a secure connector, the event can only be triggered if the message has been received by the intended destination.

```
1   event  GetPayload extends GetPayload
2     where
3         @restrictiveGetPldGrd  connectorsUsed(m) ↦ ConnectorPayloadConfidentiality ∈
          ConnectorProperty ⇒ allowedGetPayload(m) = Uses(receiver(m))
4   end
```

Listing 4.2. restrictiveGetPld constraint guard

4.2   A Representative Integrity Security Objective

According to the ISO/IEC 27000:2018 standard [9], *integrity* ensures that transmitted information is accurate and complete. In the context of message passing communications within software architectures, message integrity ensures that the content of the message received is the same as when it was sent. If a message m, sent by the component c, has a payload p then c originally sent m with the same payload p. In other words, for any message m, if a component c_2 is able to get the payload p of a message m, then p is the initial payload of m. For components $s, r \in \mathcal{C}$, we denote this representative property as $PayloadIntegrity(s, r, m)$ which is specified for all messages $m \in \mathcal{M}$ as:

$$\mathbb{H}_s(set\_pld(m, p)) < \mathbb{H}_r(get\_pld(m, p))$$

Here, $\mathbb{H}_r(get\_pld(m, p))$ is a predicate indicating that component $r \in \mathcal{C}$ has gotten the payload $p \in \mathcal{D}$ of $m \in \mathcal{M}$ and $\mathbb{H}_s(set_pld(m, p))$ is a predicate indicating that $s \in \mathcal{C}$ has set the payload of m to p. Therefore, the validity of the property $PayloadIntegrity(s, r, m))$ would show that the *PayloadIntegrity* objective is fulfilled between s and r in the system.

Formal Specification and Analysis in Event-B. Assuming a mechanism (i.e., constraint) as an abstract security mechanism called *restrictiveSetPld* is deployed, we show that the security objective (i.e., property) *PayloadIntegrity* holds. We build a new Event-B model named *CBSE MPS CIAAA Event-B model* as a refinement of the *CBSE MPS Event-B model*. The payload integrity property is represented in Event-B as an *Invariant* (see Listing 4.3) that states if a message has been injected into a connector enforcing *restrictiveSetPld* then the payload has not been changed.

```
1   invariants
2       @messageIntegrityInv  ∀ conn, m ·
3           conn ∈ Connector
4           ∧ conn ↦ ConnectorMessageInTransitIntegrity  ∈ ConnectorProperty
5           ∧ m ∈ artifact
6           ∧ m ∈ message
7           ∧ connectorsUsed(m) = conn
8           ⇒   initialPayload (m) = messagePayloads(m)
```

Listing 4.3. PayloadIntegrity property invariant

For the invariant encoding the security objective to hold, we incorporate a constraint in the model (security mechanism), as depicted in Listing 4.4. This constraint is modeled in Event-B as a guard (line 3) in the event *ChangePayload*: when the considered message is sent through a secure connector (the connector has the property *ConnectorMessageInTransitIntegrity*), the event cannot be triggered (the guard *restrictiveSetPldGrd* cannot be true).

```
1   event ChangePayload extends ChangePayload
2       where
3           @restrictiveSetPldGrd  connectorsUsed(m) ↦ ConnectorMessageInTransitIntegrity ∉
            ConnectorProperty
4       end
```

Listing 4.4. restrictiveSetPld constraint guard

4.3   A Representative Authenticity Security Objective

According to the ISO/IEC 27000:2018 standard [9], *authenticity* ensures that an entity is what it claims to be. In the context of message passing communications within software architectures, message authenticity guarantees that the source written in the message is the actual sender. If a message m has a component c_1 as its source then it was sent by c_1. In other words, for any message m, if a component c_2 is able to get source c_1 of a message m, then c_1 is the accurate sender of m. For components $s, r \in \mathcal{C}$, we denote this representative property as $MessageAuthenticity(s, r, m)$ which is specified for all messages $m \in \mathcal{M}$ as:

$$\mathbb{H}_{c_1}(inject(m)) \; < \; \mathbb{E}_{c_2}(get\_src(m, c_1))$$

Here, $\mathbb{E}_{c_2}(get\_src(m, c_1))$ is a predicate indicating that component $c_2 \in \mathcal{C}$ is able to get that the source of m is $c1$ and $\mathbb{H}_{c_1}(inject(m))$ is a predicate indicating that $c1$ has injected the message. Therefore, the validity of the property $MessageAuthenticity(s, r, m)$ would show that the *MessageAuthenticity* objective is fulfilled between c_1 and c_2 in the system.

Formal Specification and Analysis in Event-B. Assuming a mechanism (i.e., constraint) as an abstract security solution called *restrictiveSetSource* is deployed, then we show that the security objective (i.e., property) *MessageAuthenticity* holds. The message authenticity property is represented in Event-B as an *Invariant* (see Listing 4.5) that states that if a message has been injected into a connector enforcing *restrictiveSetSource* then the message has been sent by the source.

```
1   invariants
2     @messageAuthInv ∀ conn, m ·
3         conn ∈ Connector
4         ∧ conn ↦ ConnectorMessageAuthenticity ∈ ConnectorProperty
5         ∧ m ∈ artifact
6         ∧ connectorsUsed(m) = conn
7         ⇒ source(m) = sender(m)
```

Listing 4.5. MessageAuthenticity property invariant

Table 1. Analysis results of the number of events, guards and POs

Machine	Events	Guards	Automatic PO	Interactive PO
Communication	3	11	27	0
MPS	5	12	42	0
Authenticity	5	1	14	0
Payload confidentiality	5	1	24	0
Payload Integrity	5	1	5	0

For the invariant encoding the security objective to hold, we add a constraint in the model (security mechanism), as shown in Listing 4.6). This constraint is modeled in Event-B as a guard (line 3) in the event *Inject*: when the considered message is sent through a secure connector (the connector has the property *ConnectorMessageAuthenticity*), the event is only triggered if the sender identifies itself as the source (the guard *restrictiveSetSourceGrd* must be true).

```
1   event Inject extends Inject
2     where
3         @restrictiveSetSourceGrd conn ↦ ConnectorMessageAuthenticity ∈ ConnectorProperty ⇒ s =
          aSender
4     end
```

Listing 4.6. restrictiveSetSource constraint guard

4.4   Proof Obligations

Table 1 presents the count of *Events* and *Guards* used to specify both the properties and behavior of the system. It also shows the number of generated *proof obligations (PO)* to prove the correctness of the model (behavior and properties) at each refinement level. All the generated proof obligations have been discharged automatically using the integrated *SMT solvers of Rodin*.

5   Model Verification and Validation

In this section, we present an experiment using the college library website example presented in [20] where a User that has gained access to the connector connecting the Administrator and the Database attempts to impersonate the Administrator (see Fig. 2). In our modeling, the User attempting to impersonate the Administrator is represented through an Inject event where the source of the message is set to Administrator and the actual sender is set to User. We use the security property *ConnectorMessageAuthenticity* to protect against this behavior. We consider two scenarios: (1) the connector enforces the message authenticity property, and (2) the connector does not enforce the message authenticity property.

5.1 Event-B Verification

For the Event-B formal modeling, the Library structural model is defined as extension of the *CBSE MPS CIAAA Event-B context* and the Library behavioral model is defined as a refinement of the *CBSE MPS CIAAA Event-B model*.

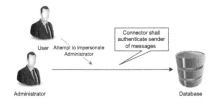

Fig. 2. User trying to impersonate the Administrator on a connector enforcing message authenticity

The *ConnectorMessageAuthenticity* property in this model is verified when the behavior of the corresponding connector is constrained by *restrictiveSet-Source* (Scenario 1), by construction thanks to the Event-B refinement mechanism. The resulting Library system behavior satisfies the security properties established in the *CBSE MPS CIAAA Event-B model*.

For the Event-B verification, we start by defining the component types and the interfaces and connectors using the software architecture metamodel concepts and their interpretations in Event-B. Listing 5.1 shows an excerpt of the Event-B context model specification of the architecture of Library application example described in Fig. 2, with respect to the functional requirements.

```
1  context SystemLibrarySecure extends Context9MPSCIAAA
2
3  constants Database Webserver Browser Administrator PortDatabaseIN PortDatabaseOUT
       PortWebserver PortBrowser PortAdministrator ConnectorBrowserWebserver
       ConnectorWebserverDatabase ConnectorAdministratorDataBase DataDatabaseIN
       DataDatabaseOUT DataWebserver DataBrowser DataAdministrator
4  axioms
5  @axmFillSystemComponents partition(Component, {Database}, {Webserver}, {Browser}, {
       Administrator})
6  ...
7  @axmFillSystemConnects partition(Connects,
8     {PortAdministrator ↦ ConnectorAdministratorDataBase},
9     {PortDatabaseIN ↦ ConnectorAdministratorDataBase}, ...)
```

Listing 5.1. Library structural model

From the security perspective, in Scenario 1 (see Listing 5.2) the *ConnectorAdministratorDatabase* linking the Administrator to the Database satisfies the *ConnectorMessageAuthenticity* property (line 2–3) while Scenario 2 does not (line 6).

```
1  // Scenario 1
2  @axmFillConnectorProperty partition (ConnectorProperty,
3      {ConnectorAdministratorDataBase ↦ ConnectorMessageAuthenticity})
4
5  // Scenario 2
6      @axmFillConnectorProperty ConnectorProperty = ∅
```

Listing 5.2. ConnectorProperty relation filled with and without the constraint applied

In addition, in the *CBSE MPS CIAAA Event-B model* we add a theorem representing the expected property of the connector between the database and the administrator (See Listing 5.3). The verification of this theorem shows that it is automatically discharged in Scenario 1 and that it cannot be discharged in Scenario 2, which verifies the intended property.

```
1  theorem @messageAuthTheorem ∀ m ·
2      m ∈ artifact
3      ∧ connectorsUsed(m) = ConnectorAdministratorDataBase
4      ⇒ source(m) = sender(m)
```

Listing 5.3. Library theorem

5.2 Validation by Animation

Moreover, to validate the resulting system model and for illustration purposes, we used ProB for simulation. In our experiment, ProB allows consistency checking of Event-B machines displaying all the states that were explored until the invariant violation was found. The goal is to demonstrate that the application of the constraint in the machine constrains the operation of the system to satisfy the corresponding security objective, while the absence of the constraint can lead to the violation of the corresponding security objective.

In these two scenarios, after creating a message to be sent, ProB allows to list all the possible parameters that an event can take to be triggered as depicted in Fig. 3 and Fig. 4. In these figures, the columns *conn*, *d*, *s* and *aSender* represent the used connector, the destination of the message, the source of the message and the actual sender.

The trace of the two scenarios is executed as follows: first we initialize the model with the INITIALISATION event, as depicted in Listing 5.4. It sets the default value of all the variables declared in the machines and sets the basis for recursive proof of the model. Listing 5.4 show the initialization of the variable used in the Authenticity invariant depicted in Listing 4.5.

```
1   event INITIALISATION
2   then
3        @sourceInit  source  := ∅
4        @senderInit  sender  := ∅
5        @connectorsUsedInit connectorsUsed  := ∅
6        @artifactInit    artifact  := ∅
7        . . .
8   end
```

Listing 5.4. INITIALISATION event

After the initialization, a message is created using the CreateMessage event. This message has a datatype that is usable in the connector between the administrator and the database. It also contains a payload representing the content of the message.

Finally, the Inject event can be triggered with different parameters depending on the scenario. In Scenario 1 (Fig. 3), the only possible parameters for the Inject event are the ones where the source of the message is the actual sender. Leading to the satisfaction of the property. In Scenario 2 (Fig. 4), where the constraint is not applied, two additional set of parameters are possible compared to Scenario 1. The set of parameters in blue shows a possibility where the User can impersonate the Administrator, the source is referencing the Administrator while the actual sender is the User violating the property.

Fig. 3. Possible events for Scenario 1

Fig. 4. Possible events for Scenario 2 (Color figure online)

6   Related Work

More than 30 years ago Burrows et al. [5] pioneered the use of formal methods applied to security. It created some basis for the use of formal methods applied to security protocols by answering a set of simple questions such as "Does this protocol work?". The authors introduced the BAN (Burrows-Abadi-Needham) logic as a set of rules to define and analyze communication protocols. They applied it to authentication protocols as a way to answer those questions. In more recent work, Rodano et al. [14] presented an axiomatic approach to security properties using first-order logic. They validated modeled architectures in different tools using a formal representation. These papers show that the use of formal methods to specify and describe the security aspect of communication has applications. Contrary to our proposed approach, these works focus mainly on the data transfer aspect of communication while we introduce a representation of the underlying behavior of connectors as part of our modeling.

Oheimb and Modersheim [12] introduced a formal specification tool named ASLan++ that specializes in the specification and analysis of distributed systems. ASLan++ uses an entity and agent specification close to what any object-oriented language may provide with classes, and it uses model checking to verify security goals and security properties described with first-order logic to verify the validity of the modeled system. Other works focused on the use of Event-B for the formal verification of system models. For instance, Babin et al. [3] used Event-B to verify the runtime compensation of web services and Graiet et al. [7] used Event-B to verify elastic component-based applications.

Other works studied the specification and verification of security threats, objectives, and policies using Alloy [17] and Coq [16]. Among these works, we also find studies on the use of Event-B for security modeling and analysis. For example, Laibinis et al. [10] used Event-B to simulate attacks on communication protocol using initial knowledge and protocol primitives. The protocol is animated by events allowing the execution of every primitive with its respective conditions stated in the Context as axioms. Additionally, Benaissa and Méry [4] created guidelines to formally describe communication protocol to support cryptography key establishment using Event-B. They used refinement to introduce the attacker's action and to identify potential vulnerabilities, events to represent the transitions of the protocols and the actions that an attacker could perform on the system and invariants to specify and verify the protocol's properties.

These papers set the basis for the theoretical aspect of our work, and we presented a metamodel for the description of security in the context of a component-based software architecture and message-passing communication, augmented with a formal interpretation in Event-B. Concretely, in our work, we provide formal support for specifying and analyzing mechanisms (i.e., security solutions), objectives (i.e., security problems) and the process of validating them, thus supporting the principles of security-by-design. The resulting Event-B model describes the functional and security aspects (structural and behavioral) of a software architecture. These aspects can be specified and verified at different levels of abstraction.

7   Conclusion and Future Work

In this paper, we proposed a formal approach to specify and verify security objectives in the context of a component-based software architecture and message-passing communication, using Event-B. The proposed approach follows two levels of abstraction: (1) logical specification of security objectives using first-order and modal logic as an abstract and technology-independent formalism; (2) formalization and verification using Event-B as a semi-automated proof assistant. For each representative CIAAA security objective, an appropriate security mechanism, acting as a constraint of the model, to make the security property hold is defined and verified. We keep the domain specifying security requirement categories at an abstract level to remain independent of any particular technology or implementation of the model. The proposed approach can help system designers rework their designs to enforce the identified security objective and/or to aid in selecting appropriate security controls.

In future work, we plan to improve the approach by including the specification of security patterns such as those used in [8] to describe security mechanisms. We would also like to study the integration of our tools with other MDE tools.

References

1. Abrial, J.R.: Modeling in Event-B: System and Software Engineering. Cambridge University Press, Cambridge (2010)
2. Abrial, J.R., Butler, M., Hallerstede, S., Hoang, T.S., Mehta, F., Voisin, L.: Rodin: an open toolset for modelling and reasoning in Event-B. Int. J. Softw. Tools Technol. Transfer **12**(6), 447–466 (2010)
3. Babin, G., Ameur, Y., Pantel, M.: Formal verification of runtime compensation of web service compositions: a refinement and proof based proposal with Event-B. In: 2015 IEEE International Conference on Services Computing, pp. 98–105 (2015)
4. Benaissa, N., Méry, D.: Cryptographic protocols analysis in Event B. In: Perspectives of Systems Informatics, pp. 282–293. Springer, Heidelberg (2010)
5. Burrows, M., Abadi, M., Needham, R.: A logic of authentication. ACM Trans. Comput. Syst. **8**(1), 18–36 (1990)
6. Crnkovic, I.: Component-based software engineering for embedded systems. In: 27th International Conference on Software Engineering, pp. 712–713. ACM (2005)
7. Graiet, M., Hamel, L., Mammar, A., Tata, S.: A verification and deployment approach for elastic component-based applications. Formal Aspects Comput. **29**(6), 987–1011 (2017)
8. Hamid, B., Weber, D.: Engineering secure systems: models, patterns and empirical validation. Comput. Secur. **77**, 315–348 (2018)
9. International Organization for Standardization: ISO/IEC 27000:2018 Information technology – Security techniques – Information security management systems – Overview and vocabulary (2018)
10. Laibinis, L., Troubitsyna, E., Pereverzeva, I., Oliver, I., Holtmanns, S.: A formal approach to identifying security vulnerabilities in telecommunication networks. In: Formal Methods and Software Engineering, pp. 141–158 (2016)
11. Leuschel, M., Butler, M.: ProB: a model checker for B. In: Araki, K., Gnesi, S., Mandrioli, D. (eds.) FME 2003: Formal Methods, pp. 855–874. Springer, Heidelberg (2003)
12. von Oheimb, D., Mödersheim, S.: ASLan++ – a formal security specification language for distributed systems. In: Aichernig, B.K., de Boer, F.S., Bonsangue, M.M. (eds.) Formal Methods for Components and Objects, pp. 1–22. Springer, Heidelberg (2012)

13. Taylor, R.N., Medvidovic, N.: Software Architecture: Foundation, Theory, and Practice. Wiley, Hoboken (2010)
14. Rodano, M., Giammarc, K.: A formal method for evaluation of a modeled system architecture. Procedia Comput. Sci. **20**, 210–215 (2013)
15. Ross, R., Winstead, M., McEvilley, M.: Engineering trustworthy secure systems. Special Publication (NIST SP) 800-160 Volume 1, Revision 1, National Institute of Standards and Technology (2022)
16. Rouland, Q., Hamid, B., Bodeveix, J.P., Jaskolka, J.: Formalizing the relationship between security policies and objectives in software architectures. In: IEEE 20th International Conference on Software Architecture Companion (ICSA-C), pp. 151–158 (2023)
17. Rouland, Q., Hamid, B., Jaskolka, J.: Specification, detection, and treatment of stride threats for software components: modeling, formal methods, and tool support. J. Syst. Architect. **117**, 102073 (2021)
18. Scandariato, R., Wuyts, K., Joosen, W.: A descriptive study of Microsoft's threat modeling technique. Requirements Eng. **20**(2), 163–180 (2015)
19. Selic, B.: The pragmatics of model-driven development. IEEE Softw. **20**(5), 19–25 (2003)
20. Thierry, L., Jaskolka, J., Hamid, B., Bodeveix, J.P.: Specification and verification of communication paradigms for CBSE in Event B. In: 27th International Conference on Engineering of Complex Computer Systems (ICECCS), pp. 157–166 (2023)
21. Tuma, K., Calikli, G., Scandariato, R.: Threat analysis of software systems: a systematic literature review. J. Syst. Softw. **144**, 275–294 (2018)

Supervisory Control of Cyber-Physical Systems Using Labeled Petri Nets Under Sensor and Actuator Attacks

Jintao Jia[1], Gaiyun Liu[2(✉)], and Zhiwu Li[3]

[1] School of Electro-Mechanical Engineering, Xidian University,
Xi'an 710071, China
[2] Groupe de Recherche en Electrotechnique et Automatique du Havre,
Université Le Havre Normandie, 76600 Le Havre, France
gaiyun.liu@univ-lehavre.fr
[3] Institute of Systems Engineering, Macau University of Science and Technology,
Taipa, Macao SAR 999078, China

Abstract. In this paper, we investigate the control problem of a cyber-physical system modeled with labeled Petri nets under malicious cyber attacks in the discrete event system framework. Attacks aim to modify sensor readings and control commands in sensor and actuator communication channels. We use transitions in labeled Petri nets as the formalism to model these attacks. Because the real states of the plant may be different from the states estimated by the supervisor, we construct the attack monitor and supervisor monitor to describe the above two types of states. Based on the concurrent composition of the two monitors, we develop a general attack structure that can describe all possible attacks. By splitting the attack structure into two parts, we give conditions for the existence of a robust supervisor. Finally, a new method for designing a robust supervisor to guarantee the security of the plant is proposed.

Keywords: Sensor attack · Actuator attack · Labeled Petri net · Supervisory control

1 Introduction

Cyber-physical systems (CPSs) represent a new generation of integrated systems blending computational and physical capabilities. They engage with system operators through diverse modalities rooted in computation, communication, and control [2,9]. Comprising plants, sensors, actuators, supervisors, and communication networks, these systems have wide-ranging applications in sensor-based communication environments such as advanced manufacturing plants, network control systems, intelligent traffic systems, maritime and port systems and so on. However, the communication networks linking the cyber and physical components of these systems are vulnerable to malicious cyber attacks [5,13,14].

© The Author(s), under exclusive license to Springer Nature Switzerland AG 2025
B. Ben Hedia et al. (Eds.): VECoS 2024, LNCS 15466, pp. 159–173, 2025.
https://doi.org/10.1007/978-3-031-85356-2_11

Attacks have the potential to compromise sensor readings, called sensor attacks, leading to inaccurate observations by supervisors. This can result in supervisors making incorrect decisions, which in turn causes erratic or unsafe behavior in the system. Furthermore, attacks might directly manipulate the actions of actuators, called actuator attacks, further impacting the system's performance and safety. It is extremely important to study the security and control issues of CPS under attacks. In reality, since discrete event systems (DESs) are driven by events, the plant of a CPS can also be modeled as a DES. At the supervisory layer, the key control objective is usually to ensure that the controlled system remains within a predefined set of safe states [1,12,21].

Within the DES framework, researchers extensively investigate attacks. In terms of detection of attacks, the work [15] shows that attacks could significantly compromise the security of controlled systems and proposes a methodology to assess the potential damage caused by attacks. In [5], Carvalho et al. divide attacks into four categories: enabling actuator, disabling actuator, sensor erasure, and sensor insertion. This study [5] proposes an embedded module within the supervisor to detect these cyber attacks. The supervisor responds by disabling all controllable events when an attack is detected, thereby minimizing potential harm and maintaining the security of a system. Gao et al. show that the problem of attack detection can be transformed into a classical state estimation/diagnosis problem for these new structures [7]. In [6], Ding et al. propose a cyber-attack detection model within the framework of DES, modeled using a deterministic finite probabilistic automaton. The model employs deep learning techniques to extract and train features from event sequences.

If cyber attacks cannot be detected in time, the security of controlled systems may be compromised. In terms of supervisory control under attacks, supervisory control of a DES within the RW-framework under attack scenarios has been proposed in [17]. In this work, a supervisor is modeled as a finite state automaton that is robust to replacement-removal attacks, where the sensor signals produced by certain events can be replaced by the signals produced by other events, or can be canceled. From the viewpoint of an attacker, Su firstly constructs a supremal intelligent attack strategy and then seeks for a robust supervisor [14]. The work [8] proposes a model of deception attack from the monitoring layer of a CPS and studies how to synthesize a covert deception attack to make the system enter unexpected states. A new structure [9] is proposed to model the closed-loop system after attacks based on [8] which contains all the possible operations that an attacker can perform on the system. Wang et al. elaborate upon the supervisory control problems using the paradigm of Petri nets [18]. It considers a system under a few types of malicious attacks from an external intruder. Based on the observation reachability graph, a novel structure is proposed to decide the existence of such a supervisor by checking whether each state in the graph satisfies a particular condition. A type of sensor-reading modification attacks [20] is considered. This work proposes a tool named a supervisor graph based on reachability graph analysis and designs a resilient supervisor to enforce the liveness of Petri nets.

Recapitulating the above discussion, modeling a system with ordinary automata increases the complexity of constructing, concomitantly diminishing computational efficiency. It is imperative to acknowledge that diverse attack types, including sensor and actuator attacks, can occur concurrently. The existence of robust supervisors requires more conditions, and few studies have comprehensively considered the efficacy of such a system under two kinds of attacks.

In this paper, we first consider the closed-loop system under sensor attacks and actuator attacks as shown in Fig. 1. The attackers aim to mislead the supervisor and affect systems by corrupting sensor channels and actuator channels. We assume that all vulnerable transitions are known and attackers have full knowledge of the plants. Since labels in labeled Petri nets (LPNs) [11] can represent observability in real events, we construct an observer of an LPN for the system to reduce the number of states to improve the efficiency of analysis and computation. A new attack structure based on the observer is proposed to analyze the security of the system under both sensor attacks and actuator attacks. We divide the attack structure into two categories: legal-zone and illegal-zone according to the definition given in this paper. If there exists the legal-zone, a robust supervisor can be designed using the method we proposed.

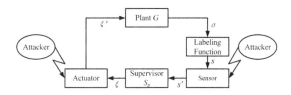

Fig. 1. Closed-loop system.

Contributions of this paper are as follows: (1) In order to deal with nondeterministic states (markings) because of unobservable transitions, an observer for LPN is computed. (2) Based on the two types of monitors we proposed, we construct a more general attack structure to describe sensor attacks and actuator attacks. (3) We propose a method to design a robust supervisor against attacks and provide the condition for the existence of a robust supervisor.

The remainder of this paper is organized as follows. The next section provides a brief introduction to Petri nets, LPNs, and attacks. In Sect. 3, a closed-loop system is considered. Firstly, based on the observer, the attacks are formally represented from the attacker's and supervisor's viewpoint, constructing the attack monitor and supervisor monitor. Then, a new attack structure is proposed to show how attackers harm the plant. Section 4 provides a new method for designing a robust supervisor to defend against sensor attacks and actuator attacks and provide a condition for the existence of a robust supervisor. Section 5 concludes this work and discusses the future work.

2 Preliminaries

2.1 Petri Net

A Petri net is a four-tuple $N = (P, T, F, W)$, where P and T are sets of places and transitions which are nonempty, bounded and disjoint, respectively, i.e. $P \neq \varnothing$, $T \neq \varnothing$, $P \cap T = \varnothing$. F is referred to as the set of directed arcs or flow relations, and $F \subseteq (P \times T) \cup (T \times P)$ denotes the directed arcs between the places and transitions. Given a set of natural numbers $\mathbb{N}$, where W is a mapping $(P \times T) \cup (T \times P) \to \mathbb{N}$ to assign weights for arcs. If $f \notin F$, then $W(f) = 0$; if $f \in F$, then $W(f) > 0$. We call W the weight function of a Petri net N.

In the context of a Petri net, a marking denoted as M is a mapping from the set of places P to the set of natural numbers $\mathbb{N}$. For a specific place p, the count of tokens at marking M is expressed as $M(p)$ and is usually represented by small black dots or a numerical value. Furthermore, a Petri net system with an initial marking M_0 is denoted as (N, M_0).

In the context of a Petri net (N, M_0), a transition $t \in T$ is considered enabled at marking M, denoted as $M[t\rangle$, if for all $p \in {}^\bullet t$, the condition $M(p) \geq W(p, t)$ holds. We denote the set of enabled transitions at marking M as $\Gamma(M)$. Upon firing an enabled transition t at marking M, a new marking M' is reached. We use $M[t\rangle M'$ to denote the firing of t yielding marking M'. The token count in each place $p \in P$ is adjusted according to the formula: $M'(p) = M(p) - W(p, t) + W(t, p)$. The language of a Petri net (N, M_0) is denoted as $L(N, M_0) = \{\sigma \mid (\exists \sigma \in T^*) M_0[\sigma\rangle\}$.

The set of all reachable markings of a Petri net (N, M_0) from the initial marking M_0 is denoted as $R(N, M_0) = \{M \mid (\exists \sigma \in T^*) M_0[\sigma\rangle M\}$. A reachability graph of a net is denoted as RG. A Petri net (N, M_0) is said to be bounded if there exists an integer $K \in \mathbb{N}$ such that $\forall M \in R(N, M_0)$ and $\forall p \in P, M(p) \leq K$ holds.

2.2 Labeled Petri Net

A labeled Petri net is a four-tuple $G = (N, M_0, E, \ell)$, where (N, M_0) is a Petri net system, E is the set of labels and $\ell : T \to E \cup \{\varepsilon\}$ is the labeling function that each transition $t \in T$ will be assigned to a symbol from $E \cup \{\varepsilon\}$. Therefore, the set of transitions can be partitioned into two disjoint sets $T_o \cup T_{uo}$, where $T_o = \{t \in T \mid \ell(t) = e \in E\}$ is the set of observable transitions and $T_{uo} = T \backslash T_o = \{t \in T \mid \ell(t) = \varepsilon\}$ is the set of unobservable transitions. The labeling function can be extended to firing sequences: $\ell : T^* \to \{E \cup \{\varepsilon\}\}^*$, i.e. $\ell(\sigma t) = \ell(\sigma)\ell(t)$, where $\sigma \in T^*$ and $t \in T$. The set of the transitions in an LPN can also be partitioned into two disjoint sets $T_c \cup T_{uc}$, where T_c is the set of controllable transitions and T_{uc} is the set of uncontrollable transitions. Let the set of labels be partitioned into two sets as E_c and E_{uc}, where E_c is the set of controllable labels with $\ell(t_c)$ and $E_{uc} = E \backslash E_c$ is the set of uncontrollable labels. Given an LPN $G = (N, M_0, E, \ell)$ and the initial marking M_0, we define the language generated by G is denoted as $L(G) = \{s \in E^* \mid (\exists \sigma \in T^*) M_0[\sigma\rangle M, \ell(\sigma) = s\}$.

2.3   Sensor Attacks and Actuator Attacks

Considering a closed-loop system as shown in Fig. 1, the plant generates a transitions sequence $\sigma \in T^*$, and a corresponding labels sequence is $s \in E^*$. For sensor attacks, an attacker can corrupt the sensor readings, such as inserting labels that did not occur (sensor insert attack) or deleting labels that have already occurred (sensor erase attack). Hence, the label sequence $s \in E^*$ becomes $s' \in E^*$ because of the attacker. The supervisor may make false estimations about the states of the plant based on the sequence with label s'. This will lead to a situation where the real plant has already reached an unsafe state (unsafe state is a state that the system does not want attackers to reach, which violates specifications) through the transition sequence σ, but the supervisor still considers the plant to enforce specifications. Besides, for actuator attacks, an attacker could re-fire the transition which is disabled by the supervisor. The control command $\xi \in T$, issued by the supervisor based on s', may become $\xi' \in T^*$ after being attacked. We can clearly recognize that both sensor attacks and actuator attacks would compromise the security of the plant.

The set of labels which are vulnerable to attacks is denoted as $E_{att} = E_{ins} \cup E_{era} \cup E_{ena}$. Where E_{ins} is the set of vulnerable labels that can be inserted, E_{era} is the set of labels that can be erased and E_{ena} is the set of labels that can be enabled. It is important to note that $E_{ins} \subseteq E$, $E_{era} \subseteq E$. To effectively characterize the states using the observer, we assume that $E_{ena} \subseteq E_c \subseteq E$. This assumption is easily satisfied in reality, as all control commands are usually observable [14] in real applications.

In order to better represent the impact produced by the attacker, we need to expand the set of labels. The set of inserted labels is defined as $E_+ = \{e_+ | e \in E_{ins}\}$, and the set of erased labels is defined as $E_- = \{e_- | e \in E_{era}\}$. We use $E_a = E \cup E_+ \cup E_-$ to describe the labels set under attacks, with the assumption that they are disjoint. The transition associated with the label that the attacker may insert is denoted as $t'(e_+)$. Similarly, the transition associated with the label that the attacker may erase by $t'(e_-)$. The transitions under attacks will be expended to $T_a = T \cup \{t'(e_+)\} \cup \{t'(e_-)\}$.

In plain words, the attacker knows the real label sequence generated by the plant, so it treats the label e_+ as ε and e_- as label e. In the view of a supervisor, the supervisor treats the fake label e_+ as a normal label e and the label e_- will be treated as ε because of the supervisor cannot observe the label e_-.

3   Closed-Loop System Under Attacks

This section initially introduces the observer of LPN. Then, we build the attacker monitor and the supervisor monitor to describe the states of the plant and supervisor under attacks. The supervisor controls the plant with the objective of preventing it from reaching unsafe states. The goal of the attacker is to prevent the supervisor from achieving its objective. Considering a closed-loop system, we construct a new attack structure with the above two monitors. The attack structure represents all possible states and shows how attackers can harm the plant and deceive the supervisor. Finally, examples are provided.

3.1   Observer of an LPN

Due to the accuracy of the DES representation, the size of its state space is usually large. To mitigate this, a reachability graph can be compactly represented by an observer [4,16], which merges transitions with the same labels and hides unobservable transitions from the reachability graph of an LPN. Accordingly, the number of states in an observer is generally less than the number of markings in a reachability graph. Since the state of the CPS is finite, in this paper we only consider bounded Petri nets.

Definition 1 ([16]). *Given an LPN $G = (N, M_0, E, \ell)$ and a marking $M \in R(N, M_0)$, the unobservable reach of M is defined as $\mathcal{U}(M) = \{M' \in R(N, M_0) | (\exists \sigma_{uo} \in T_{uo}^*) M[\sigma_{uo}\rangle M'\}$.*

In simple words, the unobservable reach of a marking M is the set of markings reachable from M by firing only unobservable transitions.

We denote by $G_{ob} = (\mathcal{M}_{ob}, E, \delta_{ob}, M_{ob,0})$ the observer of an LPN, where $M_{ob,0}$ is the initial state of the observer, E is the set of labels, $\delta_{ob} : M_{ob} \times E \to M_{ob}$ is the transition function. Each new state M'_{ob} will be calculated from the previous state M_{ob} by the equation $M'_{ob} := \bigcup_{M \in M_{ob}} \mathcal{U}(M)$. Obviously the number of observer states is bounded.

The observer can be computed by Algorithm 1 (motivated by Algorithm 7 in [4]). In this paper, we construct an LPN observer based on the reachability graph, and the initial state is based on its initial marking of the reachability graph. The markings obtained by firing the unobservable transitions will be hidden. While in [4], the initial marking of an LPN belongs to a given convex set, where an extended reachability graph is proposed and Algorithm 7 in [4] is formulated based on the extended reachability graph.

Example 1. We consider a traffic control system example from [19]. The problem consists of two vehicles a and b that must travel from the origin A to the destination B through a single one-way road. The road is partitioned into four sections, as shown in Fig. 2. Traffic lights and detectors are placed at the connections of the zones, where traffic lights are placed at the entrances of 1, 4, and B and detectors are placed at the entrances of 1, 3, 4, and B, respectively. The goal is to ensure vehicles reach B without colliding. This traffic system could be modeled by the LPN depicted in Fig. 3, where the labels of $t_1, t_2, t_3, t_4, t_5 \in T$ are a, ε, c, d, e, respectively. We have $t_1, t_4, t_5 \in T_c$, $t_2, t_3 \in T_{uc}$, $t_1, t_3, t_4, t_5 \in T_o$, $t_2 \in T_{uo}$. The specifications are $M(p_2) < 2$, $M(p_3) < 2$, $M(p_4) < 2$, and $M(p_5) < 2$.

According to Algorithm 1, the observer can be computed. As shown in Fig. 4(a), we know that the unsafe states are $M_{ob,2}$, $M_{ob,6}$, and $M_{ob,11}$. Where $M_{ob,2} = \{[0\ 2\ 0\ 0\ 0\ 0]^T, [0\ 1\ 1\ 0\ 0\ 0]^T, [0\ 0\ 2\ 0\ 0\ 0]^T\}$, $M_{ob,6} = \{[0\ 0\ 0\ 2\ 0\ 0]^T\}$, and $M_{ob,11} = \{[0\ 0\ 0\ 0\ 2\ 0]^T\}$ which contain the markings that violate the specifications.

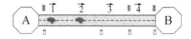

Fig. 2. Traffic control system.

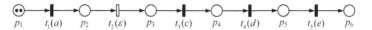

Fig. 3. LPN model.

Algorithm 1. Computation of an observer

Input: $G = (N, M_0, E, \ell)$ with $N = (P, T, F, W)$
Output: The observer of LPN $G_{ob} = (\mathcal{M}_{ob}, E, \delta_{ob}, M_{ob,0})$
1: Let $M_{ob,0} = \mathcal{U}(M_0)$
2: Let $\mathcal{M}_{ob} = \varnothing$
3: Let $\mathcal{M}_{new} = \{M_{ob,0}\}$
4: **for all** $M_{ob} \in \mathcal{M}_{new}$ **do**
5:    **for all** $M \in M_{ob}$ **do**
6:       **for all** $t \in T_o$ **do**
7:          $M_{ob,tem} := \bigcup_{M \in M_{ob}} \{M' | M[t\rangle M' \text{ is defined}\}$
8:          $M'_{ob} := M_{ob,tem} \cup \bigcup_{M \in M_{ob,tem}} \mathcal{U}(M)$
9:          Let $\delta_{ob}(M_{ob}, t(e)) = M'_{ob}$
10:      **end for**
11:   **end for**
12:   **if** $M'_{ob} \notin \mathcal{M}_{ob} \cup \mathcal{M}_{new}$ **then**
13:      Let $\mathcal{M}_{new} = \mathcal{M}_{new} \cup \{M'_{ob}\}$
14:      Let $\mathcal{M}_{ob} = \mathcal{M}_{ob} \cup \{M'_{ob}\}$
15:   **end if**
16: **end for**
17: **return** $G_{ob} = (\mathcal{M}_{ob}, E, \delta_{ob}, M_{ob,0})$

3.2   Attacker Monitor

Definition 2. *Given an observer $G_{ob} = (\mathcal{M}_{ob}, E, \delta_{ob}, M_{ob,0})$, the transition function δ_{ob} is called self-loop transition function if exists a state M_{ob} updates to state M_{ob} by firing a transition $t(e)$, i.e. $\delta_{ob}(M_{ob}, t(e)) = M_{ob}$. The corresponding transition $t(e)$ is called self-loop transition at state M_{ob}.*

When analyzing a plant under attacks, we assume the attacker has the same observation capability as the supervisor. We can build an attacker monitor G_{att} to describe the plant from the viewpoint of the attacker. G_{att} is a reachability graph with E_a based on G_{ob}. For actuator attacks, an attacker could re-fire the transitions that are disabled by the supervisor. Transitions and corresponding labels do not need to be changed in the view of the attacker. For sensor attacks, the attacker may erase the label $e \in E_{era}$, although the corresponding transition

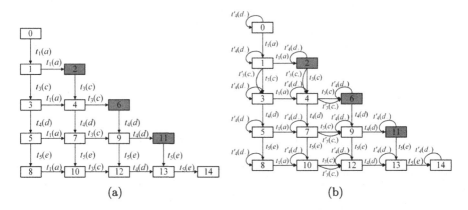

Fig. 4. (a) Observer of LPN and (b) attacker monitor G_{att}. Notation: state $M_{ob,i}$ is denoted as "i".

$t(e)$ has actually fired. We should add a transition $t'(e_-)$ parallel to $t(e)$ in the attacker monitor. The attacker may also insert the label $e \in E_{ins}$, although the corresponding transition $t(e)$ has not actually fired. A self-loop transition $t'(e_+)$ is supposed to be added at each state. The attacker monitor can be built by Algorithm 2.

Remark 1. The self-loop transition functions represent the attacker's ability which can change the labels sequence received by the supervisor.

Example 2. Considering the plant in Example 1, assume that $c \in E_{era}$, $d \in E_{ins}$ and $e \in E_{ena}$. By Algorithm 2, the corresponding attacker monitor is depicted in Fig. 4(b). Due to $c \in E_{era}$, the corresponding $t_3(c)$ has already fired in the real plant, we add parallel transitions $t'_3(c_-)$ like $t_3(c)$ in the monitor. Because of $d \in E_{ins}$, we add self-loop transition $t'_4(d_+)$ at every state in the observer. Since $e \in E_{ena}$, we do not take any action.

Now we discuss the computational complexity involved in constructing the attacker monitor G_{att}. Given an observer G_{ob} with set of states $\mathcal{M}_{ob}$. According to Algorithm 2, G_{att} has the same number of states as G_{ob}; thus the complexity of building G_{att} is $O(|\mathcal{M}_{ob}|^2|T|)$.

3.3 Supervisor Monitor

Let $G_s = (\mathcal{M}_s, E, \delta_s, M_{s,0})$ be the supervisor of the plant under no attacks, where $\mathcal{M}_s \subseteq \mathcal{M}_{ob}$, $\delta_s \subseteq \delta_{ob}$. We build a supervisor monitor, denoted as G_{sup}, to represent G_s under attacks. For each attacked label sequence s', the supervisor estimates states based on $P(s') \in E$. There are two kinds of states in G_{sup}, one is inherited from the G_s, and the other is a specially defined virtual state, denoted as $M_{sup,\varnothing}$. The supervisor considers the plant to be normal when the

Algorithm 2. Construction of an attacker monitor

Input: $G_{ob} = (\mathcal{M}_{ob}, E, \delta_{ob}, M_{ob,0})$ with $G = (N, M_0, E, \ell)$, and $E_+ \cup E_-$
Output: $G_{att} = (\mathcal{M}_{ob}, E_a, \delta_{att}, M_{ob,0})$
1: Let $E_a := E \cup E_+ \cup E_-$
2: Let $\delta_{att} = \delta_{ob}$
3: **for all** $t \in T$ with $\ell(t) = e \in E_{era}$ **do**
4:     **for all** $M_{ob} \in \mathcal{M}_{ob}$ **do**
5:         **if** exists $M'_{ob} \in \mathcal{M}_{ob}$, $M_{ob}[t(e)\rangle M'_{ob}$ is defined **then**
6:             $\delta'_{att}(M_{ob}, t'(e_-)) = M'_{ob}$
7:             $\delta_{att} := \delta_{att} \cup \delta'_{att}$
8:         **end if**
9:     **end for**
10:    **for all** $t \in T$ with $\ell(t) = e \in E_{ins}$ **do**
11:       **for all** $M_{ob} \in \mathcal{M}_{ob}$ **do**
12:          $\delta'_{att}(M_{ob}, t'(e_+)) = M_{ob}$
13:          $\delta_{att} := \delta_{att} \cup \delta'_{att}$
14:       **end for**
15:    **end for**
16: **end for**
17: **return** $G_{att} = (\mathcal{M}_{ob}, E_a, \delta_{att}, M_{ob,0})$

first kind of states occur. This is because the supervisor will not detect the presence of an attacker whether or not the observed label sequence is attacked. When the virtual state occurs, the supervisor knows that the plant is certainly under attacks. The supervisor monitor can be built by using Algorithm 3.

Example 3. The supervisor $G_s = (\mathcal{M}_s, E, \delta_s, M_{s,0})$ of Example 1 is shown in Fig. 5(a). According to Algorithm 3, the supervisor monitor is depicted in Fig. 5(b). At the initial state $M_{sup,0} = M_{s,0}$, we firstly add the self-loop transition function $\delta_{sup}(M_{sup,0}, t_1(a)) = M_{sup,1}$ like the transition function defined in Definition 2. Then, we add the self-loop transition t'_3 at state $M_{sup,0}$, i.e., $\delta_{sup}(M_{sup,0}, t'_3(e_-)) = M_{sup,0}$. Since transitions t_3, t_5, and t'_4 with labels $c \in E_{uc}$, $e \in E_{ena}$, and $d_+ \in E_+$ are not defined at state $M_{sup,0}$, it follows that $M_{sup,0}$ is supposed to reach the virtual state $M_{sup,\varnothing}$ through firing transitions $t_3(c)$, $t_5(e)$, and $t'_4(d_+)$. Similar discussions can be applied to other states and transitions of the attack monitor.

Given an observer G_s with set of states $\mathcal{M}_s$. According to Algorithm 3, the supervisor monitor G_{sup} has at most $|\mathcal{M}_s| + 1$ states thus, the complexity of constructing G_{sup} is $O(|\mathcal{M}_s + 1|^2 |T|)$.

3.4 Attack Structure

In this section, we present a notion of a new attack structure $G_{as} = (\mathcal{M}_{as}, E_a, \delta_{as}, M_{as,0})$ under sensor attacks and actuator attacks, where $\mathcal{M}_{as} = \mathcal{M}_{ob} \times \mathcal{M}_{sup}$, $M_{as,0} = (M_{ob,0}, M_{sup,0})$ is the initial state, and the alphabet is $E_a = E \cup E_+ \cup E_-$. Lastly, the transition function is a mapping $\delta_{as} : \mathcal{M}_{as} \times T_a \to \mathcal{M}_{as}$.

Algorithm 3. Construction of a supervisor monitor

Input: $G_s = (\mathcal{M}_s, E, \delta_s, M_{s,0})$ with $E_+ \cup E_-$
Output: $G_{sup} = (\mathcal{M}_{sup}, E_a, \delta_{sup}, M_{sup,0})$
 1: Let $\mathcal{M}_{sup} = \mathcal{M}_s \cup \{M_{sup,\varnothing}\}$
 2: Let $\delta_{sup} = \delta_s$
 3: Let $E_a := E \cup E_+ \cup E_-$
 4: **for all** $t \in T$ with $\ell(t) = e \in E_{era}$ **do**
 5:     **for all** $M_{sup} \in \mathcal{M}_{sup}$ **do**
 6:         $\delta'_{sup}(M_{sup}, t'(e_-)) = M_{sup}$
 7:         $\delta_{sup} := \delta_{sup} \cup \delta'_{sup}$
 8:     **end for**
 9: **end for**
10: **for all** $t \in T$ with $\ell(t) = e \in E_{ins}$ **do**
11:     **for all** $M_{sup} \in \mathcal{M}_{sup}$ **do**
12:         **if** exists $M'_{sup} \in \mathcal{M}_{sup}, M_{sup}[t(e)\rangle M'_{sup}$ is defined **then**
13:             $\delta'_{sup}(M_{sup}, t'(e_+)) = M'_{sup}$
14:         **else**
15:             $\delta'_{sup}(M_{sup}, t'(e_+)) = M_{sup,\varnothing}$
16:         **end if**
17:         $\delta_{sup} := \delta_{sup} \cup \delta'_{sup}$
18:     **end for**
19: **end for**the supervisor monitor is depicted
20: **for all** $t \in T$ with $\ell(t) = e \in E_{uc} \cup E_{ena}$ **do**
21:     **for all** $M_{sup} \in \mathcal{M}_{sup}$ **do**
22:         **if** all $M'_{sup} \in \mathcal{M}_{sup}, M_{sup}[t(e)\rangle M'_{sup}$ is not defined **then**
23:             $\delta'_{sup}(M_{sup}, t(e)) = M_{sup,\varnothing}$
24:         **end if**
25:         $\delta_{sup} := \delta_{sup} \cup \delta'_{sup}$
26:     **end for**
27: **end for**
28: **return** $G_{sup} = (\mathcal{M}_{sup}, E_a, \delta_{sup}, M_{sup,0})$

We denote the set of enabled transitions at state M_{ob}(or M_{sup}) as $\Gamma_{att}(M_{ob})$(or $\Gamma_{att}(M_{sup})$). For every $M_{as} = (M_{ob}, M_{sup}) \in \mathcal{M}_{as}$ and every $t(e) \in T_a(E_a)$, the transition function $\delta_{as}((M_{ob}, M_{sup}), t(e))$ is defined as $\delta_{as}((M_{ob}, M_{sup}), t(e)) = (\delta_{att}(M_{ob}, t(e)), \delta_{sup}(M_{sup}, t(e)))$ if $t(e) \in \Gamma_{att}(M_{ob}) \cap \Gamma_{sup}(M_{sup})$. Obviously, the function can be extended to $\delta_{as} : \mathcal{M}_{as} \times T_a^* \to \mathcal{M}_{as}$ in the same way. The attack structure outlines the state estimation calculated by the evolution of the attacker monitor and the supervisor monitor based on their respective states.

Example 4. According to the attacker monitor G_{att} and supervisor monitor G_{sup} from Examples 2 and 3. By Algorithm 4, the corresponding attack structure G_{as} is depicted in Fig. 6. At the initial state $(M_{ob,0}, M_{sup,0})$, if transition $t_1(a)$ fires, the state will update to $(M_{ob,1}, M_{sup,1})$. Since $t_3(c) \in \Gamma_{att}(M_{ob,1}) \cap \Gamma_{sup}(M_{sup,1})$, we add transition function $\delta_{as}((M_{ob,1}, M_{sup,1}), t_3(c)) = (M_{ob,3}, M_{sup,3})$. Same discussions can be applied to other states and transitions of the attack structure.

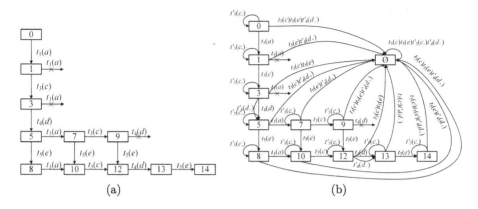

Fig. 5. (a) supervisor G_s for the observer in Fig. 4(a) and (b) supervisor monitor G_{sup}. Notation: state $M_{sup,j}$ is denoted as "j".

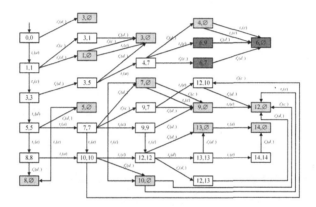

Fig. 6. The attack structure G_{as}. Notation: state $(M_{ob,i}, M_{sup,j})$ is denoted as "i, j".

Definition 3. *Let $\mathcal{M}_{us}$ be the set of unsafe states of the plant G. Given an attack structure $G_{as} = (\mathcal{M}_{as}, E_a, \delta_{as}, M_{as,0})$, the set of unsafe states of G_{as} is $\mathcal{M}_{as,us} := \{M_{as} = (M_{ob}, M_{sup}) | M_{ob} \in \mathcal{M}_{us}\}$.*

In Fig. 6, we can see that there exist three unsafe states $(M_{ob,6}, M_{sup,9})$, $(M_{ob,6}, M_{sup,7})$, and $(M_{ob,6}, M_{sup,\varnothing})$ in red because of attacks. Notably, the unsafe states in the attack structure align with those in the attacker monitor. When there exists a virtual state $M_\varnothing$ in attack structure G_{as} which is in yellow, we can certainly know that the plant has already been under attacks. For the security of the plant, the supervisor aims to prevent the appearance of unsafe states (in red) from the plant.

4   Robust Supervisor Synthesis Against Attacks

4.1   Robust Supervisor

For safe control purposes, we should design a robust supervisor $G_{sup,r}$ by further restricting the behavior of G_{sup} to keep the plant in safe states. This requires us to analyze the security of the plant and find the key that leads the plant to danger. This section tackles the problem of synthesizing a supervisor that enforces predefined control requirements under actuator and sensor attacks.

Definition 4. *Given an LPN $G = (N, M_0, E, \ell)$ with control specifications, a supervisor is called robust if the system cannot reach the states that violate the specifications whether or not the system is under attacks E_{ins}, E_{era}, and E_{ena}.*

We firstly consider an attack structure G_{as} as a plant with the attack alphabet $E_a = E \cup E_+ \cup E_-$. Then, we regard the trimming process of G_{as} as a modified partially observed supervisory control problem. In the viewpoint of the supervisor, the alphabet $E_{a,o} = E_o \cup E_+$ is observable and the alphabet $E_{a,uo} = E_-$ is unobservable. Since $t' \in T_a$ with $\ell(t') = e_- \in E_-$is followed by $t \in T$ with $\ell(t) = e \in E$, the corresponding $t(e)$ can be disabled so that $t'(e_-)$ does not fire again. We denote by $E_{a,c}^- = \{e_- \in E_- | e \in [(E_c \backslash E_{ena}) \cap E_{era}]\}$ the set of labels in E_- whose corresponding label e could be disabled by the supervisor. Thus, the set of controllable labels is $E_{a,c} = (E_c \backslash E_{ena}) \cup E_{a,c}^-$, and the set of uncontrollable labels is $E_{a,uc} = E_a \backslash [(E_c \backslash E_{ena}) \cup E_{a,c}^-]$. We divide the states set $\mathcal{M}_{as}$ into legal-zone $\mathcal{M}_l$ and illegal-zone $\mathcal{M}_{il}$. The synthesis of a robust supervisor against attacks is presented in Algorithm 4.

Now we discuss the complexity of Algorithm 4. Given an attack structure $G_{as} = (\mathcal{M}_{as}, E_a, \delta_{as}, M_{as,0})$, $\mathcal{M}_{il}$ has the same number of states as $\mathcal{M}_{as}$ at most; thus the complexity of synthesis of a robust supervisor is $O(|\mathcal{M}_{as}|^2 |T|^2)$

Theorem 1 *(Existence of robust supervisor). Given an attack structure $G_{as} = (\mathcal{M}_{as}, E_a, \delta_{as}, M_{as,0})$ with $t_{a,c} \in T_a | \ell(t_a) = e \in E_{a,c}$, there exists a robust supervisor that can enforce the control specifications to keep the plant from unsafe states if $\mathcal{M}_l$ is not empty.*

Proof. According to the steps 1–13 in Algorithm 4, we know that the transitions between $\mathcal{M}_l$ and $\mathcal{M}_{il}$ are certainly controllable. All states in $\mathcal{M}_l$ do not violate the control specifications. The supervisor can prevent the system from reaching to the states in $\mathcal{M}_{il}$ by disabling controllable transitions. Thus, a robust supervisor can be designed to enforce the control specifications, i.e. to keep the plant in safe states if there exits $\mathcal{M}_l$.

Example 5. According to the supervisor monitor G_{sup} from Example 3 and the attack structure G_{as} from Example 4, the robust supervisor monitor $G_{sup,r}$ is depicted in Fig. 7. By steps 1–13, we can easily compute that $\mathcal{M}_{il}$ in this example contains $(M_{ob,4}, M_{sup,7})$, $(M_{ob,6}, M_{sup,7})$, $(M_{ob,6}, M_{sup,9})$, and $(M_{ob,6}, M_{sup,\varnothing})$. By step 16, the transition function $\delta_{sup}(M_{sup,5}, t_1(a)) = M_{sup,7}$ should be removed. Finally, we remove all transitions $t'_3(c_-)$, $t'_4(d_+)$ and the corresponding arcs from the supervisor according to step 17. We could obtain the robust supervisor $G_{sup,r}$ as shown in Fig. 7.

Algorithm 4. Synthesis of a robust supervisor against attacks

Input: An attack structure $G_{as} = (\mathcal{M}_{as}, E_a, \delta_{as}, M_{as,0})$, and a supervisor $G_s = (\mathcal{M}_s, E, \delta_s, M_{s,0})$

Output: A robust supervisor $G_{sup,r} = (\mathcal{M}_{sup,r}, E, \delta_{sup,r}, M_{sup,0})$

1: Let $\mathcal{M}_{il} := \mathcal{M}_{as,us}$
2: **for all** $M'_{as} \in \mathcal{M}_{il}$ **do**
3:    **for all** $M_{as} \in \mathcal{M}_{as}$ **do**
4:       **for all** $t_a \in T_a$ with $\ell(t_a) = e \in E_{a,uc}$ **do**
5:          **if** $M_{as}[t_a\rangle M'_{as}$ **then**
6:             $\mathcal{M}_{il} := \mathcal{M}_{il} \cup \{M_{as}\}$
7:          **end if**
8:       **end for**
9:       **if** $|\Gamma(M_{as})| = 1 \wedge M_{as}[t_a\rangle M'_{as}$ **then**
10:          $\mathcal{M}_{il} := \mathcal{M}_{il} \cup \{M_{as}\}$
11:       **end if**
12:    **end for**
13: **end for**
14: remove the states in $\mathcal{M}_{il}$ and the corresponding transitions from attack structure
15: **if** exists $\sigma \in T_a^*$ and exists $t \in T_a$, such that $\delta_{att}(M_{ob,o}, \sigma) = M_{ob}$, $\delta_{att}(M_{ob}, t) = M'_{ob}$, and $\delta_{as}(M_{ob}, t)$ is not defined **then**
16:    remove the corresponding states M_{sup} and transitions t that $\delta_{sup}(M_{sup}, t) = M'_{sup}$ such that $\delta_{sup}(M_{sup,0}, \sigma) = M_{sup}$ from supervisor monitor, and use $\delta_{sup,r}$ to denote the pruned transition function of supervisor monitor
17:    $\delta_{sup,r} := \delta_{sup,r} \cap \delta_s$
18: **end if**
19: $\mathcal{M}_{sup,r} = \{M_{sup} \in \mathcal{M}_{sup} | \exists \sigma \in T^*, \delta_{sup,r}(M_{sup,0}, \sigma) = M_{sup}\}$
20: **return** $G_{sup,r} = (\mathcal{M}_{sup,r}, E, \delta_{sup,r}, M_{sup,0})$

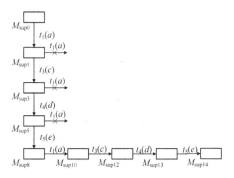

Fig. 7. Robust supervisor $G_{sup,r}$

At the end of this section, we have the following remark. Compared to the method in [18], the robust supervisor in this paper is effective against sensor and actuator attacks simultaneously. In [18], the existence of a supervisor is based on the generated language of the plant. Because of the above, it cannot deal with the signals inserted by sensor insertion attacks. We construct the new attack structure and divide the structure into $\mathcal{M}_l$ and $\mathcal{M}_{il}$ in this paper. The robust supervisor can be designed to keep the states in the legal-zone. Hence, the plant can not reach unsafe states with a robust supervisor, even if there are sensor attacks and actuator attacks.

5 Conclusion

This research details the security analysis and supervisory control of the plant-based on LPN formalism under several malicious cyber attacks. We divide the attacks into two main categories: sensor attacks and actuator attacks. For sensor attacks, the attacker primarily intrudes the communication channel between the plant and the supervisor, i.e., destroys or appropriately modifies the sensor readings. For actuator attacks, the attacker can also fire certain transitions that are prohibited from enabling by the supervisor through modifying the control commands. Since the attack structure contains both of sensor attacks and actuator attacks, we can easily analyze the security of the system. By defining legal-zone and illegal-zone, we can divide the attack structure into two distinct parts. If there is a legal-zone in the attack structure, then a robust supervisor can be designed through the algorithm proposed in the paper to ensure the security of the plant.

In the future, we will try to design a method for maximally permissive supervisor by appropriately modifying the structure of the plant [10]. In order to represent CPSs more accurately, the time factor will also be taken into account [3].

Acknowledgement. This work is supported by Région Normandie with Project RIN ASSAILLANT 2023 ref. 23E02599 and the Natural Science Basic Research Program of Shaanxi Province under Grant 2024JC-YBMS-534.

References

1. Abubakar, U.S., Liu, G., Barkaoui, K., Li, Z.: Adaptive supervisory control for a class of Petri nets with bimodal transitions. Inf. Sci. **650**, 119683 (2023)
2. Baheti, R., Gill, H.: Cyber-physical systems. In: The Impact of Control Technology, vol. 12, no. 1, pp. 161–166 (2011)
3. Boucheneb, H., Barkaoui, K., Xing, Q., Wang, K., Liu, G., Li, Z.: Time based deadlock prevention for Petri nets. Automatica **137**, 110119 (2022)
4. Cabasino, M.P., Hadjicostis, C.N., Seatzu, C.: Marking observer in labeled Petri nets with application to supervisory control. IEEE Trans. Autom. Control **62**(4), 1813–1824 (2016)
5. Carvalho, L.K., Wu, Y.C., Kwong, R., Lafortune, S.: Detection and mitigation of classes of attacks in supervisory control systems. Automatica **97**, 121–133 (2018)
6. Ding, S., Liu, G., Yin, L., Wang, J., Li, Z.: Detection of cyber-attacks in a discrete event system based on deep learning. Mathematics **12**(17), 1–21 (2024)

7. Gao, C., Seatzu, C., Li, Z., Giua, A.: Multiple attacks detection on discrete event systems. In: 2019 IEEE International Conference on Systems, Man and Cybernetics (SMC), pp. 2352–2357 (2019)
8. Góes, R.M., Kang, E., Kwong, R., Lafortune, S.: Stealthy deception attacks for cyber-physical systems. In: 2017 IEEE 56th Annual Conference on Decision and Control (CDC), pp. 4224–4230. IEEE (2017)
9. Góes, R.M., Kang, E., Kwong, R., Lafortune, S.: Synthesis of sensor deception attacks at the supervisory layer of cyber-physical systems. Automatica **121**, 109172 (2020)
10. Liu, G.Y., Chao, D.Y., Uzam, M.: A merging method for the siphon-based FMS maximally permissive controllers with simpler structures. IMA J. Math. Control. Inf. **31**(4), 551–573 (2014)
11. Qin, T., Yin, L., Liu, G., Wu, N., Li, Z.: Strong current-state opacity verification of discrete-event systems modeled with time labeled Petri nets. IEEE/CAA J. Autom. Sin. **12**, 1–15 (2025)
12. Ramadge, P.J., Wonham, W.M.: Supervisory control of a class of discrete event processes. SIAM J. Control. Optim. **25**(1), 206–230 (1987)
13. Shen, C., Liu, G., Zhong, C., Barkaoui, K.: Analysis of effectiveness and stealthiness of sensor attacks in labeled Petri nets. In: 2023 IEEE International Conference on Networking, Sensing and Control (ICNSC), vol. 1, pp. 1–6. IEEE (2023)
14. Su, R.: Supervisor synthesis to thwart cyber attack with bounded sensor reading alterations. Automatica **94**, 35–44 (2018)
15. Thorsley, D., Teneketzis, D.: Intrusion detection in controlled discrete event systems. In: Proceedings of the 45th IEEE Conference on Decision and Control, pp. 6047–6054. IEEE (2006)
16. Tong, Y., Li, Z., Seatzu, C., Giua, A.: Verification of state-based opacity using Petri nets. IEEE Trans. Autom. Control **62**(6), 2823–2837 (2016)
17. Wakaiki, M., Tabuada, P., Hespanha, J.P.: Supervisory control of discrete-event systems under attacks. Dyn. Games Appl. **9**, 965–983 (2019)
18. Wang, Y., Li, Y., Yu, Z., Wu, N., Li, Z.: Supervisory control of discrete-event systems under external attacks. Inf. Sci. **562**, 398–413 (2021)
19. Wonham, W.M., Cai, K.: Supervisory Control of Discrete-Event Systems. Springer (2019)
20. You, D., Wang, S., Seatzu, C.: A liveness-enforcing supervisor tolerant to sensor-reading modification attacks. IEEE Trans. Syst. Man Cybern. Syst. **52**(4), 2398–2411 (2021)
21. Zhang, Z., Liu, G., Li, Z.: Adaptive supervisory control of automated manufacturing systems with unreliable resources based on smart switch controllers. IEEE Trans. Autom. Sci. Eng. **21**(4), 5445–5456 (2024)

ERTMS/ETCS L3: Usable Formal Models for the "Loss of Train Integrity" Operation Scenario

Rim Saddem-Yagoubi[1]([✉]) [ID], Julie Beugin[2] [ID], and Mohamed Ghazel[2] [ID]

[1] Aix Marseille Univ., CNRS LIS, Marseille, France
`rim.saddem@lis-lab.fr`
[2] Univ. Gustave Eiffel, COSYS, ESTAS, 59650 Villeneuve-d'Ascq, France
`{julie.beugin,mohamed.ghazel}@univ-eiffel.fr`

Abstract. Railway safety standards recommend the use of formal modelling and verification techniques to guarantee processes' correctness and validate safety requirements. In this paper, we follow a generic methodology framework to produce usable formal models for the "Loss of Train Integrity" Operation Scenario.

Keywords: Railway safety · Requirement engineering · formal modelling · ERTMS/ETCS · Moving block · Verification & validation

1 Introduction

Railway signaling is a system that is responsible for managing railway traffic and ensuring a safe distance between trains at all times. The traditional signaling system operates on the concept of fixed blocks; namely, the railway line is divided into sections of track known as blocks. These blocks are separated by lineside signals that control their occupancy. A block can be occupied by only one train at a time [2]. Among other drawbacks, this system lacks flexibility because the block size is fixed, irrespective of the actual speed and braking performance of the running trains. In other words, the long safety distances required for fast trains are also imposed on slower trains, unnecessarily reducing track capacity. Today, rail transport systems are an important mode of transport for both freight and passengers, with demand growing rapidly. As a result, traditional signaling systems become insufficient to meet this rising demand. For instance, in 2019, statistics showed approximately 643 billion passenger kilometers on European railways, making Europe the second-largest market for rail passenger traffic in the world[1]. To address this growing demand, the European railway industry is looking for next-generation signaling systems that are able to manage train traffic more efficiently. In particular, Moving Block (MB) systems are being introduced in this context. These control-command and signaling systems can reduce train headways to maximize capacity utilization of existing networks. The

---

[1] https://www.statista.com/topics/8282/rail-passenger-transport-in-europe/ dossierKeyfigures.

B. Ben Hedia et al. (Eds.): VECoS 2024, LNCS 15466, pp. 174–188, 2025.
https://doi.org/10.1007/978-3-031-85356-2_12

third application level of ETCS (European Train Control System) is based on the MB principle. ETCS, the automatic train protection (ATP) component of the European Rail Traffic Management System standard (ERTMS), aims to replace the different national train Control-Command and Signaling systems (CCS) in Europe with an interoperable European CCS system [9]. Compared to ETCS Levels 1 and 2, which are based on traditional signaling systems, ETCS Level 3 introduces the innovative concept of moving block as follows: Trains could only be separated by an absolute or a relative braking distance (i.e. the distance required to reach a stopping point or the speed of the train ahead) plus a safety margin (see Fig. 1). Lineside signals (used in ETCS L1) and train detectors (used in ETCS L1 and L2) are no longer required. Consequently, ETCS L3 allows for substantial capacity gains, cost reductions (e.g., removal of trackside equipment), and increased reliability due to less trackside equipment [6].

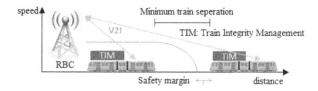

Fig. 1. Full Moving Block

One of the key issues to be tackled for implementing ETCS L3 is the Verification and Validation (V&V) of the safety and functional specifications of the MB system, developed through previous European projects (X2Rail-1, X2Rail-3, X2Rail-5, MovingRail, Astrail). These specifications comprise numerous inter-related requirements that must be consistent with each other while addressing all the safety and performance aspects of railway operations. Given the critical nature of railway CCS systems, railway safety standards recommend the use of formal modeling and verification techniques for the engineering of such systems.

This work is part of the PERFORMINGRAIL project, which aims to develop semi-formal and formal models for MB systems, among other objectives. More details are available at PERFORMINGRAIL project[2]. In this paper, formal models for the "Loss of Train Integrity" Operation Scenario (OS) are provided.

The remainder of this paper is organized as follows. Section 2 presents the methodological process used to develop formal models that accurately represent the behavior of ETCS L3 in operation. Section 3 presents the designed formal models and properties to be verified for the Loss of Train Integrity OS. Section 4 concludes and presents the future work.

2   Methodological Framework

The methodology defined within the context of the PERFORMINGRAIL project aims to produce generic semi-formal and formal models for Moving Block (MB)

---

[2] https://projects.shift2rail.org/s2r_ip2_n.aspx?p=S2R_PERFORMINGRAIL.

systems. It consists of several interrelated activities that exchange various inputs and outputs. Figure 2 provides a high-level view of this methodology framework. The bold blue items in the figure correspond to the outputs of the workflow.

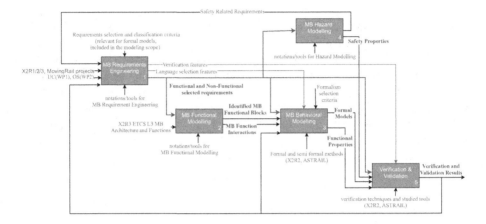

Fig. 2. Workflow structure

The first step, "MB Requirement Engineering", involves identifying and classifying the most relevant requirements for the MB system. These selected requirements can be represented using SysML requirement diagrams [7]. The second step, "MB Functional Modeling", aims at identifying the various functions within the MB scope from the selected requirements, as well as the interactions among them. The identified functions can be modeled using SysML state machines, and their interactions can be modeled using SysML sequence diagrams. The "MB Behavioral Modeling" step develops parameterizable formal models for the various MB functions and identifies functional properties. The "Hazard Modeling" step aims at modeling the identified hazards related to the MB system and at specifying the safety properties to be verified. Finally, the "Verification & Validation" step is introduced to verify and validate the formal models developed in the previous step.

This framework is adaptable to different formal languages or notations, it is scenario oriented to develop key aspects of MB complex systems, especially the safety-related aspects. In this paper, the choice of Timed Automata/UPPAAL tool [5] as a formal language/tool for "MB Behavioral Modelling" was guided by several factors: availability of a supporting tool for UPPAAL, previous experience and mastery of this tool, support of temporal aspects, modularity and parameterisation of models, which allow the composition of sub-models and configuration of the system, facilitating the modelling of complex systems. In addition, UPPAAL offers interesting possibilities in terms of model edition, generation, formal verification and simulation. An overview of formal tools used to model full moving block systems is available in [4].

3 Formal Modeling and Properties to Check for Loss of Train Integrity Operation Scenario

This section provides a detailed description of the Loss of Train Integrity (LTI) operational scenario (OS). It is important to note that we have followed the methodological framework outlined earlier to generate formal models of the LTI OS. Due to space limitations, we will focus on the "MB Behavioral Modeling" step in this paper. Some semi-formal models for LTI OS can be found in [10]. It is important to note that the way of deriving formal models from SysML state machines and sequence diagrams is not automatic.

To understand how formal models have been developed, we need to describe the result of the "MB Functional Modelling" step, which is the functional architecture of the ETCS L3 system.

3.1 Brief Description of ETCS L3 System Architecture

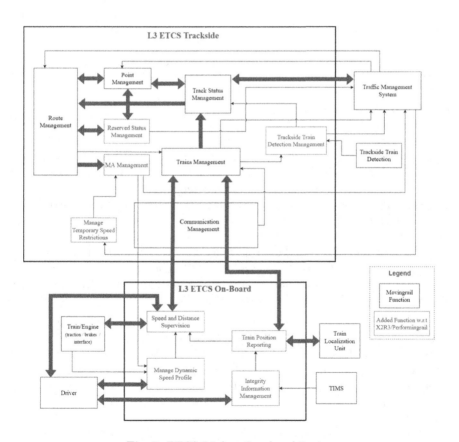

Fig. 3. ETCS L3 functional architecture

The ETCS L3 system architecture consists of two blocks: the *ETCS L3 Trackside* block and *ETCS L3 On board* block. They interact with ETCS L3 External Users (*Driver*) and ETCS L3 *External Interfaces* (*Traffic Management System, Trackside Train Detection, Train/Engine, Train Localization Unit*, and *Train Integrity Management System*).

The ETCS L3 Trackside block consists of 9 trackside functions (see Fig. 3). The ETCS L3 On-board block includes 4 on-board functions. Notably, the trackside function "Manage Low Adhesion Areas" is omitted from Fig. 3 due to the absence of a defined requirement specification [1]. Figure 3 provides an overview of the data flow between the external interfaces and the ETCS L3 systems. A more detailed representation of this architecture is available here.

3.2 Formal Modeling of LTI OS

The LTI OS is a hazardous scenario. It corresponds to the situation where some wagons are unintentionally detached from the train, potentially leading to severe accidents if not timely detected. Train integrity is considered to have been lost in either of the following cases: a loss of integrity is explicitly reported, or integrity is assumed to have been lost due to the expiry of the wait integrity timer or upon receiving new Validated Train Data. In case of unintentional train splits, the dispatcher must take appropriate measures to avoid the collision of the disconnected part of the train and some following trains. It is noteworthy that under ETCS L3 operation, the availability of train integrity information significantly influences line performance.

The on-board function "*Integrity_Information_Management*" receives Train Integrity Information (TII) either from the external device *TIMS* or from the *Driver*. Then, the "*Integrity_Information_Management*" function computes the integrity status and forwards it to the "*Train_Position_Reporting*" function (see Fig. 3). Then, the "*Train_Position_Reporting*" requests the position from the *Train Localization Unit*, which computes the train position and replies to the request. Finally, the "*Train_Position_Reporting*" sends the Train Position Report (TPR) to the "*Trains_Management*". The interactions among ETCS L3 actors and ETCS L3 internal functions depend on the integrity status stored in the variable Q_LENGTH of the TPR. The integrity status can have four states: no integrity information, integrity confirmed by the driver, integrity confirmed by an external device, and integrity lost

- Q_LENGTH = MONITORINGDEVICE (RESP. DRIVER) means that the integrity is confirmed by the TIMS (resp. Driver). The "*Trains_Management*" function restarts the wait integrity timer and computes the areas of the track that are released/occupied by the train. Then, it sends the information to the "*Track_Status_Management*" to update the track status areas.
- Q_LENGTH = LOST means that the integrity is lost, and it is reported by the TIMS. In this case, the "*Trains_Management*" function computes the area of the track that is unknown. Then, it sends the information to the "*Track_Status_Management*" to update the track status area.

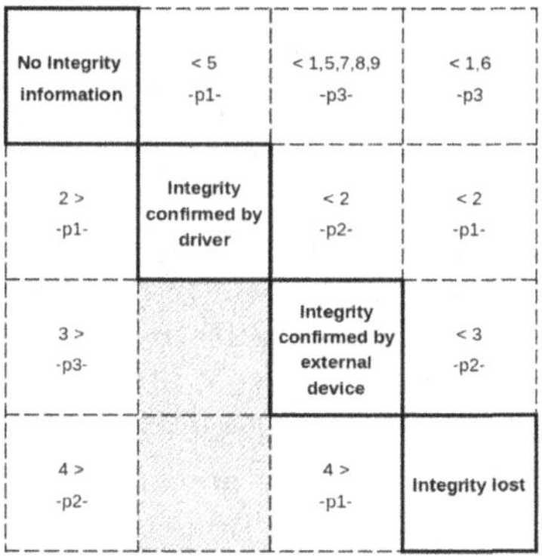

Fig. 4. States and transitions in *"Integrity_ Information_ Management"*

Table 1. Switching Conditions

ID	Content of the conditions
[1]	No valid Train data is available
[2]	(Train is at standstill) AND (valid Train Data is available and has been acknowledged by the RBC "Radio Block Center") AND (the train integrity is confirmed by the driver)
[3]	(The information "Train integrity confirmed" is received from an external device) AND (valid Train Data is available and has been acknowledged by the RBC) AND (Train Data regarding train length has not changed since the time the train was last known to be integer) AND (the train position is valid and is referred to an LRBG) AND (the train position was valid and was referred to an LRBG at the time the train was last known to be integer) AND (no reverse movement is currently performed nor has been performed since the time the train was last known to be integer) AND (the distance between the min safe rear end at the time the train was last known to be integer and the current estimated train position does not exceed the range of the safe train length information)
[4]	(The information "Train integrity lost" is received from an external device) AND (valid Train Data is available since the time the train integrity was last known to be lost)
[5]	A position report indicating that the train integrity is confirmed is sent to the RBC
[6]	The information "Train integrity status unknown" is received from an external device
[7]	Train Data regarding train length is changed
[8]	A reverse movement is performed
[9]	The distance between the min safe rear end at the time the train was last known to be integer and the current estimated train position exceeds the range of the safe train length information

- Q_LENGTH = NoInformation means that the integrity is unknown, and it is reported by the TIMS. If the wait integrity timer expires, the trackside system assumes integrity is lost. The *"Trains_Management"* function calculates the area of the track with unknown status and sends this data to the *"Track_Status_Management"* function, which updates the track status and reacts accordingly, based on its configuration.

It is crucial to explain how the integrity status is determined. The state transitions are outlined in a transition table (Fig. 4), derived from the ERA change request document CR 940_16042020 (subset-026 v3.6.0) [11].

As shown in Fig. 4, state transitions are driven by various conditions and priority levels "pi", with details listed in Table 1.

To address all switching conditions, especially conditions 3 and 9, a formal model for train movement is required. A train needs a Movement Authority (MA), sent from the MA Management function to the on-board sub-system, to proceed. Hence, a formal model of the MA Management function is essential. Additionally, if a train loses integrity, the MA for the next train must be updated.

The formal models representing the LTI OS consist of fourteen timed automata, which were identified based on the interactions depicted in Fig. 3. Additional models were necessary to account for the conditions listed in the transition table (Table 1). The behavior of each automaton is described below:

- "TIMS" automaton, represented in Fig. 5, emulates the behavior of the *TIMS* block by sending three signals for integrity unknown, confirmed and lost.

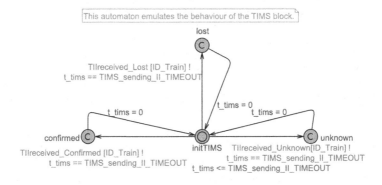

Fig. 5. "TIMS" automaton

- "Driver" automaton emulates the behavior of the *Driver* block by sending signal *'integrityDriver'*.

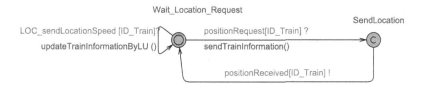

Fig. 6. "TrainLocalizationUnit" automaton

- "TrainLocalizationUnit" automaton, represented in Fig. 6, emulates the behavior of the external actor *Train Localization Unit*. It receives the train's location and speed from "TrainMovement_MAIN" automaton and responds to "TPRManagement" requests (*'positionRequest'*) by sending the last recorded information (*'positionReceived'*).
- The "TrainDataManagement" automaton (Fig. 7a) manages train data needed to compute integrity status (see Table 1). Upon request, it fills the train data structure and sends it back ("trainData").
- "TimeStep" automaton, inspired from [8] and represented in Fig. 7b, manages the increment of the integer variables. If the clock LOC_C_freq is equal to time step (LOC_freq), the channel *'LOC_NextTimeStep'* is issued.

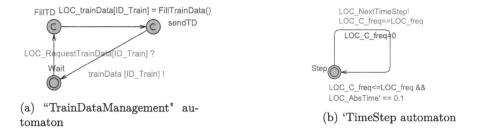

(a) "TrainDataManagement" automaton

(b) 'TimeStep automaton

Fig. 7. "TrainMovement_MAIN" and "TimeStep" automata

- "TrainMovement_MAIN" automaton, inspired by [3], models train movement behavior by initializing the value of all train movement variables, calculating acceleration, and updating movement authority. No figure is provided due to space limitations.
- "TrainMovement" automaton, based on [8], handles train acceleration, velocity, and position updates, with state changes (accelerating, braking, or constant speed) occurring at each time step. No figure is provided due to space limitations.
- "IIMStatusManagement" automaton, depicted in Fig. 8, represents a part of the behavior of the function *"Integrity_Information_Management"*. It intercepts *TIMS* and *Driver* signals, and according to the current status of integrity and other conditions described in Table 1, performs the switching from one state to another.

- "IIMUpdating" automaton, depicted in Fig. 9, represents a part of the behavior of the on-board function *"Integrity_Information_Management"*. At initial state, it waits for INTEGRITY_CHECK_TIMEOUT. Then, it sends the value of the variable $LOC\_CurrentIntegrityStatus$ to "TPRManagement" automaton through the channel '*integrityInfoRecv*'.

- "TPRManagement" automaton, depicted Fig. 10, represents the behavior of the on-board function *"Train_Position_Management"*. This automation is responsible for sending to the "TrainManagement" automaton a train position report which includes, mainly, the train position, the train speed and the train integrity information. It receives from "TrainManagement" automaton a request for Position Report '*getTPRRequest*' and it receives the integrity status from "IIM updating" automaton '*integrityInfoRecv*'. It sends a request for location to "TrainLocalizationUnit" automaton. In the state *Wait_Train_Localization_Unit_Position*, it waits for a reply. When receiving '*positionReceived*' from "TrainLocalizationUnit" automaton, it fills the variable $msgTPRReceived$ which contains the train position report and sends it to "TrainManagement" automaton using the channel '*TPRReceived*'.

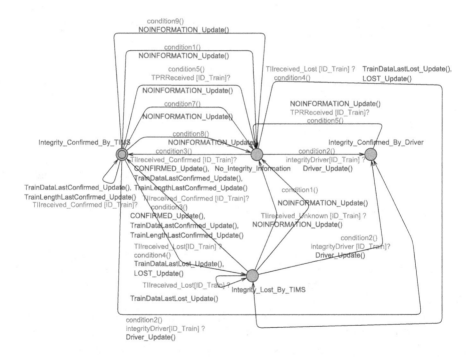

Fig. 8. *IIMStatusManagement* automaton

- "SpeedDistanceSupervision" automaton represents the behavior of the on-board function *"Speed_Distance_Supervision"* related to the train data. $LOC\_start[ID\_Train]$ is a local boolean variable allowing to receive train data for the first time. If it is false, train data are already received.

LOC_Available_Train_Data and *LOC_Ack_Train_Data_RBC* are local variables and initialized by "InitOnBoard" automaton. If no valid train data is available (!*LOC_Available_Train_Data*[*ID_Train*]) and the train is at a standstill, the "SpeedDistanceSupervision" automaton sends a request to "TrainDataManagement" automaton to re-send train data ('*LOC_RequestTrainData*'). After reception of train data ('*trainData*'), it sends validated train data ('*VTDReceived*') to "TrainManagement" automaton and waits for an acknowledgment from this latter ('*VTDAck*').

– "InitOnBoard" automaton is designed to initialize on-board variables. The current integrity status is set to confirmed by TIMS using the function *CONFIRMED_Update()*. Train data are initialized as follows: valid train data are always available and valid Train Data have been acknowledged by the RBC. To emulate the generic behavior of train data, initial values of train data are defined as parameters of the automaton. The "InitOnBoard" automaton stores the value of the variable *LOC_CurrentIntegrityStatus* representing the current integrity status in the variable *LOC_sentII* and issues a channel '*integrityInfoRecv*' to send this value to "TPRManagement" automaton. This automaton is represented in Fig. 11.

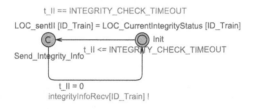

Fig. 9. "IIMUpdating" Automaton

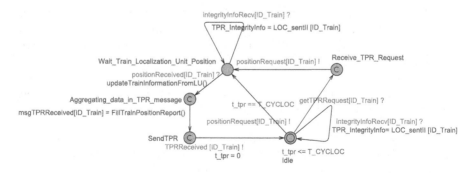

Fig. 10. "TPRManagement" Automaton

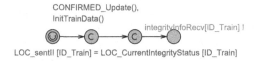

Fig. 11. "InitOnBoard" automaton

– "TrainManagement" automaton represents a part of the behavior of the track-side function *"Trains_ management"*. It receives the train position report (*'TPRReceived'*) from "TPRManagement" automaton, receives validated train data (*'VTDReceived'*) from "SpeedDistanceSupervision" automaton, sends an acknowledgment upon reception of train data (*'VTDAck'*) and sends a request for train position report (*'getTPRRequest'*) from "TPRManagement" automaton if the min safe front end of the train exceeds a specific value expressed as the destination of the train. This automaton is represented in Fig. 12.

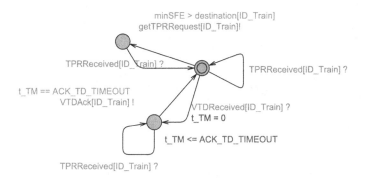

Fig. 12. "TrainManagement" automaton

– "MAManagement" automaton is designed to emulate the behavior of the trackside function *"Movement_ Authority_ Management"*. It is inspired from [3]. In "MAManagement" automaton, the Movement Authority (MA) is computed after reception of Train Position Report (*'TPRReceived'*) from "TPRManagement" automaton because MA needs the position of all trains to compute future MA. Once MA is computed, a channel *'MAupdate'* is sent to "TrainMovement_MAIN" automaton.

The models developed for the Loss of Train Integrity OS were described in details in this subsection. The results related to the main properties checked on this OS are now described in the next subsection (see Table 2).

3.3   Checked Properties

Some properties were verified on Loss of Train Integrity OS to assess the soundness of the models. The verification was performed either by simulation or by checking the properties with the verifier of the UPPAAL tool.

Table 2. Properties Description

ID	Property description	UPPAAL syntax
[1]	Is it possible that the end of authority (EoA) in the movement authority MA for the first train (Id = 0) is different from 0?	$E <> MA[0].EoA! = 0$
[2]	Is it possible to reach the state *Integrity_ Confirmed_ By_ Driver* in the automaton "IIMStatusManagement"?	$E <> IIM\_Process\_A\_Integrity$ $\_Confirmed\_By\_Driver$ $\&\&LOC\_AbsTime > 60$
[3]	Is it possible to reach the state *SendTPR* in the automaton "TPRManagement"?	$E <> TPR\_Process\_A.SendTPR$ $\&\&LOC\_AbsTime > 60$
[4]	Is it possible to reach the state *SendMA* in the automaton "MAManagement"?	$E <> MA\_Process\_A.SendMA$ $\&\&LOC\_AbsTime > 60$
[5]	Is it possible to reach the state *Failure_ ACK*" in the automaton "SpeedDistanceSupervision"?	$E <> SDS\_Process\_A.Failure\_ACK$
[6]	Is it possible that the train reaches its destination referenced by 700000?	$E <> (P\_int[0] == 700000$ $\&\&LOC\_AbsTime > 60)$
[7]	How speeds of trains evolve over time?	$simulate\ [LOC\_AbsTime <=$ $300; 1]\{V\_int[0] * 0.1, V\_int[1] * 0.1\}$
[8]	How trains speeds received by train management evolve over time?	$simulate[LOC\_AbsTime <= 300; 1]$ $\{(msgTPRReceived[0].positionReport.$ $V\_TRAIN) * 0.1, (msgTPRReceived[1]$ $.positionReport .V\_TRAIN) * 0.1\}$
[9]	How locations of trains evolve over time?	$simulate\ [LOC\_AbsTime <= 2000; 1]$ $P\_int[0] * 0.1, P\_int[1] * 0.1$

IIM_Process_A, *MA_Process_A*, *TPR_Process_A* are instances of the automata described in Subsect. 3.2 The value of 60, corresponding to 6 s, was necessary for system initialization. **The first property** means that the "MAManagement" automaton receives from "TPRManagement" automaton a train position report and computes accordingly the MA. If $MA[0].EoA == 0$ means that no MA is computed.

For the second property, the reachability of all states for all the automata composing the LTI OS were checked (see Fig. 13).

Focusing on the property: **"it is possible to reach in the automaton "IIMStatusManagement"?"** the state *Integrity_ Confirmed_ By_ Driver*. Its checking requires that condition 2 in Table 1, presented as a guard in the automaton "IIMStatusManagement", is true. $LOC\_AbsTime > 60$ is to express that time has passed, and the initial conditions are no longer valid. Condition 2 (Table 1) seems simple, but implementing and verifying such a condition, requires many interactions between many designed automata. Indeed, *Train is at standstill* means that the speed

Fig. 13. Verification of first 4 local properties using verifier

of the train is 0. This requires an interaction between "TrainMovement_MAIN" automaton, which represents a part of the behavior of train movement, the "TrainLocalizationUnit" automaton, which receives train speed from the "Train-Movement_MAIN" automaton and sends it to the "TPRManagement" automaton. The condition "Valid Train Data is available and has been acknowledged by the RBC" requires an interaction between "TrainDataManagement" automaton, which sends train data to "SpeedDistanceSupervision" automaton, this latter sends it back to "TrainManagement" automaton and waits for acknowledgment. Condition "Train integrity is confirmed by the driver" requires an interaction "Driver" automaton, which issues the channel '*integrityDriver*' received by the automaton "IIMStatusManagement". This example is just to show that verifying some reachability properties requires large interactions between designed models, and it is not a trivial activity.

For **the first four local properties**, they are all satisfied, which means that the composition of the automata works well. A trace has been generated for each satisfied property. All generated traces are checked and they produce the expected behavior.

Property 5 is not satisfied, which means that the system never moves to a failure state. This is the expected behavior. The "TrainManagement", "SpeedDistanceSupervision" and 'TrainDataManagement" automata are involved in this analysis and, hence, are instantiated in system composition to verify the property.

Property 6 can not be verified due to memory exceptions.

For **the last three local properties**, which focus on train movement, two trains are instantiated. For simulate properties, all channels are broadcast.

All trains start at position and speed zero. Positions are defined relative to the first balise: Train 0 starts at 8000 m with a destination at 16000 m, and Train 1 starts at 1000 m with a destination at 13000 m. The braking distance is 5000 m. The last three properties are satisfied.

Figure 14a depicts the speed of both trains over time, highlighting that:

– Both trains accelerate together while a safe braking distance is respected, and then they brake;

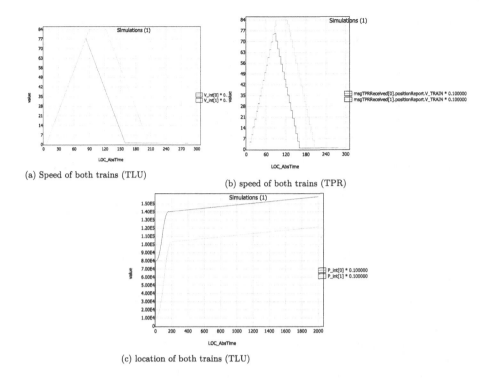

(a) Speed of both trains (TLU)

(b) speed of both trains (TPR)

(c) location of both trains (TLU)

Fig. 14. Simulate properties verification

- The first train begins braking before the second, respectively corresponding to the travelled distances of 8000 m and 12000 m;
- The speed curves are continuous as the speed is updated every 0.1 s.

Fig. 14b depicts the speed of both trains over time as received by train management. The speed curves are represented as step curves because the speed values are updated every 5 s, corresponding to the interval between two position reports.

Figure 14c depicts the location of both trains over time. The curves are continuous since the location is updated each 0.1 s, representing instantaneous positions. The location of the first train approaches 16000 m (its destination), while the location of the second train approaches 13000 m (its destination). This is the expected behavior.

4   Conclusion

In order to overcome the difficulties encountered in modeling complex rail CCS systems using the operating principles of moving blocks, a generic modeling framework leading to semi-formal and formal models and to the analysis of safety-related properties, has been proposed in the work performed during the

Performingrail project. This paper demonstrates the framework's applicability through the development of formal models for the Loss of Train Integrity operational scenario within ERTMS/ETCS L3, leading to the verification of the associated model properties.

Future work will explore additional operational scenarios to enhance the robustness of our models. We will investigate how the provided formal models and their analysis can contribute to safety proofs, thereby participating in the safety assurance of moving block systems.

Acknowledgments. Many thanks to all the partners involved in WP2 of the Performingrail project.

Disclosure of Interests. The authors have no competing interests to declare that are relevant to the content of this article.

References

1. X2Rail-5 deliverable D4.1 - moving block specification—part 3 system specification. Technical report (2022)
2. Alikoc, B., Mutlu, I., Ergenc, A.F.: Stability analysis of train following model with multiple communication delays. IFAC Proc. Vol. **46**(25), 13–18 (2013)
3. Basile, D., ter Beek, M.H., Ferrari, A., Legay, A.: Exploring the ERTMS/ETCS full moving block specification: an experience with formal methods. Int. J. Softw. Tools Technol. Transfer 1–20 (2022). https://doi.org/10.1007/s10009-022-00653-3
4. Basile, D., ter Beek, M.H., Ferrari, A., Legay, A.: Exploring the ERTMS/ETCS full moving block specification: an experience with formal methods. Formal Aspects Comput. (2022)
5. Behrmann, G., et al.: UPPAAL 4.0. In: Proceedings of the 3rd International Conference on Quantitative Evaluation of SysTems (QEST 2006), pp. 125–126. IEEE (2006)
6. Furness, N., van Houten, H., Arenas, L., Bartholomeus, M.: ERTMS level 3: the game-changer. IRSE News **232**, 2–9 (2017)
7. Hause, M., et al.: The SysML modelling language. In: Fifteenth European Systems Engineering Conference, vol. 9, pp. 1–12 (2006)
8. Himrane, O., Beugin, J., Ghazel, M.: Toward formal safety and performance evaluation of GNSS-based railway localisation function. IFAC-PapersOnLine **54**(2), 159–166 (2021)
9. Hoang, T.S., Butler, M., Reichl, K.: The hybrid ERTMS/ETCS level 3 case study. In: International Conference on Abstract State Machines, Alloy, B, TLA, VDM, and Z, pp. 251–261 (2018)
10. SaddemYagoubi, R., Beugin, J., Ghazel, M.: Verification framework for moving block system safety: application on the loss of train integrity use case. In: 11th TRISTAN Conference, pp. 19–25 (2022)
11. UNISIG: ERTMS/ETCS: System Requirements Specification - SUBSET-026, issue 3.6.0 (2016)

Towards a Model for Energy-Efficient and Flexible IoT Systems

Yassmine Gara Hellal[1]([📧])(iD), Lazhar Hamel[2](iD), and Mohamed Graiet[2](iD)

[1] Faculty Of Sciences of Monastir, University Of Monastir, Monastir, Tunisia
garayesmine@gmail.com, yasmine.garahellal@fsm.rnu.tn
[2] ISIMM, University Of Monastir, Monastir, Tunisia

Abstract. Modern IoT systems introduce unique challenges related to flexibility, resource limitations, and energy efficiency. As these IoT systems expand to incorporate more devices, ensuring reliable communication, managing energy consumption, and preventing standoff situations becomes increasingly difficult. This paper proposes a formal model to verify complex IoT systems, addressing key areas: design, coordination, flexibility and energy efficiency. Using the Event-B method, our model enables a gradual refinement of system properties, enhancing both reliability and correctness in IoT systems. The model's validity is further demonstrated through the use of powerful Rodin plugins and tools.

Keywords: IoT Systems · Design · Coordination · Flexibility · Energy Efficiency · Automated Reasoning

1 Introduction

Currently, IoT systems [1] encompass a diverse array of devices to address the evolving needs of users while leveraging technological advancements to create a more interconnected, intelligent, and efficient ecosystem. Despite this progress, the manufacturers often prioritize cost, size, and weight over holding energy and resources when designing IoT devices. Many IoT devices operate over networks characterized by intermittent connectivity, energy limitations, and reliance on battery power or strict energy requirements. Thus, they must carefully manage energy consumption to extend operational lifespan, particularly in remote or hard-to-reach locations [2].

These IoT systems involve numerous small devices that might shut down at any point in time and periodically wake up to execute particular duties. Accordingly, they often require shared cache to offload critical data prior to powering down, which assists in maintaining network connectivity and conserving energy [3]. However, operating under strict energy limits complicates the continuous and adequate functioning, especially for IoT devices requiring energy-intensive communications that quickly deplete energy sources and decrease system efficiency. Shared caches [2] should offer flexibility and energy efficiency to manage the amplified needs of IoT devices and improve the overall outcome. Energy efficiency is introduced as the ability to supply optimal use of energy resources and perform IoT interactions while minimizing power consumption and ensuring the system's sustainability. Flexibility refers to redunding shared caches in case of intense load and to adjust voltage and frequency levels of IoT devices (or their processors) based on the load to retain optimal operation.

In this context, modeling IoT systems with formal methods can provide guarantees on properties like reliability, flexibility, and energy efficiency in device interactions. We propose a model using the Event-B technique [4] that facilitates incremental model refinement and verification through mathematical proof obligations (POs) [4]. This paper outlines our methodology, structured into many verification tiers—design, coordination, and flexibility—energyEfficiency-ensuring that these systems' features are both effective and verifiable.

The below sections are arranged as follows: Sect. 2 discusses the key challenges in IoT systems, while Sect. 3 inspects prior studies. Section 4 outlines IoT systems requirements, and Sect. 5 affords a recap of Event-B. Section 6 reveals our suggested model, followed by a detailed verification and validation process in Sect. 7. Finally, Sect. 8 concludes with suggestions for future work.

2   Illustrative Example

To illustrate the challenges of IoT systems, we use a Collision Tracking System (CTS) designed to assess situations where a vehicle might be in danger of a collision. The CTS involves devices operating under restricted energy conditions that are required to interact in real time, continuously sharing critical data like vehicle positions, speed, and proximity to other objects. They must operate reliably to detect potential collisions promptly, ensuring timely responses to avoid accidents. In such setups, smaller devices should often leverage additional resources (e,g., processor voltage) to handle communication across the network and with external services while minimizing energy-intensive operations.

As the number of IoT devices proliferates, shared caches face potential issues when attempting to offload the data of energy-limited devices that may shut down at any moment. This situation becomes critical in IoT systems, as it directly impacts network efficiency, energy usage, and delay management. Specifically, challenges include:

- Non-Flexibility: As devices increase, non-flexible shared caches may lead to network congestion or energy drain as additional devices compete for limited shared cache resources. For example, adding more sensors to track additional collision metrics may overload a shared cache device.
- Shared Caches Disputes: Shared caches can only offload the data of a limited number of energy-restricted devices. When this bound is reached, additional data cannot be offloaded, leading to communication and energy management issues.
- Design Limits: IoT devices vary widely in energy capabilities, making direct communication challenging.

To address these challenges, we propose a model for IoT systems, focusing on flexible communication structures within IoT networks. The model incorporates mechanisms to balance energy consumption with network load, ensuring long-term operation and reliable device interaction. As shown in Fig. 1, the Collision Tracking System (CTS) comprises *Gyroscope*, *Accelerometer*, and *Ultrasonic* sensors that are categorized as Event energy-limited, meaning they remain in an off state until triggered by specific events and possess only a minimal energy reserve, sufficient for executing targeted duties. The following sensors and actuators are involved in the CTS:

- *Ultrasonic Sensor*: It detects the presence and proximity of objects in real-time, which is essential for preventing collisions.
- *Gyroscope Sensor*: It monitors movement, orientation, and angular velocity of objects or vehicles involved in a potential collision.
- *Accelerometer Sensor*: It tracks changes in velocity that may indicate a collision.
- *Electric Motor Actuator*: It is activated when the acceleration measurement exceeds around 4 g, which might indicate a significant impact or sudden stop.
- *Hydraulic Brake Actuator*: It is enforced when the ultrasonic detects an object within a critical distance threshold, usually 1 to 2 m.
- *Electro-Mechanical Actuator*: It engages if the gyroscope sensor value surpasses 20–30 degrees per second.

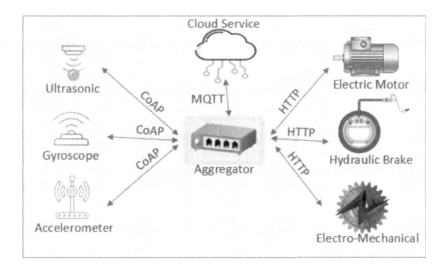

Fig. 1. *IoT-Based Collision Tracking System*

3   State of the Art

Recently, some studies have explored IoT systems, particularly with a focus on optimizing energy efficiency. This section examines significant contributions and key advancements within this domain.

In [5] a model for distribution management systems incorporating IoT and formal methods. However, the reliance on traditional models, like NFA and UML, may limit the ability to address evolving system complexities in dynamic smart grid environments. Besides, this work does not examine the energy needs of IoT systems.

In [6], the UPPAAL model-checking and formal simulation framework have been adopted to evaluate energy harvesting strategies for IoT systems and to capture their key aspects. Meanwhile, it addresses a critical gap in extending the energy profiles and operational lifespan of IoT devices while also tackling the unpredictability of environmental energy sources. This framework paves the way toward a potentially battery-independent energy solution. Real-world IoT calibrations have been used to demonstrate the framework's applicability to diverse energy harvesting configurations. In summary, this energy-focused framework is able to establish a robust foundation for assessing IoT energy harvesting. However, it may be limited in addressing system-level outcome fluctuations that arise under varying operational demands, especially in more complex or limited IoT ecosystems that require voltage adjustments.

The [7] introduces a fully digitized workflow aimed at ensuring the energy efficiency and significantly enhancing the accuracy of large-scale HVAC systems [8]. The proposed workflow integrates a developed Control Description Language (CDL) as a declarative language with existing building standards to streamline the design, formal verification, code generation, and simulation-based testing of HVAC control sequences against digital specifications. While this approach is effective for annual energy management and targets significant improvements in HVAC systems, several limitations persist. The essential challenges stem from the focus on HVAC systems and the lack of fine-grained modeling for IoT systems, which require substantial adaptation of the proposed methodology to be applicable to diverse and general-purpose IoT systems.

The [9] focuses on sustaining energy needs for IoT systems and tailoring probabilistic energy models for hybrid energy harvesting (HEH) nodes within IoT systems. As single-source energy harvesters often fail to meet the energy demands of practical IoT setups, the study emphasizes the combination of multiple energy harvesters in a unified probabilistic framework, using Gaussian mixture models (GMMs). This encapsulates the randomness and variability of ambient energy by capturing energy clusters (ESCs) based on joint distributions of both independent and correlated energy sources. A key shortcoming of this proposal is that it relies on probabilistic models to predict energy availability without explicitly implementing a formal verification framework to ensure reliability while managing energy under fluctuating environmental conditions.

In [10–12] the authors propose energy-aware methods, such as Contiki OS's power track module, that monitor and offer bounds for energy consumption to prolong the lifespan across various battery-powered IoT devices. The [10] is primarily directed at (i) identifying factors impacting energy consumption and (ii) verifying and predicting energy usage against the system's energy efficiency requirements, through the Behavior-Interaction-Priority (BIP) framework. By applying statistical model checking, the [11] formally sets precise bounds on energy consumption for specific device duties (e.g., radio interface) in order to assess how well IoT devices meet lifetime requirements. In [12], the authors use a systematic methodology to investigate formal methods, simulations and measurements with the aim of identifying if IoT devices consume less energy. While these approaches are useful for pre-deployment validation, they may not incorporate a voltage scaling mechanism, which is essential for continuously enhancing energy efficiency, especially in systems with stringent energy limits.

In [13,14], the authors initially propose a two-level model addressing mediation and horizontal scalability in IoT systems to highlight the role of intermediaries during the execution of IoT applications. Building on this, the second study later extends the prior work that presents a more granular four-level approach, covering architectural, behavioral, mobility, and scalability aspects. This scope extension offers a deeper view to address key concerns such as adaptability in evolving IoT environments. Although these studies advance scalability across multiple dimensions, our novel work diverges these efforts by integrating voltage scaling as a complementary and critical factor in enhancing energy efficiency and sustainability within IoT environments.

The [15] explores digital design methodologies using commercial CAD tools to optimize outcome and versatility tradeoffs beyond the limits of conventional wide voltage scaling. This book mainly addresses general hardware design adaptability for broader applications. However, our research goes further by formally targeting the specific needs of IoT systems, such as continuous power management, aiming for energy optimization at runtime.

Our approach addresses these gaps by integrating design, coordination, flexibility and energy management verification within a single framework using Event-B. By leveraging Event-B's refinement capabilities and proof obligations, our model incrementally manages state complexity while providing formal guarantees on energy efficiency, and correctness. This approach offers a comprehensive solution for IoT systems, combining proof-based verification with model checking for robust IoT design.

4   Modeling Requirements

To ensure reliability, flexibility and energy efficiency in IoT systems, we identify and formalize three core modeling requirements:

1. Design Requirements: IoT systems often operate in environments where network configurations vary significantly. A low-power network consists of devices that are limited in available energy as opposed to (or in addition to) being limited in available power and encounter additional limitations like intermittent

connectivity. Based on IETF Working Group documents, IoT devices are categorized based on energy capabilities. Devices in category E9 have no direct quantitative limitations to available energy. For devices with a finite energy supply over their operational lifetime, such as those with non-replaceable primary batteries, they fall under category E2 (Lifetime energy-limited). When energy limitations apply within specific timeframes, like periodic battery replacement, devices are classified as E1 (Period energy-limited). Lastly, devices limited to a set amount of energy for single events are designated as E0 (Event energy-limited).

2. Coordination Requirements: In IoT systems, the devices frequently rely on shared caches to enable reliable data exchange and synchronization across varied protocols and to ensure seamless communication between devices with differing resources and energy limits. For example, in a Collision Tracking System, the event energy-limited sensors (E0 highly energy-limited) might be energy-depleted at any moment, and data stored locally could be lost. Thus, they require shared caches to offload critical information before shutting down and efficiently relay collision data to more resource-rich devices. These requirements thus stipulate that shared caches facilitate communication based on device capabilities while minimizing delays.

3. Flexibility and Energy Efficiency Requirements: The rapid growth in IoT systems demands mechanisms to add more shared caches or increase processor voltage and frequency when needed, while optimizing energy consumption. These mechanisms will allow for additional shared caches when existing ones reach their upper bound, which prevents single points of failure and maintains reliable communication within the IoT systems. Our model includes requirements that govern when the amount of voltage, frequency, and shared caches should be increased or decreased based on system load, ensuring energy efficiency through Dynamic Voltage Scaling (DVS) and selective device activation.

Table 1 shows the design, coordination, and flexibility requirements of IoT systems. The requirements were defined based on the documents produced by the IETF WG [2,16]. They are also applicable for other forms (e.g., gateway). The gateways, while essential for routing traffic between systems and the general internet, are not optimized for the lightweight duties required for such systems.

Table 1. Design, Coordination and Flexibility Requirements

D1	An IoT system consists of devices that are categorized as E0 (*Event* energy-limited), E1 (*Period* energy-limited), E2 (*Lifetime* energy-limited), E9 (*Unlimited*), and *shared cache* devices
C1	If a device is *Event* or (*Period* energy-limited) and in a sleep mode), a *shared cache* must offload the device data
C2	If a device is *Unlimited*, a shared cache is not required
F1	When the load reaches a specified bound, the *voltage levels* of the processor shall be adjusted and enlarged based on the load to retain optimal operation
F2	The *shared caches* should redund in case of intense load

In spite of the advancements achieved in the last few years, IoT devices [1], especially sensor-like motes, may not afford to consume excessive energy [17, 18]. Besides, IoT devices may still face significant limitations regarding available energy throughout their usable lifetime [19]. In fact, they are designed to be compact and low-cost, which often leads to the use of smaller energy supplies that may not inherently provide sufficient energy density or longevity. However, most IoT devices require energy-intensive communications with cloud services or other devices to transmit complex data over long distances, which can quickly deplete ambient energy sources. In light of this, deploying sophisticated energy optimization strategies [20, 21] is crucial to ensuring the system's sustainability and durability, especially in hard-to-reach environments where frequent battery replacement is impractical. Energy efficiency pertains to cutting down on energy consumption or to extending the device's operational lifespan without compromising outcome. This will prevent spikes in energy demand and allow IoT devices to communicate across dense IoT systems with relatively high traffic without overwhelming the system's power budget.

To meet these objectives, we define a series of key requirements to optimize energy efficiency and flexibility. These requirements ensure that the system adapts to varying environmental conditions and fault scenarios while maintaining an optimal balance between energy consumption and outcome degradation. Table 2 provides a clear roadmap for implementing an energy-efficient and flexible IoT system.

Table 2. Energy Efficiency and Flexibility Requirement

F3	An IoT system must minimize the overall energy consumption to ensure prolonged battery life. This is achieved through the optimization technique of Dynamic Voltage Scaling (DVS) [22]
EE1	An IoT system must enforce that outcome deterioration remains within the lowest allowable threshold during the process of energy optimization
EE2	An IoT device should manage Pareto [23] data compression and aggregation locally or at the broker level to reduce communication delays along with energy enhancements
EE3	An IoT device should be able to trigger energy harvesting mechanisms (e.g., Stochastic Poisson [24]) when available to handle fluctuating energy streams
EE4	An IoT system must employ MDP-based adaptive duty cycling [25] to ensure the system's availability while applying energy optimization techniques

5   General View of Event-B

Event-B [4] is a formal method grounded in set theory, widely used to design and verify complex systems. Its structured approach combines formal verification and model refinement, allowing complex system properties to be decomposed incrementally.

In Event-B, models are divided into contexts and machines:

- Contexts define static elements, such as carrier sets, axioms, and theorems to capture system properties. In this work, contexts specify IoT system structures, device types, and inter-device relationships.
- Machines represent the dynamic aspects of the model, incorporating variables, invariants, and events. Events are triggered by guards and define state changes, enabling the representation of system behavior.

Event-B's refinement process allows models to evolve from abstract representations to more concrete implementations, enabling step-by-step validation of each refinement level. Proof obligations (POs) [26] generated by the Event-B model ensure that each event respects system invariants, while built-in tools like the Rodin platform automate proof and validation. Additionally, ProB provides animation capabilities to simulate system attitude and verify attitude across IoT scenarios. This makes Event-B a robust choice for verifying flexibility and energy efficiency in IoT systems.

6   The Suggested Model

Our model uses Event-B to support the construction and gradual verification of a model for complex IoT systems. The model satisfies Design, Coordination, and Flexibility requirements, while also integrating Energy Efficiency aspects.

6.1   Design Sub-model

The Design sub-model lays the groundwork for the design of IoT systems, defining essential elements such as *Lifetime* energy-limited devices and shared caches. This model ensures that the IoT system architecture aligns with core requirements for flexible and energy-efficient operations, incorporating networks, each containing a mix of energy-limited and unlimited devices.

The *"Design_Context"* in Event-B introduces these IoT components as sets, while relationships between devices are defined through constants like *EnergyLevel*. The *"Design_Machine"* introduces dynamic elements, modeling the attitude of these devices. This stage captures the static and dynamic requirements, verified through invariants that maintain network consistency and validate device categorization. The formalization of *"Design_Context"* and *"Design_Machine"* is available in [13].

6.2   Coordination Sub-model

The Coordination sub-model extends the design foundation by defining how devices interact through shared caches to communicate efficiently while considering energy restraints. It introduces events to address cases where energy-limited devices require shared caches to offload data before powering down.

Key events in this model include [13]:

– *'SharedCacheParticipation'*: This event triggers coordinator delegation for energy-restricted devices unable to communicate directly, conserving energy by managing communication via shared caches, and ensuring energy efficiency by limiting redundant communications.

The *"Coordination_Context"* adds the set *client*, and the constant *cacheSpace* that denotes the available space of a given cache. This context is seen by the refined *"Coordination_Machine"* where we introduce *cacheSharing* that indicates the number of devices shared by a *cache*. Finally, the boolean *Caching* is set to TRUE when a *cache* engages in an interaction to offload data.

Figure 2 shows the *'SharedCacheParticipation'* event. A *sharedcache* relocates the device data ($cache = TRUE$) if **C1** is respected as follows (**"grd2"**): The *client* is categorized as *Event* energy-limited (E0) or it is *Period* energy-limited (E1), but it is in a sleep mode. Nevertheless, a device that communicates directly without the engagement of shared caches, with respect to **C2** ($cache = FALSE$), should meet the requirement modeled in (**"grd1"**). Once activated, this event evaluates the variable *Caching* (**"act1"**).

6.3   Flexibility and Energy Efficiency Sub-model

The Flexibility and Energy sub-model builds on the previous layer by adding mechanisms for flexibility and energy management. This sub-model allows IoT systems to dynamically add voltage or shared caches based on load and incorporates Dynamic Voltage Scaling (DVS) to optimize energy use. We build upon the existing formalization to develop a formal sub-model for flexible and energy-efficient IoT systems.

The flexibility mechanism is a procedure termed *'InvolveNovelSharedCache'* (see Fig. 3). To implement this, we develop the *"Flexibility_Context"* to introduce the constant *novelCache* that expresses the shared *caches* to involve.

$$
\begin{array}{|l|}
\hline
\textbf{SharedCacheParticipation} \;\widehat{=}\; \\
\textbf{ANY } cache \\
\textbf{WHERE} \\
\text{grd1}: Energylevel[\{Unlimited\}]^{-1} \neq \{client\} \\
\qquad \vee (client \subseteq Energylevel[\{Period\}]^{-1}) \\
\qquad \Rightarrow cache = FALSE \\
\text{grd2}: \{client\} \subseteq Energylevel[\{Event\}]^{-1} \\
\qquad \wedge (\{client\} \subseteq Energylevel[\{Period\}]^{-1}) \\
\qquad \Rightarrow cache = TRUE \\
\textbf{THEN} \\
\qquad \text{act1}: Caching := cache \\
\textbf{END} \\
\hline
\end{array}
$$

Fig. 2. The event *'SharedCacheParticipation'*

The context is seen by *"Flexibility_Machine"* where we declare the variable *involvedCache* that refers to the novel involved *caches*. The variable *upperBound* denotes the boundary beyond which it becomes feasible to involve a novel *cache* (**"act1"**), in respect to the requirement **F2**.

InvolveNovelSharedCache $\hat{=}$
ANY clogged invol
WHERE
grd1: $clogged \in ran(novelCache) \land$
$\quad cacheSharing(clogged) >$
$\quad\quad\quad upperBound(clogged) + cacheSpace(clogged)$
grd2: $invol \in novelCache[\{clogged\}]^{-1}$
THEN
$\quad$ act1: $involvedCache(invol) := clogged$
END

Fig. 3. The event *'InvolveNovelSharedCache'*

At this stage, we present in Fig. 4 our proposed model that consists of two hierarchical levels: the *Energy Efficiency* level and the *Flexibility* level. The first abstraction level establishes foundational concepts and restrictions for managing energy consumption in IoT systems across operations. Building upon this, the second level introduces more concrete specifications, where the abstract definitions and parameters from the previous level are extended and translated into a dynamic voltage scaling technique. Through this refinement, the voltage adjustment mechanism is incorporated in a way that aligns with the *energy efficiency* objectives, enabling the system to achieve optimal or minimal energy consumption while maintaining system *flexibility* and *stability*.

Commonly, diverse techniques such as *energy harvesting* contribute to achieving *energy efficiency*, particularly in IoT systems where battery life and autonomy are critical. Energy efficiency refers to the ability of IoT systems to exploit

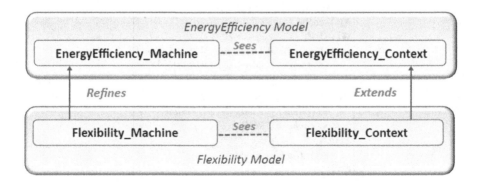

Fig. 4. *The suggested Energy Efficency and Flexibility Model for IoT Systems*

the harvested energy optimally, reducing waste and minimizing consumption. High energy efficiency ensures that harvested energy is utilized effectively, maximizing operational time and reducing dependency on external power sources. Therefore, the more energy-efficient an IoT device is, the more it can rely on harvested energy to enhance the overall functionality and sustainability of IoT systems. To model energy-efficient IoT systems using the Poisson process [27], we preliminary create in the first abstraction level the *"Energyefficiency_Context"* (Fig. 5), where we define the finite set *lambda* (**"axm1"**, **"axm2"**) that represents the average positive rates of energy arrival events for each point in time. Plus, the constant *peak* that denotes the maximum allowable energy (positive integer) to be harvested (**"axm3"**). The *"Energyefficiency_Context"* is seen by the *"Energyefficiency_Machine"*, where we define the variable *energyLevel* (**"inv1"**) that tracks the current energy stored in the system, restricted by *peak*. The **"inv1"** enforces barriers on the variable *energyLevel* to ensure it does not exceed the maximum energy capacity *peak* and is always non-negative. Besides, the **"inv2"** ensures the Poisson rate parameter remains positive within the machine.

```
CONTEXT EnergyEfficiency_Context
SETS
lambda peak
AXIOMS
axm1 : finite(lambda) ∧ finite(peak)
axm2 : lambda ∈ ℝ ∧ lambda > 0
axm3 : peak ∈ ℕ ∧ peak > 0
END
```

```
MACHINE EnergyEfficiency_Machine
SEES EnergyEfficiency_Context
VARIABLES
energyLevel
INVARIANTS
inv1 : energyLevel ∈ ℕ ∧ peak ≥ energyLevel
inv2 : lambda > 0
END
```

Fig. 5. The Event-B $EnergyEfficiency\_Context$ and $EnergyEfficiency\_Machine$

The event *'EnergyHarvest'* (see Fig. 6) models the actual harvesting process in respect to the requirement **EE3**. The (**"grd1"**) ensures energy is harvested only if capacity is not yet full. It only triggers if *energyLevel* is below *peak*. When the event occurs, it increases *energyLevel* by an amount following a Poisson distribution with mean lambda, ensuring it does not surpass *peak*. When triggered, the *energyLevel* is increased by an amount generated by a Poisson distribution with a mean *lambda*, but it cannot surpass *peak* (**"act1"**).

```
EnergyHarvest ≘
WHERE
grd1: energyLevel < peak
THEN
    act1: energyLevel := min(energyLevel + randomPoisson(lambda), peak)
END
```

Fig. 6. The event *'EnergyHarvest'*

Typically, achieving flexibility in IoT systems depends on the ability to implement a Dynamic Voltage Scaling (*DVS*) mechanism that enables the IoT system to fine-tune and adjust its computational resources (e.g., processor speed, voltage) according to varying real-time workload demands. In this context, IoT devices (or their processors) must adapt by regulating their operating voltage and frequency levels when the workload fluctuates or its conditions shift. This ensures that peak or optimal outcome is delivered during intensive tasks while energy consumption is minimized when demand decreases, conserving energy during low-demand periods. The dynamic adjustment method allows IoT devices to efficiently balance power levels based on real-time demands, optimizing resource use without sacrificing system responsiveness. In this context, we develop the *"Flexibility_Context"* (Fig. 7) to introduce the finite sets *Frequencies* and *Voltages* that denote respectively the possible or allowable frequency and voltage levels from the minimum to the maximum values (**"axm1"**). To each frequency, we have associated its corresponding valid voltage ranges denoted by the partial function *FreqVolts* (**"axm2"**), while ensuring that frequencies and voltages are non-negatives and checking the valid mapping between them. This latter is modeled through a partial function because not every frequency necessarily maps to a voltage in a practical system. This allows for some flexibility if certain frequencies are not supported. Subsequently, we have defined the set of *Duties* the device (or processor) might be running as well as their durations, respectively, via surjective relations termed *DeviceDuties* (**"axm3"**) and *dutyDuration* (**"axm4"**). Finally, we have defined the constant *EnergyProfile* that presents a mapping between frequency levels and power consumption rates while checking the consistency of the energy budget (**"axm5"**). The detailed *"Flexibility_Context"* is seen by the *"Flexibility_Machine"* where we define the variable *totalEnergy* that denotes the total energy consumed by the overall IoT system so far. **"inv1"** ensures the total energy is not decreasing. The variable *LowLimit* (**"inv2"**) denotes the limit over which the scaling of voltage should be performed to optimize the whole energy consumption. We have also defined the power consumption of a given device through a total relation called *PowConsump* (**"inv3"**). Finally, we define the variables *actualDevVoltage* and *actualDevFrequency* that denote the current voltage (**"inv5"**) and frequency (**"inv4"**) of the IoT device or processor, and we check that they are always within valid ranges.

CONTEXT Flexibility_Context	MACHINE Flexibility_Machine
EXTENDS EnergyEfficiency_Context	REFINES EnergyEfficiency_Machine
SETS	SEES Flexibility_Context
Frequencies Voltages Duties	VARIABLES
CONSTANTS	*actualDevVoltage LowLimit PowConsump*
dutyDuration FreqVolts EnergyProfile	*totalEnergy actualDevFrequency*
AXIOMS	INVARIANTS
axm1 : *finite(Frequencies)* ∧ *finite(Voltages)* ∧ *finite(Duties)*	inv1 : *totalEnergy* ∈ *Devices* ⇸ ℝ ∧*ran(totalEnergy)* ≥ 0 ∧∀*dev · dev* ∈ *dom(totalEnergy)* ⇒ (∃*d, p.(d* ↦ *p* ∈ *PowConsump* ↔ {*d*} = *dev* ∧ {*d*} ≠ ∅))
axm2 : *FreqVolts* ∈ *Frequencies* ⇸ *Voltages* ∧∀*f,v.(f* ↦ *v* ∈ *FreqVolts* ⇒ {*f*} ≥ 0 ∧ {*v*} ≥ 0 ∧ {*v*} ∈ *Voltages)*	inv2 : *LowLimit* ∈ *dom(totalEnergy)* → ℝ
axm3 : *DeviceDuties* ∈ *Devices* ⇸ ℝ	inv3 : *PowConsump* ∈ *Devices* ↔ ℝ
axm4 : *dutyDuration* ∈ *Duties* ⇸ ℕ	inv4 : *actualDevFrequency* ∈ *dom(Frequencies)*
axm5 : *EnergyProfile* ∈ *dom(PowConsump)* ⇸ *Frequencies* ∧∀*f.(f* ∈ *ran(EnergyProfile)* ⇒ *EnergyProfile*[{*f*}]⁻¹ > 0)	inv5 : *actualDevVoltage* ∈ *FreqVolts(actualDevFrequency)*
END	END

Fig. 7. The Event-B *Flexibility_Context* and *Flexibility_Machine*

When an IoT device becomes passive (**"grd2"**), the event *'OptimizeEnergyEfficiencyDVScaling'* should be automatically activated (see Fig. 8). This event minimizes the energy consumption of the IoT device as the duty progresses (**"grd1"**) based on the current frequency and voltage, while covering the requirements **F1-F3**. The (**"grd2"**) indicates that a low workload should trigger the voltage scaling. Mainly, the *PowConsump* of an IoT device or processor is approximately proportional to the square of the current voltage *actualDevVoltage* and the frequency *actualDevFrequency*. The *totalEnergy* is the integral of power over time. The (**"grd4"**) minimizes energy consumption by solving the following optimization: Minimize E = $\left[\int_0^T C \cdot V^2 \cdot actualDevFrequency\, dT\right]$ (where C is the capacitance). Once triggered, this event updates the power consumption *PowConsump* based on the new voltage level that solves optimization for minimum energy over time (**"act1:"**). Besides, the total energy consumption is updated as the duty progresses, based on the current frequency and the minimum gate-to-source voltage GSV (**"act2"**).

7 Model Assessment: Verification and Validation

To ensure the correctness and reliability of our model, we used the following two-step process.

OptimizeEnergyEfficiencyDVScaling $\hat{=}$
ANY passive V voltageLevel Capacitance
WHERE
grd1: $ran(dutyDuration) > 0$
grd2: $passive \in dom(PowConsump) \wedge passive \in dom(totalEnergy)$
$\wedge deviceDuties(passive) <$
$totalEnergy(passive) \times PowConsump(passive) + LowLimit(passive)$
grd3: $V = actualDevVoltage$
grd4: $voltageLevel := \text{argmin}_V \left[\int_0^T Capacitance \cdot V^2 \cdot actualDevFrequency\, dT \right]$
THEN
act1: $PowConsump(passive) := Capacitance \times ran(voltageLevel)^2 \times actualDevFrequency$
act2: $totalEnergy := totalEnergy + EnergyProfile(actualDevFrequency) \times dutyDuration$
END

Fig. 8. The event *'OptimizeEnergyEfficiencyDVScaling'*

7.1 Model Verification

Event-B's proof obligations (POs) provide a formal mechanism for verifying system properties. For our model, 53 POs were synthesized, covering critical aspects such as:

– Invariant Preservation: Verifying that each event sustains defined invariants, ensuring that design, coordination, flexibility and energy limits are respected.
– Well-Definedness: Ensuring that axioms, guards, and actions are well-defined, preventing illogical or undefined attitude.

Around 75% of the POs were automatically released, with the remainder verified manually to address complex logical steps. These POs confirmed consistency across refinements, ensuring each event adhered to system invariants.

7.2 Model Validation

To validate changes in attitude under different conditions, we used the ProB tool to simulate multiple scenarios. For instance, in the Collision Tracking System (CTS) scenario, we simulated the interactions between the ultrasonic sensor and the aggregator, examining flexibility and energy efficiency mechanisms. Key scenarios included:

– Shared Cache Assignment and Data Management: Ensuring shared caches manage solicitations and conserve energy by offloading data based on current load.
– Dispute Resolution: Validating that clogged shared caches reassign data or involve novel instances to maintain outcome.
– Energy Efficiency Adaptations: Simulating DVS voltage adjustments to confirm energy-saving behaviors under low-demand conditions.

8   Conclusion

This paper contributes a sophisticated model to verify flexible and energy-efficient IoT systems without drawing excessive instantaneous energy consumption. Our model provides a robust framework for IoT devices, ensuring that they stay within reliable, flexible, and sustainable operation without draining their power supplies.

Verification by proof obligations confirmed design and conduct-related correctness, while the powerful ProB plugin validated flexibility and energy mechanisms under different conditions. In future work, we plan to explore adaptive voltage and frequency scaling mechanisms in practical IoT environments. By addressing real-world limits, we aim to bridge the gap between theoretical modeling and practical solutions that respond to device demand and optimize energy consumption.

References

1. Rjoub, G., Abdel Wahab, O., Bentahar, J., Bataineh, A.: A trust and energy-aware double deep reinforcement learning scheduling strategy for federated learning on IoT devices. In: Kafeza, E., Benatallah, B., Martinelli, F., Hacid, H., Bouguettaya, A., Motahari, H. (eds.) ICSOC 2020. LNCS, vol. 12571, pp. 319–333. Springer, Cham (2020). https://doi.org/10.1007/978-3-030-65310-1_23
2. Bormann, C., Ersue, M., Keranen, A.: Terminology for constrained-node networks. Technical report (2014)
3. Wang, S., Chen, H., Wang, Y.: Collaborative caching for energy optimization in content-centric Internet of Things. IEEE Trans. Comput. Soc. Syst. **9**(1), 230–238 (2021)
4. Abrial, J.R.: Modeling in Event-B: System and Software Engineering. Cambridge University Press, Cambridge (2010)
5. Kousar, S., Zafar, N.A., Ali, T., Alkhammash, E.H., Hadjouni, M.: Formal modeling of IoT-based distribution management system for smart grids. Sustainability **14**(8), 4499 (2022)
6. Hafaiedh, I.B., Gafsi, A., Yahyaoui, M.Y., Aouinette, Y.: A model-based approach for formal verification and performance evaluation of energy harvesting architectures in IoT systems: a case study of a long-term healthcare application. Simul. Model. Pract. Theory **136**, 102990 (2024)
7. Wetter, M., et al.: OpenBuildingControl: digitizing the control delivery from building energy modeling to specification, implementation and formal verification. Energy **238**, 121501 (2022)
8. Ni, H.P., Chong, W.O., Chou, J.S.: Optimizing HVAC systems for semiconductor fabrication: a data-intensive framework for energy efficiency and sustainability. J. Build. Eng., 109397 (2024)
9. Dogay Altinel and Gunes Karabulut Kurt: Modeling of multiple energy sources for hybrid energy harvesting IoT systems. IEEE Internet Things J. **6**(6), 10846–10854 (2019)
10. Lekidis, A., Katsaros, P.: Model-based design of energy-efficient applications for IoT systems. arXiv preprint: arXiv:1807.01242 (2018)

11. Demigha, O., Khalfi, C.: Formal analysis of energy consumption in IoT systems. In: IoTBDS, pp. 103–114 (2019)
12. Oliveira, L.P., da Silva, A.W.N., de Azevedo, L.P., da Silva, M.V.L.: Formal methods to analyze energy efficiency and security for IoT: a systematic review. In: International Conference on Advanced Information Networking and Applications, pp. 270–279. Springer (2021)
13. Gara Hellal, Y., Hamel, L., Graiet, M.: An Event-B based approach for horizontally scalable IoT applications. In: Service-Oriented Computing: 22nd International Conference, ICSOC 2024, Tunis, Tunisia, December 3–6, 2024, Proceedings 22. Springer (2024)
14. Gara Hellal, Y., Hamel, L., Graiet, M.: A formal approach for scalable applications in dynamic and constrained IoT-Cloud systems. Computing (2025)
15. Jain, S., Lin, L., Alioto, M.: Conclusions. In: Adaptive Digital Circuits for Power-Performance Range beyond Wide Voltage Scaling, pp. 145–148. Springer, Cham (2020). https://doi.org/10.1007/978-3-030-38796-9_6
16. Shelby, Z., et al.: The Constrained Application Protocol (CoAP). RFC 7252 (2014)
17. Elhabbash, A., Elkhatib, Y.: Energy-aware placement of device-to-device mediation services in IoT systems. In: Hacid, H., Kao, O., Mecella, M., Moha, N., Paik, H. (eds.) ICSOC 2021. LNCS, vol. 13121, pp. 335–350. Springer, Cham (2021). https://doi.org/10.1007/978-3-030-91431-8_21
18. Aslanpour, M.S., Toosi, A.N., Cheema, M.A., Gaire, R.: Energy-aware resource scheduling for serverless edge computing. In: 2022 22nd IEEE International Symposium on Cluster, Cloud and Internet Computing (CCGrid), pp. 190–199. IEEE (2022)
19. Gara Hellal, Y., Hamel, L., Graiet, M., Balouek, D.: A formal modeling and verification approach for IoT-Cloud resource-oriented applications. In: 2024 IEEE 24th International Symposium on Cluster, Cloud and Internet Computing (CCGrid), pp. 347–356. IEEE (2024)
20. Humayun, M., Alsaqer, M.S., Jhanjhi, N.: Energy optimization for smart cities using IoT. Appl. Artif. Intell. 36(1), 2037255 (2022)
21. Heidari, E.: A novel energy-aware method for clustering and routing in IoT based on whale optimization algorithm & Harris Hawks optimization. Computing 106(3), 1013–1045 (2024)
22. Khriji, S., Chéour, R., Kanoun, O.: Dynamic voltage and frequency scaling and duty-cycling for ultra low-power wireless sensor nodes. Electronics 11(24), 4071 (2022)
23. Liu, L., Wang, A., Sun, G., Li, J.: Multiobjective optimization for improving throughput and energy efficiency in UAV-enabled IoT. IEEE Internet Things J. 9(20), 20763–20777 (2022)
24. Chu, M., Liu, A., Chen, J., Lau, V.K., Cui, S.: A stochastic geometry analysis for energy-harvesting-based device-to-device communication. IEEE Internet Things J. 9(2), 1591–1607 (2021)
25. Charef, N.: Energy sustainable reinforcement learning-based adaptive duty-cycling in wireless sensor networks-based internet of things networks (2023)
26. Abrial, J.-R., et al.: Rodin: an open toolset for modelling and reasoning in Event-B. Int. J. Softw. Tools Technol. Transfer 12, 447–466 (2010)
27. Ruíz-Guirola, D.E., LA López, O., Montejo-Sánchez, S., Mayorga, I.L., Han, Z., Popovski, P.: Intelligent duty cycling management and wake-up for energy harvesting IoT networks with correlated activity. arXiv preprint: arXiv:2405.06372 (2024)

Integrating SysML and Timed Reo to Model and Verify Cyber-Physical Systems Interactions with Timing Constraints

Perla Tannoury$^{(\boxtimes)}$ and Ahmed Hammad

University of Bourgogne Franche-Comté, France FEMTO-ST Institute
- UMR CNRS 6174, Besançon, France
{perla.tannoury,ahammad}@femto-st.fr

Abstract. Modeling Cyber-Physical Systems (CPS) with timing constraints is challenging due to the complexity of their component behaviors. We propose "Timed SysReo", a novel modeling language that extends SysML with Timed Reo to capture CPS architecture and timed interactions. Timed SysReo uses Timed Reo Internal Block Diagrams (Timed Reo IBD) and Timed SysReo Sequence Diagrams (TSRSD) to detail component interactions and message flows. Since direct formal verification of requirements in TSRSD is impractical, we automate the transformation of TSRSD into Timed Constraint Automata (TCA) using ATL rules. Requirements are expressed in Timed Scheduled-Data-Stream Logic (TSDSL), enhancing precision and rigor in CPS verification. We illustrate the efficacy of our approach through a case study involving a Smart Medical Bed (SMB).

Keywords: CPS · SysML · Timed Reo · Timed SysReo · TCA · ATL

1 Introduction

Cyber-physical systems (CPSs) are composed of software and physical components that constantly interact with one another [14]. These systems find application across various domains such as smart cities, healthcare, and autonomous vehicles [5,20,24]. Efficient modeling of CPSs is crucial for understanding and verifying functional properties, particularly in critical domains. However, modeling CPS structures and interactions with timing constraints adds complexity and challenges, risking significant errors, especially in vital sectors like emergency response and healthcare.

Several languages and formalisms are used in CPS modeling [6,10,17]. In our study, we opted for the System Modeling Language (SysML) [19] due to its capability to model heterogeneous systems, integrating both software and hardware components. SysML enhances stakeholder understanding by modeling system architecture, behavior, and requirements. In SysML, interactions between components are modeled using Internal Block Diagram (IBD) and Sequence Diagram (SD). However, these interactions adopt an "endogenous" coordination approach which complicates design and reduces "reusability", increasing project costs. Moreover, while SysML proficiently models CPS, it may not fully address formal specification and verification of intricate component interactions with timing constraints.

Alternatively, the "exogenous" coordination approach, which embeds coordination logic within connectors, is gaining traction among researchers [2,13,16]. This method enhances reusability and simplifies design. Timed Reo, as employed by scholars in [3,15], offers a circuit-like graphical representation and enables modeling interactions with timing constraints. It supports reusability, maintains synchrony during composition, and provides a formal representation through Timed Constraint Automata (TCA). However, its formal semantics may present challenges to stakeholders due to limited industrial adoption.

To our knowledge, no comprehensive study has integrated SysML and Timed Reo for CPS modelization. Previous research has focused on either SysML [12,25] or Timed Reo [3,15] separately. In our recent work, we introduced "SysReo" [21–23], combining SysML and Reo to enhance CPS validation. While "SysReo" effectively models intricate CPS requirements, structure, behavior, and interactions, it falls short in handling CPS with timing constraints.

In this paper, we first introduce "Timed SysReo" by extending SysML with Timed Reo, introducing the "Timed Reo Internal Block Diagram" (Timed Reo IBD) and "Timed SysReo Sequence Diagram" (TSRSD). Then ,we propose an approach for verifying interactions and interoperability among CPS components, relying on meta-modeling [8] and transformations [7]. This involves defining meta-models for source and target models and establishing correspondences between them. To ensure accuracy and prevent errors, we develop automated ATL rules [1] for seamless TSRSD to TCA transformation. TCAs represent CPS component behavior and coordination, facilitating verification of Timed Scheduled-Data-Stream Logic (TSDSL) requirements.

Finally, we illustrate our approach using a Smart Medical Bed (SMB) case study, showcasing the benefits of Timed SysReo and formal verification for developing robust medical CPS systems.

The paper follows this structure: Sect. 2 provides an overview of SysML, Timed Reo, and TCA. Section 3 outlines the proposed modeling approach using Timed SysReo models. The transformation of TSRSD into TCA using ATL is given in Sect. 4. Section 5 presents the SMB system case study. The paper concludes in Sect. 6, with a brief discussion on future work.

2   Background

This section provides a concise overview of SysML, Timed Reo, and Timed Constraint Automata (TCA).

2.1   Brief Overview of SysML

SysML [11], a profile of UML2.0 [18], facilitates the modeling of complex systems across industries by aligning stakeholder inputs. It offers nine diagram types for modeling CPS requirements, structure, and behavior. In our Smart Medical Bed (SMB) system modeling, we focus on the Requirement Diagram (RD), Block Definition Diagram (BDD), Internal Block Diagram (IBD), and Sequence Diagram (SD).

Requirement Diagram (RD): Illustrates system requirements and their relationships with other model elements.

Block Definition Diagram (BDD): Represents system components and their relationships, distinguishing between atomic and composite blocks.

Internal Block Diagram (IBD): Depicts the static state of the system, detailing internal arrangements through sub-blocks.

Sequence Diagram (SD): Visualizes component interactions and event sequences during specific use cases.

2.2   Timed Reo

Timed Reo [3] expands upon Reo [2], is a channel-based coordination language for concurrent and distributed systems. It introduces channels with timing constraints to regulate communication in CPS, aiming to specify exogenous protocols governing timed interactions among components. Timed Reo's formal semantics are captured by Timed Constraint Automata (TCA), extending Constraint Automata (CA) to describe behavior incorporating timing constraints.

Definition of TCA: A Timed Constraint Automaton (TCA) denoted by $A = (L, L_0, N, \rightarrow, C, ic)$ comprises:

- L: set of locations (or states).
- L_0: initial location where $L_0 \in L$.
- N: set of port names.
- $\rightarrow$: transition relation $\rightarrow \subseteq L \times 2^N \times DC \times CC \times 2^C \times L$, where DC represents Data Constraints over a finite data domain, ensuring specific conditions for data exchange between components and CC represents Clock Constraints.
- C: set of clocks.
- ic: $L \rightarrow CC$ is a function assigning to each location an invariance condition, ensuring specific timing constraints.

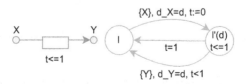

Fig. 1. Timed Reo circuit and TCA for an expiring timed FIFO channel.

Example: Consider the expiring timed FIFO channel depicted in Fig. 1. This channel extends from FIFO with a maximum time constraint for data residing in the buffer, after which the data is discarded. In the Timed Reo circuit, a clock t is declared in TCA. A time constraint $t \leq 1$ under the buffer indicates the expiration time aspect, denoted by a clock constraint $CC(t)$ as an invariance condition for location $l'(d)$ in TCA. The two edges from $l'(d)$ to l represent the event where a data item is discarded upon timer expiration and the event where Y reads the data out of the buffer, respectively.

3   Modeling Approach

In this section, we present our model-based design approach. We begin by outlining the steps for efficiently designing CPS using Timed SysReo. Then, we describe the Timed SysReo meta-models employed in the initial design phase.

3.1   Approach Steps

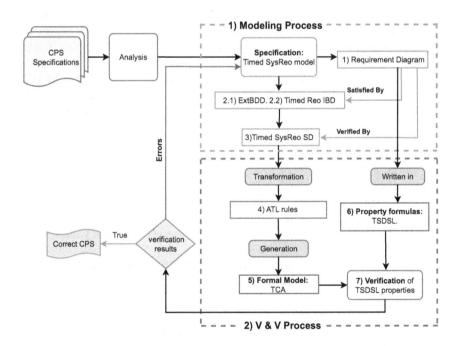

Fig. 2. Modeling and V&V processes using Timed SysReo.

This section outlines our modeling methodology, as illustrated in Fig. 2, which consists of two main processes: the modeling process and the validation and verification (V & V) process. Initially, we comprehensively model CPS components' requirements, structure, timed interaction protocols, and behavior to address critical timing constraints. Subsequently, we verify timed interactions and interoperability among CPS components.

During the initial phase, the CPS designer gathers system requirements and conducts thorough analysis. Using the "Timed SysReo" model, three main diagrams are created: (1) The requirement diagram, encompassing both functional and non-functional needs; (2.1) The ExtBDD diagram, illustrating the system's hierarchical structure through blocks, followed by (2.2) the Timed Reo IBD diagram, delineating internal structure and timed interaction protocols. Additionally, the Timed SysReo sequence diagram (TSRSD) models timed behavior and coordination of CPS components.

In the second phase, our focus shifts to the validation and verification process. We aim to accurately represent timed interactions among CPS components and verify their interoperability, modeled using TSRSD diagrams. To achieve this, we apply ATL rules to corresponding meta-models, as detailed in Sect. 4, to obtain their equivalents of Timed Constraint Automata (TCA). Additionally, we express predefined requirements in Time Scheduled Data Stream Logic (TSDSL) [3], providing a formal representation of these requirements.

Using TSDSL and TCA enhances precision and rigor in CPS verification procedures, ensuring seamless collaboration among components with timing constraints. This systematic approach guarantees the CPS system operates as intended, aligning with designer specifications. Verification results are evaluated, with any specification errors prompting a loop back to the Timed SysReo model specification phase until a precise CPS model is achieved.

3.2   Timed SysReo Meta-models

In this section, we will present the meta-models of Timed Reo Internal Block Definition Diagram (Timed Reo IBD) and Timed SysReo Sequence Diagram (TSRSD) respectively.

Timed Reo IBD Meta-model: In Fig. 3, we represent the meta-model that allows us to model Timed Reo IBD diagrams. The Timed Reo IBD serves to depict the inner structure of CPS components and the timed connections between CPS parts specified as exogenous Timed Reo protocols. These diagrams consist of parts and ports, where each part represents a CPS component. Parts are encapsulated black-box components equipped with ports for data exchange. Communication between parts is facilitated through Timed Reo connectors, which are depicted as channels. Various types of Timed Reo channels exist, each defining specific data behaviors: The Sync channel instantly transfers data from input to output. FIFO temporarily buffers data before transmission. SyncDrain receives data from two inputs simultaneously and discards them. Filter forwards data only if a specified condition is met. Additionally, Timed Reo connectors include nodes for data exchange between components and employ clocks to measure time (timeouts or delay) within the system.

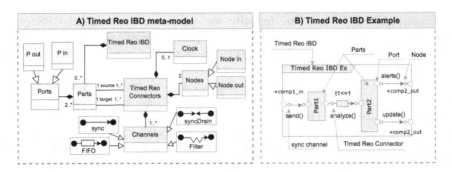

Fig. 3. Meta-model of Timed Reo Internal Block Diagram (Timed Reo IBD) followed by an example.

TSRSD Meta-model: In Fig. 4 A, we represent the meta-model that allows us to model Timed SysReo Sequence Diagrams, followed by an example in Fig. 4 B.

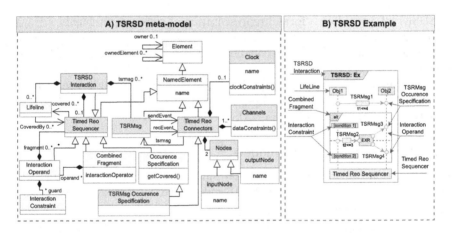

Fig. 4. Meta-model of Timed SysReo Sequence Diagram (TSRSD) followed by an example.

The main class in this meta-model is the TSRSD Interaction, which encompasses lifelines, Timed SysReo Messages (TSRMsg), and a Timed Reo Sequencer. A LifeLine represents a CPS component involved in the interaction, handling event transmission and reception. TSRMsg defines the Timed SysReo Messages exchanged between objects, with each message having a sender and receiver connected via timed Reo connectors. The Timed Reo Sequencer serves as the superclass for TSRSD Interaction, Combined Fragment, Interaction Operand, and Occurrence Specification. A Combined Fragment contains interaction operands and an interaction operator chosen from a set of options. An Interaction Operand is linked to a combined fragment, potentially with a guard condition. The

TSRMsg Occurrence Specification represents events on lifelines, marking the start or end of a timed SysReo message.

The classes Timed Reo Connectors, TSRMsg, and Timed Reo Sequencer inherit from NamedElement, which in turn inherits from Element. The 'owner' association retrieves the parent element, while 'ownedElement' retrieves child elements.

Timed SysReo, as compared to SysReo [22,23], offers a more comprehensive approach to modeling CPS. By incorporating timing notations through "Timed Reo IBD" and "Timed SysReo SD", it enables a detailed representation of CPS interactions and inner structure within specified time constraints. This enhancement ensures that all facets of CPS, from requirements to behavior to structure, are accurately captured in the modeling process.

4   Transforming TSRSD Into TCA Using ATL

In this section, we introduce the Atlas Transformation Language (ATL) and explain how to convert TSRSD diagrams into Timed Constraint Automata (TCA).

4.1   ATL Overview

The Atlas Transformation Language (ATL) is a tool in Model-Driven Engineering (MDE) used to generate target models from source models [1]. An ATL program consists of rules that match elements in the source model and create corresponding elements in the target model. These rules include a "from" section specifying patterns and constraints in the source model, and a "to" section defining how target elements are created from the source elements.

4.2   Timed Constraint Automata Meta-model

Based on the formal definition of Timed Constraint Automata (TCA), we propose a meta-model depicted in Fig. 5. The main classes are: Timed Constraint Automata, the root class containing states and transitions; State, which includes a name, type (initial or not), and an invariance condition for the maximum duration; and Transition, which specifies source and target states, node names (input/output), data constraints, and clock constraints for firing time.

4.3   ATL Transformation Rules

Several ATL rules are used to map TSRSD elements to TCA elements. Specifically, TSRMsgOccurrenceSpecification in TSRSD corresponds to State in TCA, and TSRMsg in TSRSD corresponds to Transition in TCA. Due to space constraints, we will illustrate only one rule here:

Example Rule: TSRMsg2Transition converts TSRMsg instances from TSRSD to Transition instances in TCA:

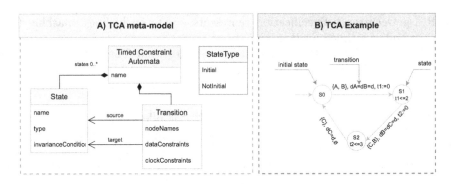

Fig. 5. Timed Constraint Automata meta-Model followed by an example.

```
rule TSRMsg2Transition {
    from
        tsrMsg : TSRSD ! TSRMsg,
        mos : TSRSD ! TSRMsgOccurrenceSpecification
    to
        t : TCA! Transition (
            nodeNames <- {tsrMsg.inputNode.name, tsrMsg.outputNode.name},
            dataConstraints <- tsrMsg.channelType,
            clockConstraints <- tsrMsg.clock.name.concat(':=0'),
            source <- thisModule.resolveTemp(mos, 's'),
            target <- thisModule.resolveTemp(thisModule
                .NextTSRMsgOccSpec(mos.getCovered(), mos), 's')
        )
    if
        not tsrMsg.outputNode.isLast
}
```

This rule maps TSRMsg to Transition, indicating message transmission, sets node names, data constraints, and initializes clock constraints. It defines source and target states based on TSRMsg specifications, using a helper function to find subsequent occurrences on a lifeline.

5   Smart Medical Bed Case Study

In this section, we present our case study on the Smart Medical Bed (SMB) system. We provide a brief overview of the SMB, gather relevant information for analysis, and use Timed SysReo models to specify requirements, design structure, and model behavior while accounting for timing constraints. The system is validated by generating TCAs from TSRSD using predefined ATL rules, enabling verification of timed properties through methods like Büchi automata [9], enhancing the validation and verification process.

5.1   SMB Overview

A Smart Medical Bed (SMB) integrates sensors to monitor vital signs like temperature, transmitting data to a Remote Terminal Unit (RTU) within 1 Time

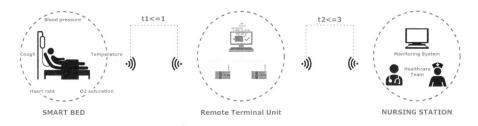

Fig. 6. Smart medical bed architecture.

Unit (TU), as shown in Fig. 6. The RTU manages data flow between the Smart Bed (SB) and Nursing Station (NS), deciding whether to update patient information or alert healthcare teams within 3 TUs. The SMB system consists of the SB, RTU, and NS components.

Our study focuses on modeling and validating the SB-RTU interaction within the SMB. Using Timed SysReo, we analyze requirements and model architecture. We employ Timed Reo IBD and Timed SysReo SD to represent internal structure and manage timing constraints, enhancing efficiency in modeling complex components and interaction protocols within the SMB environment.

5.2   Modeling Process Using Timed SysReo

Requirements: During the modeling process, it is vital to ensure system functionality and usability. This starts with identifying specific system needs, outlining functional requirements of the SMB system. For instance, requirement R1 in Table 1, emphasizes the necessity for the Smart Bed (SB) to send the collected patient vital signs data (e.g., heart rate, blood pressure, temperature, and oxygen saturation) to the Remote Terminal Unit (RTU) within a latency of no more than 1 Time Unit (TU). This requirement is satisfied by the Smart Bed (SB) component and verified by the "sendTempData()" message.

Table 1. Requirement table of SMB.

ID	Requirement Description	Satisfied by	Verified By
R1	The SB shall send the collected patient vital signs data to RTU within a latency of no more than 1 TU	SB	sendTempData()
R2	The RTU must send an "emergencyAlert()" message to the NS within 3 TU for abnormal data or transmit an "updatePatientInfo()" message within the same time-frame for normal data	RTU	emergencyAlerts(), updatePatientInfo()

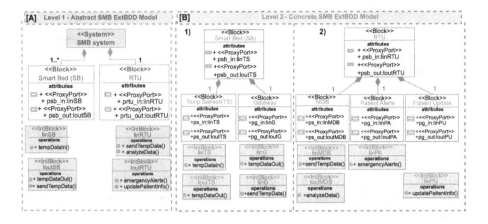

Fig. 7. The ExtBDD model of the SMB system.

Extended Block Definition Diagram (ExtBDD): The ExtBDD diagram displays the hierarchical structure of the SMB system, with each component from the requirement diagram (Table 1) depicted as a block. These blocks detail a component's internal operations, offered and required services, with input and output proxy ports. In Fig. 7 [A], we show an abstract overview of the system, featuring main components like "SMB", divided into "Smart Bed (SB)" and "Remote Terminal Unit (RTU)". In Fig. 7 [B], the concrete level illustrates subcomponents within primary components. For instance, the smart bed includes "Temperature Sensor" and "Gateway", with the former responsible for data measurement and transmission to the latter.

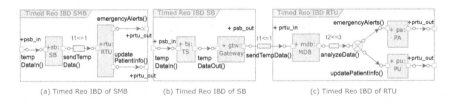

(a) Timed Reo IBD of SMB   (b) Timed Reo IBD of SB   (c) Timed Reo IBD of RTU

Fig. 8. Timed Reo IBD of the SMB system.

Timed Reo Internal Block Diagram (Timed Reo IBD): Figure 8 presents the Timed Reo IBD of the smart medical bed system. The purpose of Timed Reo IBD is to enhance the modeling of system architecture by replacing the SysML Internal Block Diagram (IBD) with Timed Reo connectors, allowing for the precise specification and analysis of timing properties and synchronization patterns within the system.

In Fig. 8(b,c), internal structures of SB and RTU components are illustrated, including their timed interaction protocols. For instance, the gateway (gtw) component sends "sendTempData()" to the medical database (MDB) component through a timed FIFO channel, constrained by $@t1 <= 1\ TU$. This channel imposes a deadline, $t1 <= 1$, where data availability follows a structured pattern: each data item in the FIFO buffer has a maximum duration of $t1 <= 1$ before removal. Similarly, the MDB sends "analyzedData()" to the Exclusive router (EXR) via a timed FIFO channel with a deadline of $@t2 <= 3\ TU$. Following that, the EXR determines whether to dispatch "emergencyAlerts()" via a sync channel for immediate transmission to the patient alert (PA) component, or to send "updatePatientInfo()" via a sync channel directly to the patient update (PU) component.

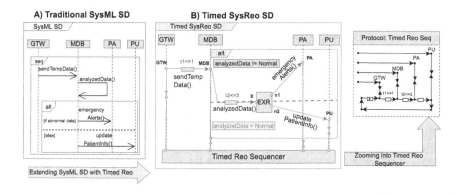

Fig. 9. Difference between traditional SysML SD and TSRSD of the SMB system.

Timed SysReo Sequence Diagram (TSRSD): The purpose of TSRSD is to enhance traditional SysML Sequence Diagrams (SD) by integrating Timed Reo, providing a comprehensive representation of complex timed interactions among CPS components. By extending SysML SD with Timed Reo, TSRSD effectively models both behavior and timed interaction protocols within CPS. TSRSD facilitates exogenous coordination among CPS components, enhancing flexibility, adaptability, and cost-efficiency in CPS modeling. Additionally, TSRSD enables the validation of predefined requirements, ensuring CPS interoperability and design precision through formal verification processes.

In our recent work [23], we enhanced traditional SysML SD by integrating Reo, creating SysReo SD. This effectively captures CPS component behavior and coordination but lacks adequate handling of timing constraints. Therefore, we introduced Timed SysReo SD (TSRSD), extending SysML SD with Timed Reo to enhance the representation of complex timed interactions among CPS components. Moreover, TSRSD serves as a starting point for the verification phase. Using predefined ATL rules outlined in Sect. 4, we directly produce Timed

Constraint Automata (TCA) from TSRSD. Subsequently, we formally verify predefined requirements, expressed in TSDSL logic, on the generated TCA to guarantee CPS interoperability and design precision.

In Fig. 9, we illustrate the contrast between traditional SysML SD and TSRSD, highlighting the detailed message flow with timing constraints among components. While SysML SD aids in understanding system behavior, it lacks explicit coordination details. TSRSD, adopting an exogenous approach, provides a precise representation of system behaviors and timed interactions. Exogenous methods like Timed Reo offer a modular approach to define protocols. In the scenario shown in Fig. 9 A, the GTW component sends the "sendTempData()" message to the MDB component. An endogenous approach would involve directly implementing the message within their respective code. However, Fig. 9 B illustrates a different strategy, where a separate component called the "Timed Reo sequencer" explicitly defines the message exchange protocol between GTW and MDB with a time constraint of $t_1 \leq 1$. For example, GTW sends "sendTempData()" to MDB using timed Reo ports {GTW, MDB} (depicted as orange circles), and the Timed Reo sequencer coordinates this message exchange. This decoupling allows for easier protocol modifications without affecting the implementation of GTW and MDB. Employing Timed Reo connectors in exogenous approaches provides more flexibility and simplifies the specification and adjustment of complex protocols in CPS. Another notable aspect of TSRSD is its capability to verify predefined requirements, as depicted in Table 1. For instance, the "R1" requirement is verified using a timed FIFO channel, coordinating the "sendTempData()" message within a time constraint of $t_1 \leq 1$.

The subsequent step involves formally representing TSRSD and outlining the method for automatic TCA generation.

5.3   Validation and Verification Process

By applying ATL rules to the Timed SysReo sequence diagram (TSRSD) of SMB, we generate the corresponding Timed Constraint Automata (TCA) shown in Fig. 10. We chose ATL to automate the transformation of TSRSD to TCA due to its efficiency and ability to reduce user errors. For example, in Fig. 9 B, the "sendTempData()" message in TSRSD is translated into a transition "t" using the ATL rule "TSRMsg2Transition" from Sect. 4.3. This transition "t" involves nodes {GTW, MDB}, with data constraint $d_{GTW} = d_{MDB} = d$ and clock constraint t1:=0. Applying ATL rule to TSRSD facilitates the creation of its corresponding TCA, depicted in Fig. 10.

Verification of TSDSL Properties on TCA: To ensure the correctness of the SMB system's behavior and coordination, we express predefined requirements using Timed Scheduled-Data-Stream Logic (TSDSL) [3], which integrates temporal logic with timing constraints. These TSDSL specifications are verified against the Büchi automata [9] of the Timed Constraint Automata (TCA) using Arbab's method [3,4].

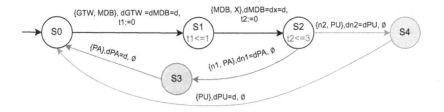

Fig. 10. The generated TCA from the smart medical bed TSRSD.

For example, consider requirement R1 in Table 1, which specifies that if data transmission occurs from the Smart Bed (SB) within 1 time unit, it is always (□) accompanied by data reception at the Remote Terminal Unit (RTU) or no observable data transmission within the subsequent 1 time unit:

$$\Box \, [[SB]] \, (\langle \, \langle \, RTU \, \rangle^{\le 1} \, \rangle) \vee \neg \langle \, \langle \, . \, \rangle^{\le 1} \, \rangle$$

Arbab's method, detailed in [3], ensures that a given TCA satisfies a specified TSDSL formula. It involves transforming the TSDSL formula into its negation, constructing a Büchi TCA for this negation, merging it with the original TCA, and checking the emptiness of the resulting combined TCA.

Checking the emptiness of the combined TCA involves determining if there exists a run (sequence of states and transitions) that satisfies the negated formula. For requirement R1, this means verifying if there is no sequence where data transmission from SB occurs within 1 time unit without either a corresponding reception at RTU within the same time or no transmission at all within the subsequent 1 time unit. If the combined TCA is empty, meaning no such run exists, then the original TCA satisfies the TSDSL formula for requirement R1. This verification step ensures that the CPS model adheres to the specified timing and temporal logic requirements, thus confirming its correctness and reliability.

6   Conclusion and Future Work

In this paper, we present a novel approach for modeling and verifying Cyber-Physical Systems (CPS) interactions with timing constraints using Timed Sys-Reo. Our method enhances CPS designs by incorporating precise timing considerations through the integration of Timed Reo into SysML diagrams. This allows for an accurate representation of system requirements, behaviors, and interactions under specified timing constraints. Timed SysReo uses two key diagrams: the Timed Reo Internal Block Diagram (IBD) and the Timed SysReo Sequence Diagram (TSRSD). The Timed Reo IBD focuses on the structural aspects of CPS, offering a static view of the system architecture. In contrast, the TSRSD emphasizes dynamic behaviors and timed interactions, providing a dynamic perspective on system operations. Together, these diagrams offer a comprehensive depiction of both the static and dynamic elements of CPS with respect to timing constraints. Additionally, we demonstrate the automation of transforming TSRSD diagrams into Timed Constraint Automata (TCA) using ATL, which significantly enhances the precision and ease of verifying CPS requirements specified in TSDSL logic. Our approach is exemplified through a case study involving a Smart Medical Bed (SMB), highlighting the practical application and benefits of Timed SysReo in real-world scenarios.

In our future efforts, we will assess Timed SysReo's performance across diverse sectors like automotive and aerospace CPS, moving beyond its current focus on healthcare. This evaluation aims to determine its suitability and address specific challenges and opportunities in each domain. Additionally, we intend to enhance Timed SysReo by modeling both discrete and continuous CPS behaviors. Currently, the Timed SysReo framework primarily handles discrete behaviors, but our expansion will integrate parametric diagrams and incorporate Reo connectors to model differential equations for continuous dynamics. This approach will enable comprehensive modeling of CPS hardware components, considering physical constraints to ensure robust system designs across different operational scenarios.

References

1. Eclipse ATL. https://eclipse.dev/atl/. Accessed May 02 2024
2. Arbab, F.: Reo: a channel-based coordination model for component composition. Math. Struct. Comput. Sci. **14**(3), 329366 (2004). https://doi.org/10.1017/S0960129504004153
3. Arbab, F., Baier, C., de Boer, F., Rutten, J.: Models and temporal logical specifications for timed component connectors. Softw. Syst. Model. **6**, 59–82 (2007)
4. Arbab, F., Baier, C., De Boer, F., Rutten, J.: Models and temporal logics for timed component connectors. In: Proceedings of the Second International Conference on Software Engineering and Formal Methods, 2004. SEFM 2004, pp. 198–207. IEEE (2004)
5. Barroso, S., Bustos, P., Nunez, P.: Towards a cyber-physical system for sustainable and smart building: a use case for optimising water consumption on a smartcampus. J. Ambient. Intell. Humaniz. Comput. **14**(5), 6379–6399 (2023)
6. Bouskela, D., et al.: Formal requirements modeling for cyber-physical systems engineering: an integrated solution based on form-l and modelica. Requirements Eng. **27**(1), 1–30 (2022)
7. Czarnecki, K., et al.: Classification of model transformation approaches. In: Proceedings of the 2nd OOPSLA Workshop on Generative Techniques in the Context of the Model Driven Architecture, vol. 45, pp. 1–17. USA (2003)
8. De Lara, J., Vangheluwe, H., Alfonseca, M.: Meta-modelling and graph grammars for multi-paradigm modelling in ATOM 3. Softw. Syst. Model. **3**, 194–209 (2004)
9. Gastin, P., Oddoux, D.: Fast LTL to Büchi automata translation. In: Berry, G., Comon, H., Finkel, A. (eds.) CAV 2001. LNCS, vol. 2102, pp. 53–65. Springer, Heidelberg (2001). https://doi.org/10.1007/3-540-44585-4_6
10. Genius, D., Apvrille, L.: Hierarchical design of cyber-physical systems. In: Modelsward (2023)

11. Hause, M., et al.: The SYSML modelling language. In: Fifteenth European Systems Engineering Conference, vol. 9, pp. 1–12 (2006)
12. Huang, P., Jiang, K., Guan, C., Du, D.: Towards modeling cyber-physical systems with SYSML/MARTE/PCCSL. In: 2018 IEEE 42nd Annual Computer Software and Applications Conference (COMPSAC), vol. 1, pp. 264–269. IEEE (2018)
13. Ivers, J., Clements, P.C., Garlan, D., Nord, R., Schmerl, B., Oviedo-Silva, J.: Documenting component and connector views with UML 2.0 (2004)
14. Kim, K.D., Kumar, P.R.: Cyberphysical systems: a perspective at the centennial. Proc. IEEE **100**(Special Centennial Issue), 1287–1308 (2012). https://doi.org/10.1109/JPROC.2012.2189792
15. Kokash, N., Jaghoori, M.M., Arbab, F.: From timed REO networks to networks of timed automata. Electr. Notes Theor. Comput. Sci. **295**, 11–29 (2013)
16. Lau, K.K., Ornaghi, M., Wang, Z.: A software component model and its preliminary formalisation. In: International Symposium on Formal Methods for Components and Objects, pp. 1–21. Springer (2005)
17. Mallet, F.: MARTE/CCSL for modeling cyber-physical systems. formal modeling and verification of cyber-physical systems: 1st International Summer School on Methods and Tools for the Design of Digital Systems, Bremen, Germany, September 2015, pp. 26–49 (2015)
18. Miles, R., Hamilton, K.: Learning UML 2.0: a Pragmatic Introduction to UML. O'Reilly Media, Inc., Sebastopol (2006)
19. OMG: OMG System Modeling Languag. https://www.omg.org/spec/SysML/. Accessed 09 Apr 2024
20. Panahi, V., Kargahi, M., Faghih, F.: Control performance analysis of automotive cyber-physical systems: a study on efficient formal verification. ACM Trans. Cyber-Phys. Syst. (2022)
21. Tannoury, P.: An Incremental model-based design methodology to develop CPS with SysML/OCL/Reo. In: Journées du GDR GPL. Vannes, France (2022), https://hal.science/hal-03893454
22. Tannoury, P., Chouali, S., Hammad, A.: Model driven approach to design an automotive CPS with SysReo language. In: Proceedings of the 20th ACM International Symposium on Mobility Management and Wireless Access, pp. 97–104 (2022)
23. Tannoury, P., Chouali, S., Hammad, A.: Joint use of SYSML and Reo to specify and verify the compatibility of CPS components. In: International Conference on Formal Aspects of Component Software, pp. 84–102. Springer (2023)
24. Tartarisco, G., et al.: An intelligent medical cyber-physical system to support heart valve disease screening and diagnosis. Expert Syst. Appl. **238**, 121772 (2024)
25. Xie, J., Tan, W., Yang, Z., Li, S., Xing, L., Huang, Z.: SysML-based compositional verification and safety analysis for safety-critical cyber-physical systems. Connection Sci., 1–31 (2021)

A Reliable and Resource-Aware Federated Learning Solution by Decentralizing Client Selection for IoT Devices

Mohamed Aiche[1]([⊠])(iD), Samir Ouchani[2](iD), and Hafida Bouarfa[1](iD)

[1] LRDSI Laboratory, Faculty of Science, University Blida 1,
Soumaa BP 270, Blida, Algeria
`aiche1mohamed@gmail.com`, `hafidabouarfa@hotmail.com`
[2] LINEACT research laboratory Ecole dIngénieur CESI, Aix-en-Provence, France
`souchani@cesi.fr`

Abstract. Federated learning (FL) is a distributed machine learning approach where each participating node is referred to as a client. Clients are expected to use only local data to train their local machine-learning models. Nevertheless, a client's poor participation can have a significant impact on FL quality. Therefore, the clients should be carefully chosen, and the selection process should be dynamic and efficient. The majority of proposed methods depend on centrally gathering resource information from nodes, and then selecting clients accordingly. To overcome the drawbacks of the centralization selection paradigm, we propose a decentralized approach in which neighboring nodes cooperate under the guidance of a leader to gather data about a node's resources. Further, the leader uses a *lightweight deep learning model* on the collected data to select clients. Compared to the conventional client selection method, our approach speeds up the convergence of the model and consumes less energy by minimizing the number of rounds.

Keywords: Federated Learning · Client selection · Leader election · Lightweight Deep Learning · IoT

1 Introduction

The Internet of Things (IoT) is a field that, at present, has firmly gained a place amongst other advanced technologies, with the potential to alter our daily lives significantly. This topic's popularity has recently grown as a result of increased research and study. The integration of IoT networks is expected to substantially boost the volume of generated data [1]. By 2025, several IoT nodes should produce upwards of 70 Zettabytes of data, according to research done by the International Data Corporation (IDC) [2]. Additionally, the development of smart IoT infrastructure based on machine learning is possible as a result of this massive amount of data. Most often, all data are saved in the cloud [3] that converts them into a source of power for building machine learning (ML) models. As a result, intelligent services are deployed based on the outcomes of the ML model within the IoT infrastructure. However, because sensitive data may be stored on the cloud, users' privacy may be threatened [4]. Thus, the communication cost might drastically rise when transmitting data to the cloud.

Due to these shortcomings, Google introduced a novel strategy called Federated Learning (FL) [5]. The method avoids sending data to the cloud and instead lets each node train its own model locally, preserving privacy and lowering communication overheads. However, for each round, FL selects a group of clients to use in training their local model until they reach the necessary measure of global accuracy. Nevertheless, choosing the incorrect clients can slow down convergence and lead to more rounds, which use up resources on the node. Consequently, a number of solutions were put forth to reduce this risk and enhance the client selection process. Hence, almost all of them concentrated on concepts based on centralized information collection concerning node characteristics. Therefore, a central server will choose clients using the gathered information on characteristics. However, when every node begins transmitting the information to the server and depends only on it, failures including bottlenecks, single points of failure, and increased latency are possible [6].

The flaws mentioned above serve as proof that our solution is necessary. Indeed, our approach is based on decentralizing the client selection phase, which is managed without the requirement for a central entity. Decentralization is handled by electing leaders on each local network. Therefore, each leader will be responsible for coordinating the mission to gather information about each node. At last, the leader applies a lightweight deep learning model [7] to the collected data to assess whether or not the nodes are eligible to participate in Federated Learning. The main contributions of this paper are illustrated as follows.

- Offering a decentralized approach to client selection that helps to accurately gauge each client's participation eligibility. The objective is to reduce the number of learning rounds, which will speed up convergence and use fewer resources.
- Describing the impact of decentralization on federated learning. Hence, the concept of leader coordination is introduced in FL to present a vision for how it might be applied in later FL phases.
- Discussing our method's application and evaluation in various settings, as well as the outcomes in terms of accuracy, energy use, and latency.

The structure of this document is organized as follows. In Sect. 2, we review and discuss the previous works of FL and the client selection step. Section 3 outlines and details our approach's steps. Finally, Sect. 4 presents the outcomes of simulations and experiments, while Sect. 5 illustrates our future plans.

2   Related Work

The reviewed literature presented in this section is divided into: 1) federated learning, which is the core topic of our contribution; 2) client selection, which is the particular step we enhance; 3) our motivation, and the research that inspired us.

2.1   Federated Learning

Federated learning (FL) is the outcome of research carried out by McMahan et al. [5] in 2017. FL's primary objective was to overcome the drawbacks related to privacy and communication costs. Unfortunately, some limitations might have a negative effect on the effectiveness of FL, which encouraged researchers to delve deeper into this concept.

Various works, including [8,9], addressed a variety of issues in FL, including communication, privacy, and data distribution and sharing. Due the limits of earlier works on common subjects, Wahab et al. [10] emphasized client selection, focusing on which nodes should be selected to participate in FL.

Client selection, in accordance with [11], is a crucial phase that can significantly affect how the learning proceeds. As stated by Nour et al. [12], the selection is very important and directly affects both the model convergence and communication costs. Given its importance and the significant impact it can have, we focused our efforts on it in order to improve this step.

2.2   Client Selection

This step was initially presented in [5], where the selection of nodes was random. Indeed, this kind of selection is luck-based, having the probability of getting bad clients that alters our learning model. VanillaFL is the name given to this fundamental method in the literature. Moreover, Cho et al. [13] have quantified how selection bias impacts convergence speed. They showed that fewer quality clients can provide better service than a greater number of unqualified and random ones. Nishio and Yonetani [14] described how poor communication and computational capabilities of some clients can make VanillaFL learning ineffective. The authors have then developed a revised protocol that focuses on choosing clients depending on their state of resources. The candidates who can complete the FL steps by a predetermined deadline are chosen.

Another protocol known as FedMCCS was proposed by AbdulRahman et al. [15]. In FedMCCS, a variety of factors, like processor power, memory, and energy capacity, are required to determine a client's eligibility for FL. Although, none of the aforementioned methods took the clients' data quality factor into consideration, which was then treated and referred to by Wang et al. [16]. Data quality was previously assumed to be a highly relevant selection factor, which can considerably alter the model's accuracy. Hence, the authors have suggested a brand-new client selection technique depending on dataset contents. Considering the same factor, another strategy was put up by Taik et al. [17], to select the most data-intensive clients. This technique also takes into account how much each client contributed to the global model in each round.

All of the aforementioned methods require the nodes to communicate information about their resource usage to the server, and client selection is done from a single point. However, using this methodology and relying on a single location carries significant risks, including bottlenecks, single points of failure, and security threats. Furthermore, managing the dynamic variation of the resources will be challenging [18], calling for frequent monitoring of each node's state.

2.3 Discussion

The previously stated weaknesses of centralization were mentioned by [19–21]. According to the mentioned studies, BlockChain technology should be incorporated into Federated Learning to decentralize it. As an alternative, Saha et al. [22] suggested a decentralized technique by placing a fog node as a local aggregator in each location. Local Aggregators are responsible for aggregating models for clients who only live in their area. However, they addressed only the aggregation process and did not consider the client selection.

In the present work, we take advantage of the potential of decentralization to improve client selection, as well as federated learning as a whole since client selection is a significant part of FL, and centralized approaches have their drawbacks.

3 Decentralized Leader-Based Client Selection

Decentralizing the selection process and getting rid of server-client dependence are the foundations of our approach. The goal is to avoid the disadvantages of a centralized approach. Additionally, the strategy will emphasize lowering server demand so that it is only required for computations that are greedy.

The method seeks to enable nodes in each local network to collaborate to understand the status and circumstances of each node. Therefore, the devices will jointly determine each network node's eligibility. However, each network needs to elect a leader for decentralization and inter-node collaboration to succeed. The task synchronization amongst the nodes will be the leader's responsibility. The proposed approach's architecture is briefly shown in Fig. 1, and it takes the following presumptions into account.

- The environment is stationary, and there are no moving nodes.
- Every node in the network needs to have an identifier that is visible to all other nodes.

We describe each phase of our suggested approach in the subsections that follow.

3.1 Electing the Network's Leader

In this part, we will explain what a leader is and how it is used in our approach. Furthermore, we will go through the benefits of employing a leader and the reason behind its choice as a crucial element in our approach. At last, we will look at how nodes choose their leader by employing a Leader Election algorithm.

Overview. The leader principle has been widely applied to several issues. For instance, Amazon employs a leader in its distributed systems [23] for the reliability of its infrastructure. Amazon often uses an algorithm like Paxos [24], to elect its leaders. In another case, Blockchain technology often uses the leader

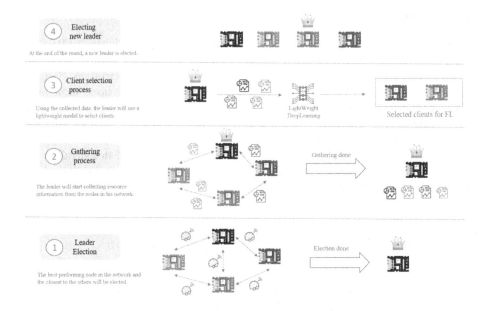

Fig. 1. Decentralized leader-based client selection overview.

concept for the consensus stage [25]. It uses the Raft algorithm to elect leaders, which is an alternative to Paxos.

Electing a leader is the most important part of our approach. It enables the nomination of the leader who will be in charge of coordinating the nodes to gather neighboring states. Then use them as metrics to select FL's clients by relying on a machine learning model. Finally, it has been broadly adopted to coordinate a group of IoT nodes with a leader in decentralized systems [26]. The leader in such an aspect was called a coordinator node [27], it was also used for coordination between UAVs [28], which illustrates the effectiveness of the leadership concept for inter-IoT node coordination. Thus, it enhances the validity of using the leader for coordination in our election mechanism.

Role of the Leader in Client Selection. The leader is the node in charge of organizing the task of gathering resources and working with the helpers alongside other nodes. It also makes sure that the process runs smoothly. It is simple for it to manage the state of its neighbors. The leader's reasoning is similar to that of the fog. However, due to how easy it is for the nodes to change the leader dynamically, it is an effective way to use a fog node. Additionally, having a leader is less expensive than deploying a fog. Lastly, a leader's ability to tolerate faults is well-known in the literature. According to [29], leader nodes can achieve higher levels of performance, dependability, and decreased latency, as well as offer users affordable computational IoT services.

The role of a leader is significant in our approach. It ensures that the nodes are properly coordinated. Its unique privilege among the nodes makes this control easier. Hence, it makes certain that each member of the group adheres to the coordinating procedures. In another case, the fog was not used for coordination, but rather to process a large amount of data.

Leader Election. In our environment, by running the leader election algorithm, every local network will have a single leader, chosen by nodes in a decentralized manner.

For the election, several solutions were proposed. The Minimum Finding algorithm is the most popular solution [26,30]. The latter considers the node with the smallest identifier as the leader. However, this approach is not ideal for our circumstances considering our leader's obligations. Particularly in an IoT scenario where nodes have constrained capacity. In our scenario, the node that is nearest to the other nodes and most resource-efficient is the optimal leader. Indeed, resources are a crucial factor for our leader because he needs to use an intelligent model. Furthermore, fast coordination and connectivity depend on the leader's position as the closest.

In the general case of leader election, each network node will initially identify himself as a leader and assign a specific criterion value to a variable *lead_value*. Following that, the nodes will begin to broadcast this value throughout the network while keeping track of the values of other nodes. When a node receives a value greater than its own, it updates *lead_value* and distributes it throughout the network. Then, when a particular node does not receive any value that is greater than its own, the election will end, and that node will be declared as a leader.

In our approach, the criterion that is put into the values is the average performance of the resources, as well as the delay. The delay is used to find the node that is closest to the others. Each node broadcasts the transmitting time as well as the average performance of its resources. The remaining nodes will estimate the delay based on the transmitting time received by comparing it with the arrival time. The estimation delay for a node i is denoted as D_i, it will be applied to the final election value.

The performance value is indicated as P_i. Moreover, it is a weighted value between the CPU (C_i), RAM (R_i), and energy capacity (E_i); so that, the user has the option to choose the resources' priorities. Equation 1 expresses P_i, where w_1, w_2, and w_3 are the weights factors for priorities.

$$P_i = w_1 C_i + w_2 R_i + w_3 E_i \qquad (1)$$

Here, *lead_value* will be evaluated as Eq. 2, and the node with the highest *lead_value* will be the leader.

$$lead\_value = \frac{P_i}{D_i} \qquad (2)$$

3.2 Decentralized Gathering Step

In our contribution, gathering data about the nodes is a server-independent task. Thus, the nodes will be in cooperation and managed by a leader to accomplish this task and know the status and conditions of each device. Such nodes are known as assistants or helpers. At the beginning of the task, the leader is the only helper. Afterward, a request for assistance is sent to the leader by each node with low resource utilization or in an idle state. The leader will then randomly assign a set of clients of $1/nA$ to the new helper, where nA reflects the number of helpers in the environment. Then, the address of this helper will be transmitted by the leader to the involved nodes.

The nodes are requested to send their characteristics and resource states for each variation of the latter. Indeed, each node must send the states only to its helper. The helper must gather the necessary information to predict the device's eligibility. The information contains the transmission date and time, hardware details, resource utilization rate, and the amount of data gathered since the previous transmission. This process is carried out by all nodes up until the predetermined deadline. Next, to move forward with selecting the clients, the helpers should submit to their leaders all the gathered information.

Whenever a node sends a message to a helper and discovers that the helper is unavailable, the node notifies the leader, who then divides the helper's nodes into other nodes. By employing this technique, the system can continuously monitor changes to node resources and gather trustworthy data for use in upcoming selection policies.

3.3 Lightweight Deep Learning for Selection

This part will outline the Deep Learning model that the leader will use to forecast the nodes' upcoming behavior. We will also explain the design and concepts of the used model.

Overview. Once the leader has gathered all of the information about the neighboring nodes, it uses them to know which nodes are the best. Therefore, we will employ a Deep Learning model to determine whether the node of concern will have adequate resources during the FL process. Deep Learning will use the obtained data to forecast how nodes will use their resources in the future.

Nevertheless, the IoT context's resource limitations may prevent the leader from performing extensive computing, and he may find it difficult to deal with this [31]. Hence, we propose using a Lightweight Deep Learning technique where our leader can easily support it for computation. Lightweight Deep Learning (DL) refers to the process of condensing neural network models into smaller ones that nonetheless perform as well as the original models. Using the perception of history and the transmitting time that was obtained during the gathering process, a recurrent neural network will be constructed. RNNs will be used to build a time series forecasting model. Nevertheless, RNN gets some constraints, which can be overcome by incorporating it with LSTM [32].

Following some studies such as [31,33], lightweight LSTM models displayed excellent forecasting performance for IoT devices, due to lightweight's lower power consumption. Thus, we propose a lightweight model architecture using LSTM, to forecast the utilization of node resources.

Recurrent Neural Networks (RNN). RNNs can extract temporal information from sequential data. Additionally, it can recognize sequential features in the data and use patterns to anticipate an upcoming probable outcome. RNN is the basic version of LSTM that will be used as a model for our selection approach.

Long Short Term Memory (LSTM). Long Short-Term Memory (LSTM) is an improvement of RNN designed by Hochreiter and Schmidhuber [32]. LSTM can store information for an extended period. It is composed of multiple memory cells and four neural networks. LSTM lets us solve the problem of gradient explosion.

Time Series Forecasting. Time series forecasting is the method of predicting future values using a model and observed values from the past. In our case, this model allows us to predict the future resource usage of the nodes that intend to participate in FL. These forecasts will aid our systems in making decisions.

This type of LSTM forecasting model has also been used to predict CPU utilization [34], as well as for forecasting the future uses of a cloud server's resources [35]. They also demonstrated that LSTM outperforms ARIMA [36] and HoltWinters [37] in predicting future resource usage.

Proposed LightWeight Time Series Model. In our design, the model uses a shallow structure, with a minimal number of neurons and no more than two hidden layers. The architecture of our model is illustrated in Fig. 2.

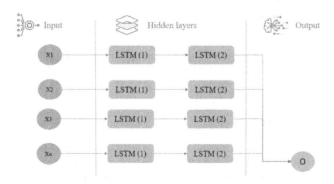

Fig. 2. The Architecture of our Lightweight Time Series.

Figure 3 shows how our Lightweight Model for time series will perform. The input of the model is a sequence of data obtained on the nodes. The information in the data includes a node's resource utilization statistics, including those for memory and CPU usage, energy usage statistics, data size, etc. The model's output is a forecast of future node resource usage. Following that, the nodes are ranked according to the average of their predicted future consumption. Based on a pre-configured selection percentage, the best-ranking nodes will be chosen for FL.

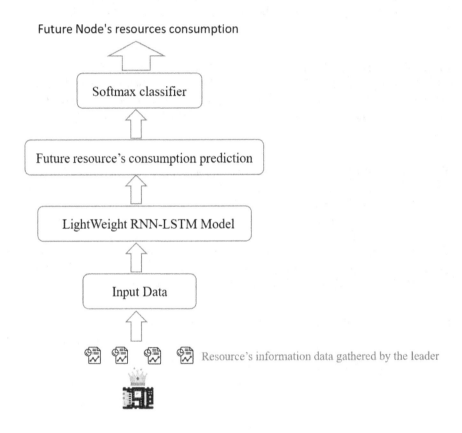

Fig. 3. Lightweight RNN-LSTM Model for future resource prediction.

3.4   Re-electing Leaders

Following each round, a new leader will be chosen, and the helper who collects the most information about the node's characteristics will take over as the new coordinator. The address of the newly elected assistant will then be broadcast throughout the network by the outgoing leader. In each round, a new leader must be elected to avoid overloading a single node.

3.5   Fault-Tolerant

Periodically, the leader's helpers send a heartbeat to it to check its status. When the leader falls, his helper will replace him. A network node will take over if no assistants are available. A fault-tolerant process [38] requires this operation to ensure smooth operation and prevent interruptions.

4   Experiments

We demonstrate the effectiveness of our method in this section by implementing it and showing the simulation results obtained from real data. As an open-source tool, the tool is implemented in a modular way, using the Python programming language. Based on a stochastic process, the implementation simulates FL client selection and determines resource consumption during the process. Our simulation software is available at: https://github.com/mohamediniesta/CLiS-FL. The Github also contains complete documentation on how the framework works. In the simulation setting, we focus on the following metrics.

- **Global accuracy:** The proof of the quality of federated learning.
- **Energy Consumption:** The goal is to determine whether the approach consumes less energy than other approaches.
- **Rejected Clients:** The quality of FL can be adversely affected by client rejection. As a result of their resources, many IoT clients may be powered down during the process, or those who are unable to finish the learning process. These nodes are called rejected clients.

Simulations were run on a machine configured with an Intel i7 processor, 16GB of RAM, and a GeForce GTX 1660Ti graphics card.

4.1   The Simulation Setup

We set up our simulation as follows. In the environment, we have configured 1000 nodes that are classified into three categories and are distributed fairly. Table 1 illustrates the categories, which are nodes with powerful, medium, and weak capabilities and capacities.

4.2   Data Distribution

Our simulation environment is based on a well-known dataset for object classification, the MNIST handwritten digits dataset. The overall capacity is made up of 60,000 training and 10,000 test data entries.

The training data was randomly assigned to all clients in the environment. Each client takes a random amount of data between the range of [100, *data_ size / number_ of_ nodes*]. We set the requirement that each data entry requires 200 *kilobytes* of storage space in the node. We can also change the amount of data in each node to adjust the simulation speed.

4.3 ML Setup

PyTorch is used to design the ML models. The model is built on a convolutional neural network (CNN) of two fully connected layers, with an output generated by a softmax function. The learning rate is set to 0.1, and MOMENTUM is the used optimizer with a value of 0.5. Ten mini-batches and epochs are used for training this model for each client, with a maximum number of rounds of 1000. The desired completion accuracy for FL is set at 90%.

Table 1. The node categories' capacity.

	Powerful nodes	Medium nodes	Low nodes
Energy (mAh)	6000	2000	600
Storage (GB)	50	15	2

4.4 Results

In this part, the various results, which followed our experimentation are presented.

FL's Quality and Energy Consumption. In this experiment, we evaluate global accuracy, energy consumption, and the total number of rejected clients. These metrics are measured based on the number of rounds of FL. To evaluate this part, we compared our approach with the conventional VanillaFL method.

Figure 4a illustrates the accuracy of the global model. The total energy consumed by the nodes is illustrated in Fig. 4b, and finally, the number of rejected clients is shown in Fig. 4c. The overall accuracy score, expressed as a percentage, is obtained at the end of federated learning. The total energy consumed during the entire FL process is measured in mAh. The nodes that couldn't finish their local learning owing to a lack of resources or other issues are the rejected clients.

4.5 Discussion

In this part, we discuss the various outcomes that have been demonstrated in the results section.

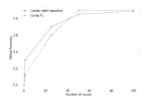

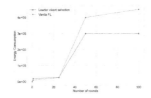

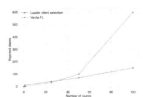

(a) Global accuracy measurement of approaches.

(b) Measurement of the energy capacity of the approaches.

(c) The rate of rejected clients for each approach.

Fig. 4. The performance of the selection using our approach (Leader client selection).

In our experiment, we compared our approach to the conventional method of client selection. Our method enables us to select the best nodes in terms of performance and data. As a result of these criteria, there has been a significant improvement in global accuracy in round variation. Due to the performance of the chosen nodes, it will be rare that a node fails or is rejected. This fact explains the minimization of rejected clients on the curve of our approach on the third graph.

Compared to VanillaFL's fundamental selection process, our strategy enables quicker model convergence, leading to fewer rounds. Therefore, shorter rounds equal reduced resource consumption. Hence, the energy consumption was reduced and illustrated in Fig. 4b.

In a large-scale system, the leader election procedure may consume some energy. However, this energy use is negligible in comparison to the reduced energy consumption caused by federated learning's quick convergence.

5   Conclusion

In this research, we proposed a decentralized approach to the federated learning client selection stage, enabling nodes to autonomously determine their eligibility for participation in federated learning. The primary objective of our method is to enhance the quality of FL by ensuring optimal client participation and mitigating the issues related to server-dependent selection stages. Our experimental results confirm that the proposed method offers considerable advantages over traditional methods, as it reduces the number of rejected clients, accelerates the convergence process, and consequently lowers energy consumption.

Looking towards the future, we intend to refine and expand upon the concept underlying our approach. By leveraging decentralized technologies such as Blockchain, we aim to apply the principle of leader selection to further stages of FL. We also intend to address additional issues like privacy and security through node-leader coordination. Finally, a key focus of our future work will be to tackle the issue of node mobility, which our current solution does not address, along with the challenges it poses to our decentralized approach.

References

1. Lakshmanna, K., et al.: A review on deep learning techniques for IoT data. Electronics **11**(10), 1604 (2022)
2. Rydning, D.R.J.G.J., Reinsel, J., Gantz, J.: The digitization of the world from edge to core. Framingham: Int. Data Corporation **16** (2018)
3. Karimipour, H., Derakhshan, F. (eds.): AI-Enabled Threat Detection and Security Analysis for Industrial IoT. Springer, Cham (2021). https://doi.org/10.1007/978-3-030-76613-9
4. Yunlong, L., Huang, X., Dai, Y., Maharjan, S., Zhang, Y.: Blockchain and federated learning for privacy-preserved data sharing in industrial IoT. IEEE Trans. Industr. Inf. **16**(6), 4177–4186 (2019)
5. McMahan, B., Moore, E., Ramage, D., Hampson, S., y Arcas, B.A.: Communication-efficient learning of deep networks from decentralized data. In: Singh, A., Zhu, J., (eds.) Proceedings of the 20th International Conference on Artificial Intelligence and Statistics, Volume 54 of Proceedings of Machine Learning Research, pp. 1273–1282. PMLR (2017). https://proceedings.mlr.press/v54/mcmahan17a.html
6. Kim, H., Park, J., Bennis, M., Kim, S.-L.: Blockchained on-device federated learning. IEEE Commun. Lett. **24**(6), 1279–1283 (2019)
7. Karakanis, S., Leontidis, G.: Lightweight deep learning models for detecting COVID-19 from chest X-ray images. Comput. Biol. Med. **130**, 104181 (2021)
8. Li, Q., et al.: A survey on federated learning systems: vision, hype and reality for data privacy and protection. IEEE Trans. Knowl. Data Eng. (2021)
9. Li, T., Sahu, A.K., Talwalkar, A., Smith, V.: Federated learning: challenges, methods, and future directions. IEEE Sig. Process. Mag. **37**(3), 50–60 (2020)
10. Wahab, O.A., Mourad, A., Otrok, H., Taleb, T.: Federated machine learning: survey, multi-level classification, desirable criteria and future directions in communication and networking systems. IEEE Commun. Surv. Tutorials **23**(2), 1342–1397 (2021). https://doi.org/10.1109/COMST.2021.3058573
11. Du, Z., Wu, C., Yoshinaga, T., Yau, K.L.A., Ji, Y., Li, J.: Federated learning for vehicular internet of things: recent advances and open issues. IEEE Open J. Comput. Soc. **1**, 45–61 (2020)
12. Nour, B., Cherkaoui, S., Mlika, Z.: Federated learning and proactive computation reuse at the edge of smart homes. IEEE Trans. Netw. Sci. Eng. (2021)
13. Cho, Y.J., Wang, J., Joshi, G.: Client selection in federated learning: convergence analysis and power-of-choice selection strategies. arXiv preprint: arXiv:2010.01243 (2020)
14. Nishio, T., Yonetani, R.: Client selection for federated learning with heterogeneous resources in mobile edge. In: ICC 2019-2019 IEEE International Conference on Communications (ICC), pp. 1–7. IEEE (2019)
15. AbdulRahman, S., Tout, H., Mourad, A., Talhi, C.: FedMCCS: multicriteria client selection model for optimal IoT federated learning. IEEE Internet Things J. **8**(6), 4723–4735 (2020)
16. Wang, S., Liu, F., Xia, H.: Content-based vehicle selection and resource allocation for federated learning in IoV. In: 2021 IEEE Wireless Communications and Networking Conference Workshops (WCNCW), pp. 1–7. IEEE (2021)
17. Taïk, A., Moudoud, H., Cherkaoui, S.: Data-quality based scheduling for federated edge learning. In: 2021 IEEE 46th Conference on Local Computer Networks (LCN), pp. 17–23. IEEE (2021)

18. Yoshida, N., Nishio, T., Morikura, M., Yamamoto, K.: Mab-based client selection for federated learning with uncertain resources in mobile networks. In: 2020 IEEE Globecom Workshops (GC Wkshps), pp. 1–6. IEEE (2020)

19. Li, J., et al.: Blockchain assisted decentralized federated learning (BLADE-FL): performance analysis and resource allocation. IEEE Trans. Parallel Distrib. Syst. **33**(10), 2401–2415 (2021)

20. Ma, C., et al.: When federated learning meets blockchain: a new distributed learning paradigm. IEEE Comput. Intell. Mag. **17**(3), 26–33 (2022)

21. Zhao, Y., et al.: Privacy-preserving blockchain-based federated learning for IoT devices. IEEE Internet Things J. **8**(3), 1817–1829 (2020)

22. Saha, R., Misra, S., Deb, P.K.: FogFL: Fog-assisted federated learning for resource-constrained IoT devices. IEEE Internet Things J. **8**(10), 8456–8463 (2020)

23. Marc Brooker. Leader election in distributed systems (2019). https://d1.awsstatic.com/builderslibrary/pdfs/leader-election-in-distributed-systems.pdf

24. Lamport, L.: Paxos made simple. ACM SIGACT News (Distributed Computing Column) **32**, 4 (Whole Number 121, December 2001), 51–58 (2001)

25. Wei, F., Wei, X., Tong, S.: An improved blockchain consensus algorithm based on raft. Arab. J. Sci. Eng. **46**(9), 8137–8149 (2021)

26. Méndez, M., Tinetti, F.G., Duran, A.M., Obon, D.A., Bartolome, N.G.: Distributed algorithms on IoT devices: bully leader election. In: 2017 International Conference on Computational Science and Computational Intelligence (CSCI), pp. 1351–1355. IEEE (2017)

27. Zhang, B., Liu, G., Hu, B.: The coordination of nodes in the internet of things. In: 2010 International Conference on Information, Networking and Automation (ICINA), vol. 2, pp. V2–299. IEEE (2010)

28. Zuo, Y., Yao, W., Chang, Q., Zhu, X., Gui, J., Qin, J.: Voting-based scheme for leader election in lead-follow UAV swarm with constrained communication. Electronics **11**(14), 2143 (2022)

29. Kanwal, S., Iqbal, Z., Irtaza, A., Ali, R., Siddique, K.: A genetic based leader election algorithm for IoT cloud data processing. Comput. Mater. Contin **68**, 2469–2486 (2021)

30. Rahman, M.U.: Leader election in the internet of things: challenges and opportunities. arXiv preprint: arXiv:1911.00759 (2019)

31. Agarwal, P., Alam, M.: A lightweight deep learning model for human activity recognition on edge devices. Procedia Comput. Sci. **167**, 2364–2373 (2020)

32. Hochreiter, S., Schmidhuber, J.: Long short-term memory. Neural Comput. **9**(8), 1735–1780 (1997)

33. Yun, M., Hong, S., Yoo, S., Kim, J., Park, S.M., Lee, Y.: Lightweight end-to-end stress recognition using binarized CNN-LSTM models. In: 2022 IEEE 4th International Conference on Artificial Intelligence Circuits and Systems (AICAS), pp. 270–273. IEEE (2022)

34. Rao, S. N., Shobha, G., Prabhu, S., Deepamala, N.: Time series forecasting methods suitable for prediction of CPU usage. In: 2019 4th International Conference on Computational Systems and Information Technology for Sustainable Solution (CSITSS), vol. 4, pp. 1–5. IEEE (2019)

35. Sarikaa, S., et al.: Time series forecasting of cloud resource usage. In: 2021 IEEE 6th International Conference on Computing, Communication and Automation (ICCCA), pp. 372–382. IEEE (2021)

36. Perone, G.: An ARIMA model to forecast the spread and the final size of COVID-2019 epidemic in Italy. MedRxiv (2020)

37. Chatfield, C.: The holt-winters forecasting procedure. J. Roy. Statist. Soc. Ser. C (Applied Statistics) **27**(3), 264–279 (1978). ISSN: 00359254–14679876. http://www.jstor.org/stable/2347162
38. Rafailescu, M.: Fault tolerant leader election in distributed systems. arXiv preprint: arXiv:1703.02247 (2017)

DRL Based SFC Orchestration in SDN/NFV Environments Subject to Transient Unavailability

Wiem Taktak[1(✉)], Mohamed Escheikh[1], and Kamel Barkaoui[2]

[1] Syscom Laboratory, ENIT, University of Tunis El Manar, Tunis, Tunisia
{wiem.taktak,mohamed.escheikh}@enit.utm.tn
[2] Cedric Laboratory, Paris, France
kamel.barkaoui@cnam.fr

Abstract. In this paper, we address how complex and dynamic environments characterized by variable and limited capacities and subject to transient unavailability may pose significant challenges for Deep Reinforcement Learning (DRL) agents. The investigation concerns the context of the Service Function Chaining (SFC) orchestration problem in Software-Defined Networking (SDN) and Network Function Virtualization (NFV)-based environments using the DRL approach, implemented through Deep Q-Network (DQN), and aims to maximize Quality of Experience (QoE) while meeting Quality of Service (QoS) constraints. We show through numerical results how limited capacity in the Physical Substrate Network (PSN) complicates the training process in terms of finding a suitable compromise between performance and convergence. We highlight how replay buffers may mitigate the transient unavailability of PSN nodes and what the limits of such a solution are when the unavailability becomes more prolonged in time or more severe (simultaneous unavailability of more than one node).

Keywords: Transient unavailability · DQN · Replay buffer · QoE · NFV · SFC Orchestration

1 Introduction

Dynamic SFC orchestration is crucial in SDN and NFV environments with limited capacity and subject to transient unavailability. This flexibility aims to enable efficient resource utilization, improve network resilience and fault tolerance and ensure that services can adapt to changing conditions and requirements. Transient unavailability due to network capacity limitations, failures, or any other disruptions can affect service delivery, and in this regard, dynamic SFC orchestration may be useful to detect these issues and automatically reroute traffic or instantiate backup services in order to ensure service continuity and minimize downtime. In SDN and NFV environments, the dynamic nature of services means that service chains may need to adapt quickly. For example, a low-latency service chain may be required for real-time applications, while a high-throughput chain may be needed for data transfer. In such a context, dynamic SFC orchestration is crucial to adjust the service chain based on these requirements, minimize operational costs, maintain QoS and Service Level Agreement (SLA) compliance, This may also be decisive in simplifying the management process by quickly deploying new services through automating the allocation, scaling, and maintenance of service functions.

DRL [1] algorithms such as DQN [5] are important for dynamic SFC orchestration because they offer a powerful mechanism for learning and making real-time decisions in complex network environments. They can also optimize SFC configurations, enhance adaptability and ensure that services meet their performance and policy requirements in evolving network scenarios. DQN evaluates various actions and their consequences to determine the optimal sequence of service functions for the current network conditions. It can adapt to changes in the network, such as transient unavailability or variations in network load, by continuously learning from the environment. It can react to changes and adjust SFCs accordingly, ensuring that services continue to meet their objectives. Through maximizing a cumulative reward signal over time, DQN can optimize resource allocation, network function selection, and the routing of traffic to minimize latency, maximize throughput, or meet other objectives. Also, self-learning from historical data and experiences is of paramount importance to be more proficient at making decisions and to allow it to adapt and improve its orchestration strategies as it encounters different network scenarios. Furthermore, automating the decision-making process for SFC orchestration is particularly valuable in dynamic environments with a large number of possible sequences and configurations where rapid decision-making and adaptability to find the best SFC configuration based on its learned policies are pivotal to ensure in real time. On the other hand, DQN and its variants may be very useful to learn to orchestrate SFCs in a way that enhances network resilience [3,4,7,8]. It can quickly respond to network failures and reconfigure SFCs to maintain service availability. It can be helpful to adapt and accommodate changing network conditions and resource availability.

In this paper, we investigate how PSN in SDN/NFV environments characterized by limited PSN nodes' capacities and subject to transient unavailability of PSN node(s) may affect the training reliability of a DQN agent used to optimize SFC orchestration. The optimization problem is formulated through a DRL approach that maximizes QoE while meeting QoS constraints. We focus on the learning process of the DQN agent, seeking to optimize SFC orchestration through three different scenarios. The first one deals with PSN nodes having unlimited capacities, whereas the second one considers PSN nodes with limited capacities. The last scenario addresses the case where PSN nodes have unlimited capacities and are subject to transient unavailability. In this regard, we establish a detailed comparison between the three scenarios in order to examine how limited capacity in PSN nodes complicates the training process in terms of finding a suitable compromise between performance and convergence. We also highlight how replay buffers may mitigate the transient unavailability of PSN nodes and what the limits of such a solution are when the unavailability becomes more prolonged in time or more severe (simultaneous unavailability of more than one node).

The rest of this paper is organized as follows: In Section, we provide first in Sect. 2 the main challenges a DQN agent may face whenever a PSN component is subject to transient unavailability's. Section 3 delves into SFC orchestration based on DRL and how experience replay may handle transient unavailability in PSN. Section 5 presents performance evaluation and numerical results for selected scenarios before concluding this paper in Sect. 6.

2 DQN Subject to Transient Unavailability

In this subsection, we detail in a first step how transient unavailability which can arise in PSN environment may affect DRL agents behavior along the training phase. We examine next the main strategies that may be adopted to mitigate these transient unavailability.

2.1 Transient Unavailability and Main Challenges for DRL Agents

Transient unavailability due to several factors, such as PSN node/link failures, may pose significant challenges for DRL agents during training process. These factors can affect DRL agents in several ways. Indeed, in such environments, it can be difficult for DRL agents to explore effectively. This can lead to sparse and non-stationary reward signals, making it challenging for DRL agents to learn optimal policies and leading to slower convergence. Also, transient unavailability may introduce non-Markovian aspects into the environment, where the current state may not fully capture the necessary information to make optimal decisions. DRL agents, which often rely on MDP, may struggle to handle these complexities. Moreover, learning in complex and dynamic environments may require a large number of samples, which can be impractical or costly. Additionally, DRL algorithms may require substantial data to adapt to changing conditions, leading to more difficulty for DRL agents to generalize well since they may become overly specialized to particular scenarios. This means that agents may have to deal with partial observability, given that they cannot directly observe some aspects of the environment.

2.2 Strategies to Mitigate Transient Unavailability for DRL Agent

Dealing with transient unavailability in the environment for DRL agents is an important aspect of developing robust and stable RL systems. To tackle these issues, several strategies may be adopted and may concern:

- **Reward Engineering**: Careful design of reward functions can help guide the learning process, making it more robust to variable capacities and transient unavailability.

- **Transfer Learning**: Pre-training on related tasks or environments and fine-tuning in the target environment can expedite learning and improve generalization.
- **Advanced Exploration Strategies**: Implementing advanced exploration techniques like curiosity-driven exploration or Bayesian optimization can help agents explore efficiently.
- **Adaptive Learning Rates**: Adjusting learning rates or using adaptive learning rate schedules can help DRL agents adapt to changing conditions.

Also, these strategies may involve implementing a retry mechanism to enable the agent wait for a brief period and retry the action or episode. They may also rely on setting timeouts for environmental interactions. Indeed, if an environment response takes too long, the agent can assume unavailability and take appropriate action, like retrying or choosing a default action. In addition, redundancy and fail over mechanisms can be implemented to ensure that multiple instances of the environment (PSN nodes/links) are available, and the agent can switch to a backup environment if the primary one becomes temporarily unavailable. Furthermore, in DQN algorithms, experience replay can help in mitigating the impact of transient unavailability and stabilizing learning via storing experiences and replaying them during training. This can smooth out the learning process. We focus in this paper on experience replay and its ability in DQN algorithms to handle transient PSN nodes' unavailability.

3   SFC Orchestration Based on DRL

DRL-based SFC orchestration combines the concepts of SFC orchestration and DRL to optimize network service delivery in dynamic and complex network environments. DRL is a sub-field of machine learning that deals with decision-making problems. It involves an agent learning to interact with an environment to achieve specific goals. The agent takes actions based on the environment's state and receives feedback (rewards) based on the consequences of its actions. Over time, the agent learns to make better decisions to maximize the cumulative reward. Combining SFC orchestration with DRL involves training an agent to dynamically decide the sequence of service functions to be applied to network traffic, considering the current network conditions, service requirements, and user demands. The goal is to optimize service delivery by learning a policy that results in the best overall performance and resource utilization. The main benefits of SFC orchestration based on DRL are adaptability, optimization and scalability. Indeed, DRL-based agents can adapt to changing network conditions and traffic patterns, leading to more efficient service delivery. They can also learn to optimize the SFC to minimize latency, improve throughput, and enhance overall network performance. Furthermore, they are able to handle complex and large-scale networks, making it suitable for modern network environments. However, it's worth noting that building and deploying such a system requires careful consideration of the network's architecture, potential risks, and challenges like training time, exploration-exploitation trade-offs, and generalization to unseen scenarios. Additionally, DRL models might require significant computational resources for training and inference, which may impact their feasibility in certain environments.

3.1 DQN Based SFC Ochestration Maximizing QoE While Meeting QoS Constraints

In this paper, DQN is used to implement SFC orchestration maximizing QoE while ensuring that QoS constraints. SFC orchestration involves the dynamic chaining of network services in a way that optimizes the user experience while adhering to network performance requirements and ensuring reliable and high-quality service delivery. This objective is achieved through careful design and considerations involving:

- **Problem Formulation**: We define the SFC orchestration as an optimization problem maximizing QoE while meeting QoS constraints. The QoE formulation is based on a combination of the standard models WFL and IQX [6] describing correlation between QoE and QoS and is used to create reward function based on QoE.
- **State Representation**: We define a state space by accounting for information about available PSN nodes/links resources and SFC request.
- **Action Space**: We specify the action space representing the possible decisions the orchestrator can make including embedding VNFs on suitable PSN nodes, mapping virtual links on appropriate PSN links and aborting the process of SFC request placement whenever QoS requirements are not met.
- **Reward Design**: Reflects the goal of maximizing QoE while meeting QoS constraints. It penalizes unsuccessful deployment of SFC request due to lack of resources or QoS violations in terms of end to end delay and end to end bandwidth.
- **DRL Algorithm**: We focus in this paper on DQN.
- **QoS Constraints Handling**: We implement mechanisms in the DQN algorithm to ensure that QoS constraints in terms end-to-end bandwidth/delay are met through adding constraints to the optimization problem.

3.2 How Experience Replay in DQN Algorithms Can Handle Transient Unavailability

Experience replay is a critical component of DRL algorithms, such as DQN and its variants, and plays a significant role in ensuring robustness and stability, especially in NFV environments characterized by limited capacities and transient unavailability. It stores past experiences in a replay buffer. These experiences typically consist of tuples (state, action, reward, next state), representing the agent's interactions with the environment. They allow the agent to learn more effectively in scenarios where certain states or experiences are temporarily unavailable from a broader range of data over time. In similar scenarios, experience replay may bring several advantages, such as:

- **Data Efficiency**: In NFVefficiency, environments with limited capacities, collecting real-time experiences for training can be challenging. Experience replay stores past experiences in a replay buffer, allowing the agent to learn from a broader range of data over time. This improves data efficiency as experiences can be reused multiple times for training, making better use of the available data.
- **Sample Efficiency**: In NFV environments where resources may be limited or transiently unavailable, training DRL agents can be time-consuming and resource-intensive. Experience replay helps by allowing the agent to learn from a diverse set of past experiences while using them more effectively. This reduces the number of interactions the agent needs with the environment, making learning more sample-efficient.
- **Stability and Robustness**: NFV environments can be highly dynamic and subject to frequent changes, including resource fluctuations and network disruptions. Experience replay helps stabilize training by providing a more consistent and less noisy learning signal. The replay buffer acts as a memory of past experiences, preventing the agent from overfitting to recent, possibly anomalous experiences. This leads to more robust and stable learning, even in the face of transient unavailability or sudden changes in the environment.
- **Policy Improvement**: Experience replay enables the agent to revisit and learn from its past actions and their outcomes. This iterative process of learning from past experiences can help the agent gradually improve its policy, adapting to changing conditions and resource constraints in NFV environments.
- **Exploration**: DRL agents often require exploration to discover optimal or near-optimal policies. In NFV environments with limited capacities, exploration can be costly. Experience replay can store and replay experiences where the agent explored and learned from, even if the exploration was inefficient or sub-optimal. This allows the agent to focus on exploiting known good policies while still benefiting from past exploration.
- **Off-Policy Learning**: Experience replay facilitates off-policy learning, which means the agent can update its policy using experiences generated by previous policies. This is particularly valuable in NFV environments where the agent may need to adapt to resource constraints and transient unavailability over time.

4   Main Assumptions

The definition of the simulation environment and the input parameters involves specifying the main assumptions related to the workload (the incoming SFC requests (SR)) and PSN topology.

- SR **assumptions**:
  - SR is composed by 5 VNFs are assumed to require equal PSN node capacity (1 unit) to be deployed and chained through 4 Vlinks.

- SR End-to-End bandwidth varies randomly in the range of $[16 - 256]$Mbps.
- SR End-to-End delay varies randomly in the range of $[50 - 90]$ms.
- **PSN assumptions**:
  - **PSN nodes**: The number of nodes in PSN is 5. PSN nodes are assumed fully interconnected via PSN links. Each PSN node can host one or more VNF(s) and two cases are considered:
    * **Unlimited capacity:** PSN nodes capacities' is fixed to 5 units so as to ensure that there is always enough capacity available to handle the worst case (all VNFs belonging to the same SR may be deployed on the same PSN node).
    * **Limited capacity:** PSN nodes have a same capacity equals to 3 units.
  - **PSN links:** Each PSN link is assumed with limited bandwidth capacity and non zero transmission delay. It may handle one or more Vlink(s). Bandwidth capacity is randomly chosen in the range of $[768 - 1280]$Mbps and link delay is randomly selected in $[10 - 20]$ms.
- **Evaluation metric for online DRL**: Is used for evaluation during training (learning) phase. It measures the quality of the learned policy (or RL algorithm) and is quantified by the average learning level (i.e., QoE_{Sc_Th}) or the cumulative reward to be reached by the DRL agent in the last 100 runs of the training phase.
- The attributes of each incoming SR and the PSN change rapidly over time and the agent needs to adapt quickly and dynamically to these new conditions.

5   Results and Discussion

We investigate in this section results and discussion related to performance evaluation of DQN agent aiming to optimize SFC orchestration by maximizing QoE while meeting QoS requirements. This performance evaluation is based on a similar approach as in [2] but considers extended assumptions and different metrics. A DRL agent is implemented in this paper by the DQN algorithm [8], which is compared to two baseline algorithms (Violent, Random). In this regard, we consider three scenarios dealing respectively with PSN where nodes capacities are unlimited (Fig. 1), PSN with limited nodes capacities (Fig. 2) and PSN having nodes with unlimited capacities subject to transient unavailability (Figs. 3 and 4). Through the first scenario (Fig. 1), we examine how DRL agent attempt to find suitable performance-convergence trade-off. Whereas, in the second (resp. third) scenario, we intend to understand how limited nodes capacities (resp. transient node(s) unavailability) affect DRL agent learning process. In the rest in this section, we first investigate each scenario described above separately and then we conduct a detailed discussion about comparison between the three scenarios.

Scenario1: We consider in this scenario PSN with unlimited nodes capacities and links limited capacities. In order to reach good training level, it is important for DRL agent to find at the end of the training phase convenient compromise between performance and convergence. In this respect, we gradually increase (sub-figures of Fig. 1) QoE threshold score (QoE_{Th-Sc}) until reaching acceptable performance learning level without sacrificing convergence. We notice that by increasing the desired performance level to be reached and expressed in terms of QoE_{Th-Sc}, DQN agent converges less rapidly. Indeed, as DQN agent attempts to reach higher QoE_{Th-Sc} values, it strives to attain better, near-optimal solutions. The solution providing the best policy is obtained for $QoE_{Th-Sc} = 2,25$ (Fig. 1f), where the DQN agent reaches a satisfactory learning level. In fact, beyond this, the QoE_{Th-Sc} DQN agent does not produce better performance, and convergence is not assured even for relatively long episodes (even with an episode size equal to 20000 runs).

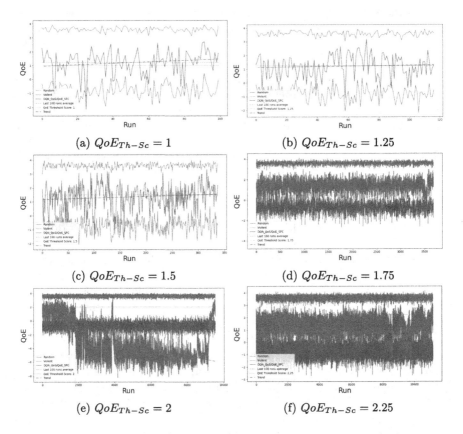

(a) $QoE_{Th-Sc} = 1$

(b) $QoE_{Th-Sc} = 1.25$

(c) $QoE_{Th-Sc} = 1.5$

(d) $QoE_{Th-Sc} = 1.75$

(e) $QoE_{Th-Sc} = 2$

(f) $QoE_{Th-Sc} = 2.25$

Fig. 1. *QoE* vs runs (unlimited PSN nodes capacities 5, 5, 5, 5, 5)

Scenario2: We investigate in Fig. 2 how limited node's capacity affects the DQN agent training process in terms both of performance and convergence. By comparing scenario2 with scenario1, we see that tangibly limiting nodes capacities significantly delays the convergence of the agent. This is illustrated for $QoE_{Th-Sc} = 1,25$ (resp. $QoE_{Th-Sc} = 1,5$), where the required number of runs to achieve DQN agent convergence goes from 120 (Fig. 1b) to 3030 (Fig. 2c) (resp. from 350 (Fig. 1c) to 4207 (Fig. 2d)). Such behavior may be explained by the fact that the problem complexity for scenario1 is easier to solve than that for scenario2. Indeed, limiting node capacity associates more constraints to solving the SFC orchestration problem and makes it more difficult. This is illustrated by both severe oscillations along training and longer time to converge.

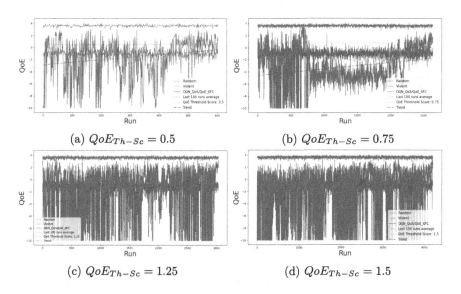

(a) $QoE_{Th-Sc} = 0.5$ (b) $QoE_{Th-Sc} = 0.75$

(c) $QoE_{Th-Sc} = 1.25$ (d) $QoE_{Th-Sc} = 1.5$

Fig. 2. QoE vs runs (limited PSN nodes capacities $3, 3, 3, 3, 3$)

Scenario3: This scenario adopts similar assumptions as in scenario1, but also considers the transient unavailability of PSN node(s) and their impact on DQN agent learning. In this regard, we carry out performance evaluation analysis comparing DQN [8] to baseline algorithms (Violent and Search) (Figs. 3 and 4).

In Fig. 3, we consider respectively three different cases ($N = 0$, $N = 1$ and $N = 2$) where N is the number of PSN node(s) being temporarily unavailable. Node unavailability is triggered during a limited period of time composed of 10 consecutive runs between run 60 and run 69 of the learning process. When comparing the case where only one PSN node is temporarily unavailable ($N = 1$) to the case where all PSN nodes are fully available ($N = 0$), we notice that baseline algorithms are sensitive to PSN node failure, whereas DQN algorithm behaves as if there is no failure. This behavior may be justified by the fact that DQN agent uses experience replay by maintaining a replay buffer for storing past experiences and replaying them during training. This helps the DQN agent learn more effectively in scenarios where certain states or experiences are temporarily unavailable. For the case where two PSN nodes are temporarily unavailable ($N = 2$), we observe that all algorithms (DQN, Violent, Random) are sensitive to nodes unavailability. This may be explained by the fact that the scale of the failure is beyond the capacity of the experience replay to allow the DQN agent to learn from past experiences. We can conclude that experience relay may handle limited transient unavailability and as soon as this unavailability extends beyond a given threshold, this will be directly reflected on the DQN agent's behavior.

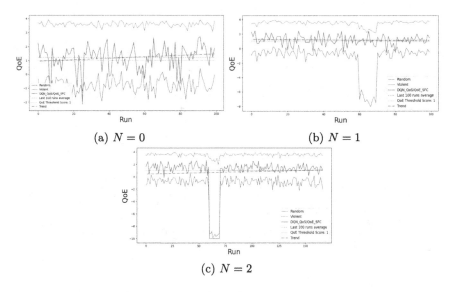

(a) $N = 0$ (b) $N = 1$

(c) $N = 2$

Fig. 3. QoE vs runs (unavailability (60–69) and unlimited PSN nodes capacities $5, 5, 5, 5, 5$) $QoE_{Th-Sc} = 1$

In Fig. 4, we consider the same cases as in Fig. 3, however, the period of time where PSN node(s) is/are unavailable is longer (20 runs instead of 10 runs). Node(s) unavailability (in Fig. 4) is/are provoked between runs 60 and 79 of the learning process. As soon as only one single node becomes unavailable for 20 consecutive runs in Fig. 4b the DQN agent behavior is partially affected. This is not the case for unavailability during 10 consecutive runs in Fig. 3b. Such behavior is very likely interpreted by the inability of experience replay to fully handle such a long unavailability, even for a single node among the five making up the PSN. Furthermore, we notice that DQN agent is partially affected by one-node unavailability, whereas baseline algorithms are fully affected. This highlights the role of replay buffer in partially mitigating unavailability for DQN. As soon as simultaneous unavailability of two PSN nodes ($N = 2$) is triggered, a sharp drop in the DQN agent reward quantified by QoE value during the downtime is immediately noticed for all algorithms including DQN.

Notice that all the previous experiences are executed with replay buffer size equal to 512. To further highlight the role of replay buffer in improving DQN

agent training efficiency and stability, we conduct simulation experiment in Fig. 5
with assumptions similar to those considered in Fig. 3b (Scenario3) but with the
replay buffer size reduced from 512 to 1. We investigate the behavior of the
different algorithms along the time period where only one node is unavailable
temporarily between run 60 and run 69. We notice that DQN agent performance
is drastically deteriorated (when compared with Fig. 3b) and becomes very close
to that of the Random algorithm. In other words, transient node unavailability (along with 10 consecutive runs) may be handled by replay buffer with

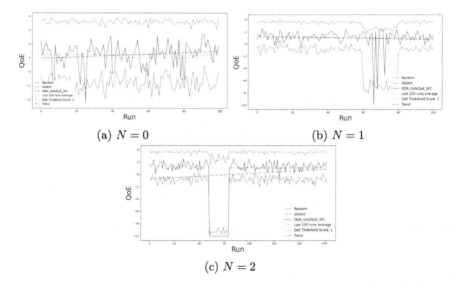

(a) $N = 0$ (b) $N = 1$

(c) $N = 2$

Fig. 4. *QoE* vs runs (unavailability (60–79) and unlimited PSN nodes capacities
$5, 5, 5, 5, 5$) $QoE_{Th-Sc} = 1$

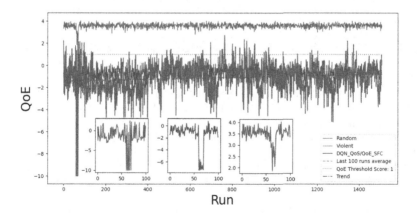

Fig. 5. Replay Buffer Memory Size $=1$

suitable configuration thanks to its ability to store trajectories of experience when executing a policy in the environment.

6 Conclusion

We focus in this paper on investigating the application of DRL, specifically using DQN, to address the SFC orchestration problem in SDN and NFV environments, maximizing QoE while meeting QoS requirements. The emphasis on the challenges posed by dynamic, capacity-limited environments and transient unavailability and the need to balance performance and convergence provides valuable insights into the complexities of implementing DRL solutions in real-world networking scenarios. We provide several insights and comprehensive understanding on how experience replay based on replay buffer can mitigate the impact of transient unavailability and limited capacity of PSN nodes during the learning process of a DQN agent managing SFC orchestration on training reliability. We assess also the limitations of the replay buffer solution, particularly when the unavailability becomes more prolonged or severe (simultaneous unavailability of more than one node). In future works, we intend to investigate solutions that enable us to strengthen availability in DRL based SFC orchestration context, such as implementing redundancy for critical components of the SFC orchestration system, including controllers and orchestration modules or using load balancing mechanisms to distribute traffic and tasks evenly across redundant components, preventing overload on any single node. We plan to leverage fail over mechanisms to swiftly switch to backup components or nodes in case of failures.

References

1. Kai, A., et al.: Deep reinforcement learning: a brief survey. IEEE Sig. Process. Mag. **34**(6), 26–38 (2017)
2. Xi, C., et al.: Reinforcement learning-based QoS/QoEaware service function chaining in softwaredriven 5G slices. Trans. Emerg. Telecommun. Technol. **29**(11), e3477 (2018)
3. Escheikh, M., Taktak, W., Barkaoui, K.: Testing quality of training in QoE-aware SFC orchestration based on DRL approach. In: IFIP International Conference on Testing Software and Systems. Springer Nature Switzerland, Cham (2023)
4. Escheikh, M., Taktak, W.: Online QoS/QoE-driven SFC orchestration leveraging a DRL approach in SDN/NFV enabled networks. Wireless Pers. Commun. **137**(3), 1511–1538 (2024)
5. Volodymyr, M., et al.: Human-level control through deep reinforcement learning. Nature **518**(7540), 529–533 (2015)
6. Peter, R., et al.: The logarithmic nature of QoE and the role of the Weber-Fechner law in QoE assessment. In: 2010 IEEE International Conference on Communications. IEEE (2010)
7. Taktak, W., Escheikh, M., Barkaoui, K.: A QoE driven DRL approach for network slicing based on SFC orchestration in SDN/NFV enabled networks. In: International Conference on Verification and Evaluation of Computer and Communication Systems. Springer Nature Switzerland, Cham (2023)

8. Taktak, W., Escheikh, M., Barkaoui, K.: DRL approach for online user-centric QoS-Aware SFC embedding with dynamic VNF placement. Comput. Netw. **251**, 110637 (2024)
9. Wang, Y., et al.: Flexible transmission network expansion planning based on DQN algorithm. Energies **14**(7), 1944 (2021)

Author Index

B. Ben Hedia et al. (Eds.): VECoS 2024, LNCS 15466, pp. 249–250, 2025.
https://doi.org/10.1007/978-3-031-85356-2

Printed in the United States
by Baker & Taylor Publisher Services